WALTER PERRIE
in Conversation with
Scottish Writers

WALTER PERRIE
in Conversation with
Scottish Writers

Donald Campbell

Duncan Glen

Tessa Ransford

Trevor Royle

William Hershaw

Alasdair Gray

Margaret Bennett

John Herdman

WALTER PERRIE
in Conversation with Scottish Writers
First published in 2021 as a complete collection of interviews
Grace Note Publications

Grange of Locherlour,
Ochtertyre, PH7 4JS, Scotland
www.gracenotepublications.com

books@gracenotereading.co.uk

ISBN: 978-1-913162-17-7 (PBK)

British Library Cataloguing-in-Publications Data

A catalogue record for this book is
available from the British Library

CONTENTS

Eight Conversations with Scottish Writers

Acknowledgements: vi

❋

Introduction:1

❋

1. Donald Campbell: 5

❋

2. Duncan Glen: 43

❋

3. Tessa Ransford: 83

❋

4. Trevor Royle: 111

❋

5. William Hershaw: 155

❋

6. Alasdair Gray: 187

❋

7. Margaret Bennett: 219

❋

8. John Herdman: 259

❋

Select Bibliographies: 299

ACKNOWLEDGEMENT

This collection was only possible with the trust and friendship of all those who took part and that has been my good fortune. In particular, I want to thank Gonzalo Mazzei for his unstinting labours, and encouragenent.

INTRODUCTION

Eight Conversations with Scottish Writers

The eight interviews in this collection were recorded over a period of fifteen years between 2006 and 2020 and cover the whole gamut of Scottish literary life across the second half of the twentieth century and into the present. They include leading figures in our national poetry, drama, the novel, short-story, history, and folk-studies, as well as publishing, education and broadcasting. The oldest of the interviewees, Duncan Glen, was born in 1933 and the youngest, William Hershaw, in 1957: two, Trevor Royle and Tessa Ransford, were born in India, reflecting the deep entanglement of Scotland and Empire. With the exception of the youngest, what they have in common is that they comprise a generation growing up in the shadow of war through the austerities of the forties and fifties, but unlike the generation immediately preceding theirs, that of Hamish Henderson, Alexander Scott, Sorley MacLean, none of them saw active service. What they did see was the end of Empire and the growing prosperity and gradual liberalisation of social attitudes through the sixties and seventies.

John Herdman and I founded *Fras* Magazine and Publications in 2004. We had first met in Edinburgh in 1970 where we were both leading active literary lives: John was editing *Catalyst* magazine and was involved with the Heretics, a group of like-minded musicians and writers, while I was editing *Chapman* magazine. By 2004 we were both living in rural Perthshire; John in Blair Atholl and I in Dunning and both felt, I think, that we had become rather isolated from contemporary literary life and that the achievements of some of our own generation were being lost in the political and cultural turmoil that had happened since.

In retrospect, I believe the later sixties and seventies marked a decisive turning point in our history. The shift begins with the first Wilson government in 1964, the first Labour administration since Attlee's in 1945, and ends with the election of Thatcher's Tories in 1979. There has not been a Scottish majority for the Conservative Party since 1955, which may in part explain the dramatic rise of the SNP in the late sixties and through the seventies. The two great wars of the twentieth century momentarily consolidated and heightened a sense of Britishness in which genuine Scottish cultural elements became all-but invisible. It was perhaps emotionally difficult for generations who had lived through Britain's wars to oppose its political clichés and unfairness, but the combination of prosperity and a resurgence of Scottish identity, helped produce a brief period of heightened cultural activity.

Scotland in the 1970s seemed small enough for its cultural activists to know each other as people we met at readings, drinking sessions or literary receptions: people we may have liked or, in keeping with Scottish tradition, detested, but whom we knew as individuals, not just as literary figures. So I had come to know not only John Herdman but Donald Campbell, Duncan Glen, Trevor Royle, Tessa Ransford and many another no longer extant. To follow but one instance: Duncan Glen, as editor of *Akros* and *Akros Publications* had published my first (pseudonymous) poetry pamphlet, and we were both involved in the *Scottish Association of Magazine Publishers*, an organisation sponsored by the Scottish Arts Council, then under the literary direction of Trevor Royle. I had visited Duncan at his home in Preston. I had also invited him, along with Donald Campbell and Sorley MacLean, to be part of a Scottish contingent to the first International Cambridge Poetry Festival in 1975, an expedition again partly funded by the Scottish Arts Council. Throughout this period, and although living in 'exile' in Preston, Duncan was a central figure in publishing Scottish literature, especially in the Scots language, and in bringing to national and international attention the then neglected figure of Hugh MacDiarmid. MacLean was finally being recognised as the genius who renovated Gaelic poetry, its most important poet since the 18th century, and Donald Campbell, a pamphlet of whose poetry I had already published, was to go on to establish himself as a major figure in Scottish theatre, a genre which had until then, thanks to the bigots of the Kirk, only the shallowest of roots in Scottish culture.

In due course, in 2008 in Kirkcaldy, I was to attend the obsequies for Duncan. Having returned from 'exile' he had arranged that the anthem for the occasion be not one of the traditional psalms but the Jacobite "By Yon Bonnie Banks", in which a rebel to be hanged in the morning tells his comrade who is to be freed, that he will be first home. These relationships, both personal and literary, were in some degree the norm rather than the exception, so that, I would suggest, there existed a sense of historic community across Scottish literary and cultural life where an older generation of writers, such as Edwin Morgan, Iain Crichton Smith, Maurice Lindsay, William Montgomerie, J.K. Annand, George Bruce, interacted with their younger peers. That continuity seemed to dissipate through the 1980s and in 2021 no longer exists. So it is that these interviews, apart from their intrinsic interest, also mark a moment in our history, Trevor Royle, of course, went on to become one of Britain's leading historians of all matters military. Alasdair Gray achieved international reputation with his novel *Lanark*. Tessa Ransford was the most persistent and dedicated founder of the Scottish Poetry Library; Margaret Bennett became internationally recognised as folklorist and performer of traditional songs and stories. John Herdman has established himself as novelist, short-story writer and scholar, whose tales are translated into French and Italian. William Hershaw is a leading Scots-language poet and musician and it would be invidious of me not to mention the youngest of those involved in creating these interviews, Richie McCaffery, whose knowledge of Scottish literature is both wide and deep and who is in his own right already a fine poet.

Walter Perrie,
Dunning, 2021

WALTER PERRIE 1949: Poet, critic, editor and publisher. Co-founder of *Chapman* magazine and *Fras* Publications.

I. DONALD CAMPBELL

Donald Campbell (1940-2019): Poet, playwright & theatre historian

This conversation took place at Donald's home in Edinburgh on June 20th. 2006. Present were John Herdman and Walter Perrie.

JOHN HERDMAN: I think I first met you in 1970 and among the things I learned about you then was that you had a mixed background from Edinburgh and Caithness, both of which were, in different ways, very important to you. I think I'm right in saying that on both sides your parentage was Caithness?

DONALD CAMPBELL: That's right. My father came from a Caithness family that had emigrated to Edinburgh a generation before my mother's. Both sides were Highland.

JH: You were born in Pultneytown, Wick because your father was away at the War at the time and you went and stayed with your mother's people?

DC: Well, my grandmother brought me up for the first five years of my life. And it's only when the War was over and when I started school, that I went back to Edinburgh after my father came home and a normal sort of lifestyle could begin. Although I remained in touch with Caithness for ten years after that, from then on my home was in Edinburgh.

JH: And when you came to Edinburgh you lived first of all in the Cowgate, is that right?

DC: My father's mother's house was in the Cowgate. But then we moved to Dalry Road and I grew up in Gorgie-Dalry.

WALTER PERRIE:What was your granny's name?

DC: My granny's name was Jean Mowat and she married a man called Campbell. On my mother's side it was Jane Sutherland and she married a man called Mackenzie.

WP: Do you ever think of yourself as a Highlander at all?

DC: Half the time I do, yes.

JH: You went to Boroughmuir, I think, where you were taught by Sam [Sorley] Maclean?

DC: That's right. I was very lucky because when I was at primary school I was taught by Norman MacCaig and when I was at secondary school I was taught by [Sorley] Maclean – very briefly, though. I was not in one of his regular classes.

JH: Do you think the fact that you had two very prominent Scottish poets as teachers had any influence on your own desire to write?

DC: It made me think that writing poetry was maybe a normal thing. It sort of demystified the whole thing for me. Generally speaking, though, my school days were a total disaster. On the other hand, it has to be said that there were pluses and minuses – and coming into contact with Norman and Sam can certainly be placed on the plus side. Later on, of course, they both became friends. It took me some time to become friendly with Norman, but eventually we did, towards the end of his life. But I was always on very good terms with Sam. But the very important thing was that it demystified that whole idea of writing from the beginning and for good too. And they were good teachers.

JH: You said your school career was a disaster and you didn't go to university.

DC: Yes, I'd like to say something more about that. I left school without any qualification whatsoever and, for a long time, I felt guilty about that. I felt that I had somehow let my teachers down. It was only after I began to work in education myself that I realised that the truth was the complete opposite. I hadn't let anyone down. They had let me down. I was a child, a pupil; for whom they were responsible – and most of them didn't even try to fulfil that responsibility. They simply decided I wasn't worth the effort. Well, if I've achieved nothing else in my writing career, I've proved them wrong.

JH: Had you by that time formed plans to be a writer?

DC: Oh yes, I think so.

WP: And when was this, in your late teens?

DC: That's right – back in the mid-fifties. One of the things they did at that time at Boroughmuir as a sort of detention was to send you to the library. One day I found myself there for some reason and I picked up a copy of *Sangschaw*. I remember reading it and thinking: well, this is for me! From then on I was really devoted to the whole MacDiarmid thing. At about the same time, though I can't remember the exact year, I became interested in Dylan Thomas because I heard *Under Milk Wood* on radio and radio has always been one of my big things. I still think that Under Milk Wood is the greatest radio play that's ever been written and so I became devoted to Dylan Thomas as well. But then of course a great hero of that time who also came to me via radio was Ewan McColl. He was touring the folk clubs and all the rest of it and also recording his radio ballads. I bought a few copies of them just the other day. He was very inspiring for me, what he and Peggy Seeger were doing, and that was an awful lot to do with the beginning of my writing.

WP: And was this also tied up with the growth of Scottish nationalism or, at least, Scottish self-consciousness?

DC: Yes, with Scottish self-consciousness. You know, in those days we were kind of suspicious of nationalism, for all sorts of reasons after the War. But it did have to do with a growth of our Scottish identity. The big thrill was in discovering things that had been a closed book to our generation. And I kind of discovered the whole range of Scottish folk art when there was that big *ceilidh* that Hamish Henderson organised at one of the first Edinburgh Festivals. Lots of singers came along and I heard new songs.

WP: Including the like of Jeannie Robertson?

DC: That whole thing was very invigorating.

WP: And was that in some way making popular culture respectable in a way it had not been by removing it from its working class contexts?

DC: It was also a reaction against the mass media. The folk revival coincided, more or less, with the emergence of television, the box in the corner. And which in some ways, though people were quite thrilled by it, de-humanised entertainment. And it destroyed the cinema eventually, though, of course, the thing was staggering by then. Live entertainment, variety for instance, was destroyed by television. People do have a need, I believe, to congregate and I think that the folk revival tried to fill that need and at least went some way towards it.

WP: What they need, surely, is community and it's that that the folk revival is a substitute for. What television really abolished was the ceilidh, with people knowing each other.

DC: Yes, that's absolutely right. Dennis Potter has an essay about television watching; suggesting that the reason people watch soap operas is that they provide a substitute for the communities that they have lost. A lot of that, at the beginning of my writing career, motivated what people were doing then.

JH: It was in 1961, I think, that you went to London, staying there for four years?

DC: That's right.

JH: What was behind that? Was it just the general desire of any person of your age and that era to have a new kind of experience?

DC: Partly, it was a wish to try to put right the damage that had been done at school – a substitute education, if you like. Mostly, though, I think it was just a need to get away, to get myself into some sort of order, to not be my father's son, to not live in a particular place. Just to go and find out something about myself. It was a voyage of self-discovery really.

JH: And you found that that happened? Did you change a lot when you were away?

DC: Oh, yes, I did. No two ways about it. I think the importance of the Scottish identity comes to me from that time because I was living in bedsit land in London and I was trying to make up the deficiencies of my education, simply by reading as much as I could get my hands on. And I became very much aware that other people that I knew had an identity they were relaxed about, served them well, whereas mine was a bit uncomfortable. I was aware of this particularly for the period of two years I stayed with a Lithuanian community in Ladbroke Grove. And, of course, at that time, people from the Baltic communities seemed to have lost their identity completely. The Lithuanians and the Letts and Estonians I met at that time had no hope of ever going home, of ever living again in a society in which their language was spoken. They thought that this was all gone, so they celebrated

9

their identity and literature. It was really quite interesting for somebody like me, particularly when a group of Lithuanians who were miners in Tranent used to come down to London, usually for the football internationals. They used to come down to Lithuanian House and as soon as they walked through the door they became Lithuanians again. Seeing that sort of thing, that was very inspiring. It was in a sense because of that experience that I wanted to get back to my Scottish roots.

WP: Was Scotland a single place or was it two places?

DC: Oh, it was more than that. It was Caithness and Edinburgh and also Glasgow. I have relatives who live in Glasgow.

JH: It was also, presumably, a literary place by this time, a place which had an existence in those poets you were reading?

DC: Of course.

JH: And when did you first meet MacDiarmid?

DC: Well, I have never been quite sure of that. I think the first time I actually had a conversation with him, I seem to remember, would be about 1970 and it was, I think, at the establishment of the Lallans Society. It is now the Scots Language Society. He was speaking at it and I spoke to him afterwards. But I seem to have a memory of meeting him in the same company a few years earlier – although I didn't know him then. I didn't really get to know him until I could speak to him, until he knew who I was. I remember one particular encounter I had with Chris was at Stirling. A young female American student came over and asked me to sign a copy of my book and I found I didn't have a pen. I turned to Chris who said: "Here, have one of mine." And he produced one of his own pens. I was just about to sign the book when the girl said to me: "Mr. Campbell, could you write – signed with Hugh MacDiarmid's pen?"

WP: It has been suggested that some degree of dislocation from the mainstream of a language is important in the writing of good poetry, so, for example, Dylan was Welsh, Yeats was an Irishman. That you need something which gives you the capacity to stand back a bit from the language you are using, so as to become aware that it is not merely a transparent window through which you look on a world. Do you agree?

DC: Yes, in terms of using language as material. I think that's an element in the best poetry, because poetry is about language really, about words.

WP: Many writers, poets in particular, are associated with one particular sense. Keats has a strong sense of smell. For Hardy it is kinetic, he can make your spine twitch, make you feel uncomfortable. Do you favour any particular sense?

DC: The only thing for me is sound. It has always been the way that people speak. Even when I am using language artificially, very often I am using Scots, I try to put that artificial language into the speech patterns that I hear in my head. It has always been sound for me. I actually think my best work has been done for radio because there you have nothing but sound. One of my ambitions and regrets was that I didn't ever get the chance to write radio ballads. But I did write two radio features that went on to win many awards, The Miller's Reel and The Year of the Bonnie Prince, and they are probably to be counted as being among my best work. Both rely, of course, entirely on sound.

WP: I try to persuade writing students that if they are to write well, they have to make their poems and prose sound like something someone might actually say.

DC: Of course, as far as that's concerned, in terms of a play, it goes further than that. Somebody actually has to say it. And right there. And they have to say it as though they had only just thought of it.

WP: And that is much more difficult.

DC: That's one of the attractions of making plays. The difficulty. The challenge.

JH: I'm interested in the progress that you made from poetry to drama and, obviously, what you were saying about the primacy of sound for you. There's an almost seamless movement there from your poetry, which was very much sound orientated, and also was very much a poetry that could be delivered, a poetry for performance. From the early 1970s you were primarily a poet and then, in the mid 1970s, you turned increasingly to drama.

DC: That's right.

JH: Two questions obviously occur here: did you feel that you had done all that you could do in Scots poetry or were you just inexorably drawn to a more expansive medium?

DC: I just stopped. I couldn't understand how that could happen, that you could stop writing poetry. Hamish Henderson once told me that he'd done the same. He had just stopped, too. It was just after I had published a collection called Blether. I think I was writing Widows of Clyth, I was getting quite a lot of work and that had a lot to do with it. I didn't lose poetry altogether. I also wrote Murals. I was spending an awful lot of my time advising poets. A lot of the satisfaction I had had from writing poetry – and I do think I wrote poems for that satisfaction. I've always enjoyed writing lyrics. But also, about the time I stopped, I discovered Rob Donn and I was working on his poems. And now that I am not getting any commissions and that the whole professional side of my career is over, I have gone back to that. I always felt that

I wanted to write poetry but I always sort of put it on the back burner. As far as my own work was concerned, I think I stopped from about 1979. The last time I wrote a poem was in 1992 and I remember it was a good poem and I enjoyed writing it.

WP: I don't think I ever enjoy writing a poem. Can you see any relevance in Jung's notion that you spend the first half of your life establishing who you are? So that, as a younger man, you are interested in the content and what you want to say. You want to hear what you have to say.

DC: Yes.

WP: But thereafter, you can't get anywhere with poetry unless there comes a transformation, a turning away at mid-point and you begin to become interested primarily in what the language has to say. So later poetry flows out of the language. Rather than the language being some kind of accident of a preconceived content, the content almost becomes an accident of the language.

DC: That's right. That's fundamental for poetry.

WP: Almost everyone who starts out as a writer wants to be a poet, and many who fail to make the transformation turn into third rate novelists.

DC: But you see, a lot of people start out by wanting to be poets because as Norman used to say: Poetry is shorter. And he never went on to anything else at all.

WP: No. But then, he never went anywhere else with his poetry either.

JH: Yes, it was very static.

WP: Once you get to the MacCaig of 1958, say, there is no difference between that and the MacCaig of 1988.

DC: That's right.

WP: And that is just the opposite from Yeats. MacCaig is like John
      Wayne always playing John Wayne.

DC: But, of course, Norman did have a great sense of that himself. I
      recall one time in Dundee. We'd done this reading and we'd both
      been invited for a meal with the University people. We had some
      time to spare so we went for a walk down by the river. When it
      was time to go, Norman gave a huge sigh and said: "Come on. It's
      time for me to be MacCaig again." But to go back to what you
      were saying about my own development, the bridge for me was
      the performance. Poetry was fundamentally for me something
      to be performed. And that's when I started moving on to drama,
      because that's a logical next step.

JH: I remember that the first play you wrote was The Jesuit, which
      is in some ways still your best remembered play. What was it
      interested you in John Ogilvie?

DC: Oh, well that was quite easy. There was an article in the
      Edinburgh Evening News in which Alex Reid wrote that with
      the anniversary of The Reformation coming up, there ought to
      be a competition for Scottish playwrights on the subject of John
      Knox. This was the most stupid suggestion I had ever heard. The
      one thing that Scottish playwrights don't need to be encouraged
      to do, is to write a play about John Knox. So I thought, I am going
      to write a play about something that's completely different from
      John Knox and I actually set out to find somebody who I could
      write about. And I found Ogilvie's story. I was actually helped
      quite a lot by Robin Lorimer at the time, who put me on to some
      material that wasn't readily available, and that's how I wrote The
      Jesuit. The problem with The Jesuit was that I knew all the big
      set pieces. They had all been recorded. All that dialogue I had.
      But I had to link them up in a way that would appear seamless
      to the audience and that's why I devised the soldiers as a kind of

14

chorus. And of course they all began to take on characters of their own and the play came on from there. Just before The Jesuit was produced, I met Sandy Neilson and it was working with Sandy that really brought me on as a playwright, because he is a very fine director. A good playwright needs that. You need somebody to tell you that something works – or doesn't. I think that if I've got any regrets in my life, it's that I've done so little directing myself. I could have been a very good director, I think. And if I'd pushed myself earlier, I might have done more directing.

JH: Would you have directed your own plays or other people's plays as well?

DC: I did direct both. My first production was a play by John McGrath called Plugged into History, and later on I directed plays by Tom Wright and a Swedish writer, Malin Lagerlof. Then I directed my own Blackfriars Wynd and the Scott adaptations, Heart of Midlothian and St Ronan's Well. I also wrote and directed a play about McGonagall called An Audience for McGonagall. But I never got to direct really top talents. Although I did direct David Hayman and Phyllis Logan with the actors that took part in The Miller's Reel on radio. I just wish that I had done more.

WP: Do you read much classical drama – by which I mean Shakespeare and Marlowe?

DC: Oh, yes, I have done. That was when I was in London. And the interesting thing about that is that people think of that, particularly Shakespeare, as high literature. But you can look at the plays from the point of view of the director, about how you can move them, how you can light them, how you can develop the performance, etc, and that's how they interest me. What I mean is that you very often find yourself in conversation with somebody about Shakespeare and they're talking about Hamlet, say, and they're discussing it as if it were a poem and they are talking simply in terms of text. A play has always got more to it than that.

WP: I do teach Act I, scene I of Hamlet as a poem because, I say to students: You need something which will do this (shouting) "Who's there? / Nay, answer me. Stand and unfold yourself."

DC: How do you say it? That's it, you see.

WP: The great poems have a voice.

DC: But a play is more flexible. The best plays have many voices. They are attractive to write for that reason.

JH: When you were writing poetry and performing it extremely finely with, for instance, The Heretics, I always felt that you had a particular rapport with an audience and that that was possibly part of what turned you towards drama.

DC: Oh, yes. As far as my own performances were concerned, I think it has something to do with my genes. There's a sense in which I come from a family of entertainers. My grandfather in the days prior to the First Wold War appeared in the Free and Easies, which was a sort of basic type of music hall. He was fairly well known in Edinburgh for his singing. His daughter was also a performer. And in my mother's family I had an aunt who used to play regularly in the Rifle Hall in Wick. There was a lot of that sort of thing going on in my family. They were all bloody theatre critics. I mean, my Granny was the most acerbic theatre critic I have ever known. She was worse than Joyce McMillan.

JH: But the relationship between the playwright and the audience is much less direct in a way than this thing of performing poets. How did you find that transition?

DC: Well you have to do it through the actors, that's the real problem. You have to rely on actors to get that. One of the things I find very interesting is what we call the Convention, the relationship between the audience and the play. You know about Brecht and the alienation effect? Well, that's the same sort of idea. Brecht thought if you could present somebody with something familiar in unfamiliar circumstances, you would get a big effect – and you do. But that's part of play writing for me as well.

WP: So it's the stage, the bracketing by the stage, which is what makes it a play?

DC: Well, you have to pay attention to the context – and, please bear in mind, most of my plays were commissioned for a specific space, a particular theatre. If I'm writing for, say, the Lyceum, I know that we're going to have tabs, I know that we're going to have a safety curtain. I know that the audience are going to come in and sit down in these rows. I know that they probably want an ice-cream in the interval. And it's a familiar place. So I write in a particular way. More than at the Lyceum, at the King's. When my last play, Glorious Hearts was on, I knew there was a football crowd coming in to the King's. The play is about the Hearts football club, and there's one scene in which Jake, who is the archetypal supporter, suddenly turns his back on the team, throws his scarf away, saying: "They're useless. I'm not supporting them any more." It's a very, very difficult scene – but it was essential for the play. And the actor who played it, Lewis Howden, is known to be a devoted Hearts supporter. As a playwright, you're really on a knife edge in that scene – but I knew that I could get away with it. I know Hearts supporters. I know my audience. And when I was leaving the theatre, I heard people talking about that scene – and I know that I did get away with it.

WP: I suppose, thinking about classical Greek theatre, Athens was a relatively intimate town where Euripides, Sophokles or Aristophanes would know personally a fair proportion of their audience; would know what would get a laugh, which politician was on the make, and so on.

DC: All the best theatre is like that. It's even true in the West End, with the big musicals. They know that they're playing to sponsored audiences, they know they're playing to tourists, and that changes the way things are presented. Scientists talk now about something we've always known in the theatre; that once something is observed, it is changed. And that's the secret at the heart of theatre actually, it's knowing how the change will take place and how the audience will react to a play.

WP: And presumably you never want your audience to react as though they were witnessing real events, so that when Polonius is stabbed by Hamlet, you don't want anyone 'phoning the police.

DC: They make that suspension of disbelief. That's part of the deal.

JH: In the last few years you have spent a lot of your energy in writing a history of the Scottish theatre. I wondered if you wanted to air any thoughts on the present state of Scottish theatre?

DC: It's pretty much in a mess. In a way it's a victim of its own success. In the 70s when I started, a bit of fresh air was coming through the Scottish theatre and everybody was doing new things. Even then, though, we had our problems. I can remember having a conversation with Tom McGrath and John Byrne at the Traverse. We all had plays on there at the time. Somebody said: "If you don't have a full-house every performance, you've failed." That sort of overtook the Scottish theatre, a situation where it was so successful that if it wasn't successful commercially, it had failed. That I think is part and parcel of what is wrong today. Commercial success is equated with artistic success – so the people who are regarded as successful are those writers who play it safe, with the consequence that there's a great absence of risk taking and, therefore, genuine achievement. I feel that in all the arts but particularly in theatre and literature, the people who are getting the opportunities today are people whose work is derivative, who are to a certain extent part of the cosmopolitan agenda. That makes it very difficult for a Scots playwright to start even thinking about doing something original. The big problem with our generation was that the people who had gone before us, all their work had vanished, so that they didn't have any influence. I know of people who were writing in the twenties and thirties, like George Reston Malloch. I managed to find and read a play by George Reston Malloch but it wasn't easily available to me. Joe Corrie wasn't particularly available to me. So we didn't have a sense of continuity; we had to start from scratch really. I suppose the beginning of the modern Scottish theatre came with Bill Bryden's play Willie Rough. But now we're getting to the stage where what we did in that time, it is being forgotten too.

WP: But not the same forgetting. What matters perhaps is where the language of authority lives; the language of the Court, of law, of Parliament, of the Church, of education. After the loss of the Court, Scotland never had a theatrical tradition associated with the language of authority.

DC: That's true.

WP: So that the work you're talking about was always going to disappear. It wasn't going to be published or played in the West End. Political power and the language of authority are Siamese twins. Scottish theatre was always peripheral to the mainstream of British cultural life.

DC: Yes, that may be true. But there's always been an underground culture as well. It's the underground that commands my loyalty – and always has. Of course, when you bring that underground culture up before the public, you get this alienation effect. Alex Scott used to say – for the simple and good reasons you've just given – that's why we have to go to the Music Hall, to Variety, and, to a certain extent, we did. When you look at Hector MacMillan's earliest plays, the sort of approach he's taking is the sort of approach you would get from somebody like Johnnie Victory or Lex Maclean, although it's for serious and not comedy purposes.

WP: From The Three Estaites there is a huge gap because the Kirk rules Scotland and there is no secular literature to speak of. After about 1711, associated with the Acts of Toleration and the Kirk no longer having a veto on Chairs in the Scottish universities, literature begins to revive. But it has nowhere to go for its models, no classical sources. So you get Allan Ramsay and The Tea Table Miscellany and the Border Ballads and Burns collecting material in the Highlands. There is a return to popular and folk traditions. So perhaps after the dead time of the 19th century, you have go to the Music Hall.

DC: Exactly. But the other thing too is that theatrical practicalities have to be observed, irrespective of the size of the theatre you are in. For instance, during most of the 19th. century, the most popular theatre in Scotland was the Theatre Royal in Edinburgh. And it was very much made a success by adaptations of Walter Scott classics and by plays like The Gaberlunzie Man by Ballantyne. And the reason for that was that William Murray, who was running the theatre, realised he could make money from that kind of theatre. I have written about that in my book Playing for Scotland. But of course, anything I say about Scottish theatre today could change with a production that opens tomorrow. You never know.

WP: Are you disappointed in how you find the Scottish cultural world now?

DC: I would like people to be a bit more inventive, a bit more imaginative. I think it is unfortunate, to say the least, disgraceful that someone like Eddie Morgan is regarded as our greatest living poet. I have always been very fond of him and I do like his verse – but I never thought he was a great poet.

WP: Is it not just that people will say that for a while because he is very old?

DC: That's probably it.

WP: I think it is Ezra Pound who says somewhere that to be acclaimed as a great poet, at least for a while, the secret is to live to a great age.

JH: I wonder also what you think about the tendency in Scottish culture – probably in world culture – to regard more and bigger as better. For instance, the Edinburgh Book Festival. We are told that because the E.B.F. is bigger than ever, therefore this is a cultural advance. To me, this has nothing to do with culture at all. It is all to do with promoting commerce.

DC: Of course it is.

JH: I find a fatal confusion between culture and commercial promotion in contemporary cultural activity. I wonder what you feel about that?

DC: Well, I think small is beautiful. The great thing about Scottish culture, which has kept me interested for so long, is its diversity. There are so many different aspects you can explore and think about. I quite enjoy blockbusters and bestsellers. I quite enjoy reading these sort of things. I am entertained by them. In fact, there's got to be room for all that as well. There's got to be room for diversity. Something that I did feel was an achievement, without any doubt whatsoever, was Irving Welsh's Trainspotting. It was an achievement because at the time it was published, it was exemplary for a particular generation – people that had been touched by drugs. It went a long way to explain to people what drug addiction was about. But it is not a great novel, I don't think. It is not a brilliant piece of writing – but it is an achievement. On the other hand, our best young playwrights – the likes of David Greig and Anthony Neilson – probably write better, but achieve less.

WP: Is there a confusion in our talk of "great writing" and commerce? Important art, surely, is something which generates and requires a certain intensity of attention focused on a core of values. When you read, say, John MacDonald of Keppoch, or Rob Donn or any of the major Gaelic poets, their audiences were minimal by any standards. Nor was it meant to be otherwise. Their work was delivered orally to an audience with which the author was intimate. There is a set of clear, quasi-tribal, traditional values briskly set forth with whatever panache and aplomb, within a well-understood set of conventions. And so they were celebrated and were celebrating a culture. They had, if not direct payment, role and status. It is not easy now, by comparison, for a writer to know what he or she is about.

DC: I wonder about the question of motivation. What I can tell you about Rob Donn is that I know that from the age of four improvising verses was something he did. He might have been a singer, he might have played the fiddle or whatever but he improvised verses and he never lost that gift and he was always in demand.

WP: Do you mean that in the Gaelic tradition that was what they were brought up to do?

DC: No, I mean that the tradition allowed such talents to flourish. It is not the individual.

WP: Is it, then, impersonal?

DC: Well, it is certainly not a matter of vanity. Just being given the opportunity to do it is what really matters. You don't actually say: "I am going to be a celebrity". Some people think: "I would like to be a celebrity." But it's not something I think most writers would aim for, though most would be quite happy if it happened.

WP: But what about those like MacDiarmid or Yeats whose aim is explicitly to shift the bias of a whole cultural tradition?

DC: They are usually hated of course. You know MacDiarmid was deeply hated. I got a piece of that when I wrote a radio programme called The Root to a Tree about MacDiarmid to celebrate the centenary of his birth. You wouldn't believe the amount of abuse and hostility I received! And it had nothing to do with me, it was to do with MacDiarmid – and it was all very childish. "You say he was great but he wasn't. He was horrible, a nasty piece of work" and all this sort of thing. But he always knew that would happen. And he knew it would happen to those who wrote about him. I mentioned that the last time I met him and he said: "What you're doing now, it will bring you nothing but trouble." And he was right.

WP: Did he have a sort of emotional ability to deal with that which most of us, I think, don't?

DC: He was tough enough to take it.

WP: It was a kind of vanity, but strangely impersonal. It was, I think, that he felt at some level that he had been touched by Destiny.

DC: Yes. He saw his aggressiveness as a duty. It was a persona. Ewan McColl was a great hero of mine. Towards the end of his life, McColl was being interviewed on television: "All these causes you have followed, you know, the miners, socialism, all the rest, all these fights you have taken part in, they've all failed, haven't they, they've all come to nothing?" And McColl's reply to that was extremely dignified: "Well," he said, "It's been a good fight." I thought; that says everything. It was something worth doing and

23

he was proud to have done it. And John Maclean and people like that, MacDiarmid included, they would all have said the same.

JH: Do you feel that, for your own work, what you've done has been worth it? Do you feel that you have achieved what you wanted to achieve when you set out as a writer?

DC: I think I probably achieved more than I set out to. What I do know is that as far as my own work is concerned, there's not very much more I'd like to do. I mean, I'd like to finish my work on Rob Donn and show its importance, apart from anything else. And I do get a lot of satisfaction from it. But as far as my drama's concerned, all my plays are written.

WP: That's an extraordinary thing to say.

DC: Well, it's true. I can't think of anything I would want to write now.

WP: Does that not sound alarmingly like a happy man?

DC: Yes, well I am. I am happy because the books that I wanted to write, my book on Scottish theatre, my book about Edinburgh, they're written. I have a degree of pride in my history of the Lyceum. But all these things I've done, all the radio programmes, the television – I've done very little television, but I have done some – I mean, apart from the experience and the money, there's nothing would give me much satisfaction left.

WP: But all that comes to a lot of work.

DC: That's right, yes. My stage-plays alone number twenty-nine – including contemporary plays, historical plays, adaptations, solo plays and musicals. They have all been professionally produced, a number of them have received awards, one or two of them have been published and some of them have even enjoyed the privilege of revival. More importantly, though, they have all been written in the teeth of intense opposition. People have been trying to undermine my writing since the very beginning but they haven't succeeded. In spite of them, I've survived.

WP: Do you think of yourself as a religious man?

DC: Well, I hesitate to answer that because in some ways I am and in other ways I'm not. I'm not a churchgoer but I am aware of spiritual dimensions in my life. And also in the things I've been writing about, the things we've been talking about, there's always a spiritual dimension.

WP: But if you are a Highlander, you see...

DC: Well, that's part of it. I was also baptised into the Free Church. I grew up in it. I had the experience of sitting through the sermons and that's important too. I think Ian Grimble makes this point too about Rob Donn. One of the reasons his elegies are so finely honed is because of these sermons he had to sit through. I remember Sam saying that as well.

WP: He said something similar to me as well.

DC: You remember when we were in Cambridge?

WP: Yes, that extraordinary night...

DC: That's what he said then.

WP: He said too that but for the translations of the Old and New Testaments into Gaelic, Gaelic would not have survived, that it would have lost too much of the range of its vocabulary.

DC: I'm sure that's true.

WP: That was an important occasion for Maclean.

DC: Yes, he really came into his own then.

WP: It has to be said that you were partly responsible for it. You recall, the first readers were, I think, Roy Fuller and David Gascoyne. You couldn't hear them. They were so quiet, reading as understated, English academic poets – and tedious. And Maclean came on. And he dropped his papers and muttered and he fumbled and he read brilliantly, passionately. As he so often did, with this hwyl, this wonderful Celtic noise. And he had his audience – and this is broadcast on the Third Programme – hypnotised. And, of course, Sam could do that. And at the end of his first reading, there was a silence. And Donald, you were seated next to me or one along from me, and started to do that (stamping foot slowly) and gradually it was taken up and the whole audience eventually rose – and it was Donald who began it. And Sam was always grateful for that because he knew that...

DC: Because I shouted Curaidhean (Heroes) across to him. He just picked up the book and said: "This is a poem called Heroes. It's about an Englishman but it's not an anti-English poem." And he read it, first in English, then in Gaelic. And they were spellbound. When I met him afterwards, I said: "Well, that was good, Sam. It was the right one to read." I'm not sure he was too pleased. He said, rather irritably: "I heard you. I heard you."

WP: He was an extraordinary creature. We were privileged to know Maclean and MacDiarmid.

DC: Yes, and it's worth remembering no other generation could know them as we did. I mean, their contemporaries could not know them as we did for their work had yet to be accomplished and no generation after ours can know them at all. And, of course, it wasn't just MacDiarmid and Maclean. There was Geerie (Robert Garioch) as well, and Sydney Smith.

WP: And they were all part of a fabric.

DC: Great changes were brought about by them and I don't think people realise nowadays how much of a change was effected. One of my colleagues when I was at Napier, was the poet Jim C. Wilson. We were talking about MacDiarmid one time and it became clear to me that Jim had never actually been exposed to the charisma that was Chris. To him MacDiarmid was just another poet and I tried to explain to him exactly why Chris was so important. I thought of that time Lady Antonia Fraser had done a book of Scottish love poems and there was this big reception in the Demarco Gallery and I was a bit reticent about going because I wasn't in the book but Alan Bold dragged me along. We all had to go and meet Lady Antonia and she was very nice and polite and said: "How pleasant of you to come," and there was a whole group of poets standing round her. And then Chris came in. He walked in the door and immediately the whole room went 'whoosh', like that, all the poets crossed the room to meet MacDiarmid, so that Lady Antonia was left stranded and had to push her way through and introduce herself.

WP: Because here, suddenly, is the real thing.

JH: There's a sense in those years that even if they didn't get on – and poets and novelists were extremely diverse, often loathed each other – yet there was a sense of their all being part of a cohesive literary scene. And not just a literary scene but also it merged into a political scene.

DC: That's right, with a sense of family.

JH: The watershed, I would say, was the Referendum of 1979. After that, there was a sense of everybody going off and doing their own thing. And that cohesive sense of communal identity that there was, disappeared. That must have affected us all in some degree. Do you think it affected you as an individual writer?

DC: I think it certainly affected the way that people looked at me.
      Before that, I was known as a dramatist. After that happened, I
      became a local Edinburgh playwright. That's the way I like to put
      it, anyway. When I went to the Lyceum first in the 1970s, there
      was a sense that we were going to do something very distinctive
      in Scottish theatre. I was promised that by the director who was
      not really all that committed but he did have the idea, as we did,
      and we were going to try and make some sort of impact and it
      wasn't just me. There was Hector MacMillan as well and Stuart
      Conn and Sue Glover. We were all going to have our plays done in
      the Lyceum; to Hell with this whole idea of National Theatre, we
      would make our own National Theatre in the Lyceum. And then,
      of course the Referendum and Mrs. Thatcher comes to power and
      there is that huge sense of disillusion, of a bubble bursting, that's
      when it all went wrong. I was able to influence things to some
      extent up till that point.

WP: Yes, it was that sense of a loss of influence which was so damaging
      in Scotland then.

DC: For instance, Joan Bakewell, the 'thinking man's crumpet' as
      she used to be known. She offered to help. She approached me
      one night, right out of the blue, gave me her telephone number
      and said "Remember to 'phone me if there are any sudden new
      developments." Unfortunately, there never were.

WP: Of course, if the Referendum had gone through, the political
      set-up we would have had, would have been immensely less
      legislatively powerful, even given the squad of fourth-raters we
      got, than what we have now.

DC: Yes. But I don't think the political thing is the difficulty. The
      difficult thing as far as artists are concerned is that what we're
      having, witnessing in Scotland at the moment, is the creation
      of an Establishment. Now, I remember, years ago, we used to

get these visits from Irish poets. There was an Irish poet called Martin O' Direan who I met in Stuart MacGregor's house.

JH: Yes, I remember him.

DC: We had a long conversation about Ireland and the situation there. And Martin said to me – we were talking about O'Casey and people like that – "Of course, that was all in the good old, exciting days before the Treaty and before we started to get an Establishment." That's what's happening in Scotland now. Its new Establishment is coming into being. And they're going to set the agenda as far as a lot of things are concerned.

WP: For a while. So this is the transitional phase?

DC: They have to be attacked.

JH: But it is an Establishment this is completely lacking in cultural values.

WP: But what would you have said of De Valera?

JH: The same.

WP: And, of course, Yeats did say it: "Had De Valera eaten Parnell's heart." His standard, De Valera's ambition for Ireland was a feeble, rural Catholic primitivism.

DC: I wonder if this is a stage every country has to go through? I think we have to have this. The thing that strikes me about the devolutionary settlement is that although we've got a parliament and an executive and a first minister and all of that, the politicians still behave as though they were under a Secretary of State. They have to be got out of that. They have to start taking initiatives. Allan Massie had a rather strange article in The Scotsman last week-end. He made a comparison between Scotland and the Republic of Ireland, which ignores the fact that Scotland's parliament has absolutely no responsibility for industrial and economic policy. And what he was saying was that the Scottish Executive is failing and they could learn some lessons from Ireland. But the thing was, Haughey, whose death provoked the article, was Taoiseach of an independent country having to deal with its own industrial and economic problems, problems which no first minister has ever even had to think about.

JH: That logic is bound to penetrate the consciousness of other commentators and is already beginning to do so.

WP: Since when did Massie support any aspect of any Scottish Executive?

JH: My friend, Willie Archibald used to say, "Of course, after independence, these people will say: 'We were always nationalists'."

DC: It's happening now. That's what's happening with the National Theatre now. It's people sticking their snouts into the trough, saying, "Yes, well we've always wanted a Scottish National Theatre."

WP: Do you think we are on an inevitable track to some sort of severance – from England?

DC: I don't know about that. It has struck me, that, strangely enough, the creation of a Scottish executive has in some ways invigorated the whole idea of a British identity.

JH: Has it not, in fact, invigorated the idea of an English identity?

DC: Well, that's part of it. Prior to this the notion of English identity was so unhealthy. It got in the way of any sense of Britishness. You know, the English insisting that the terms Britain and England were interchangeable, so that everyone was really English and the other British identities were nothing more than meaningless conceits. And now they've got to ask: "Well, am I really English?" And I think that's a good thing. It appears to me that English people, when they settle in Scotland, certainly when they settle in Edinburgh, within ten minutes they suddenly start assuming a Scottish identity. When I was writing the Edinburgh book, the editor, James Fergusson, asked me to write a chapter about the various nationalities that live in the city. He said to me, "And don't forget the English." Well there are Greeks and Italians and Palestinians and Frenchmen, but with English people it's not really possible to write about them in the same way. They don't form English societies, they don't form a distinctive English community. They just try to blend in as much as they can. When I was visiting schools a lot, I found that English parents would often complain about their children being taught Scottish literature because they came from Kent or wherever. I don't know if that still happens. On the other hand, I remember giving a reading in Balintore and the publican's accent would not have been out of place in East Enders, kept saying, (in a marked London accent) "Well, we've got so much culture up here. We've got the Gaylick language, and we got all this mewsick."

WP: To return to what you said earlier about folk music and the Scots language coming back periodically, don't they come back as something different, as nostalgia, a kind of substitute authenticity. And the debate about authenticity goes back to the eighteenth century, with Diderot and Le neveu de Rameau. After all, when you no longer have court poets or composer-musicians, or painters, how do you establish your credentials, your bona fides, if nobody is hiring you?

DC: Well, I have to point out here that, over the past thirty years, people did hire me. As I said earlier, most of either theatre companies, publishers or the B.B.C. commissioned my work. That was drama, of course. I've only ever had one poetry commission – from the Guardian in 1990 I think. However, I do take your point.

WP: So it's fair to ask, what are you doing it for and what are your standards of authenticity? If you no longer have a chief for whom you are to write praise poems or elegies, so you no longer have a direct social role. Well, what do you do? If you're a romantic? Well, in that case, your standard of authenticity becomes some kind of notion of sincerity, which very soon falls apart because there's nothing to it, a mere egotism, or it can become some kind of technical brilliance. So you, I mean serious writers, are caught in this terrible dilemma. The last of the great eighteenth century English poets to have a sense of real power, was Byron – and I do think he was an 18th. century figure – because he was a member of the House of Lords. The sense of power and status didn't have to come from the poetry. The sense of authority came from his life and got translated into the poetry – into satire and denunciation and a sense of range and freedom and influence.

DC: And Wordsworth for other reasons.

WP: Wordsworth is doing a kind of English Burns in Lyrical Ballads, where strong, apparently ordinary, popular language becomes a kind of source of authority and authenticity, or integrity.

DC: What do you make of someone like John Clare who has never had the same impact as Burns?

WP: But then Clare was never attempting the kind of social impact Wordsworth aimed at.

DC: But to be fair to Clare, he wasn't all that in control of himself. He's always been a poet I wanted to look more closely at. That's one of the things I'll maybe get round to now. I think one of the things I've done as a writer recently which I found quite interesting was writing a number of entries for the Dictionary of Scottish Women – I did some of the actresses. And I quite enjoyed doing that because it meant research.

WP: You're going to turn into a scholar!

DC: The thing is there are no scholars as far as Scottish Theatre History is concerned.

WP: Grieve once said to me: " Real scholarship is a far rarer thing than genius."

DC: Lots of people have talent but to get by in the Theatre, you need genius. Barrie said that Talent and Genius are different things. Grieve used to say talent is the enemy of the best.

JH: And talent is the enemy of genius. He said that as well. Someone you often used to mention in your youth, as having a key influence on you, that you haven't mentioned today is Mayakovsky. Where does he come in and what did he mean for you?

DC: I read Mayakovsky in English translation of course. What I found exciting about him was his success as a performer – his idea of spoken verse – and Yevtushenko was another. I actually saw him. I think his poetry is attractive too. Mayakovsky had charisma.

WP: So did Yevtushenko for a while.

DC: Yevtushenko very definitely had.

WP: Yes, he was a kind of pop star of the sixties.

WP: What about the friends you made in your time in London. Did it include any of the writers?

DC: Well, it was mostly musicians. In Lithuanian House my best friend was a cartoonist called Sax. He was actually a Latvian, one of their aristocracy, so he was ethnically German. He did cartoons for The Weekend magazine. He had been all through the war. And there was another guy in Lithuania House at the same time as him, called Theo, also a Latvian and a cartoonist but not an ethnic German, and during the war he had fought with the partisans in the forests in Latvia while Sax had been in the German army. So you can imagine the relationship – don't mention the war! And they had both gone to the same school. Theo gave me a present when I left, a recording of Smetana's Ma Vlast. At the end of the war he had been captured by the Americans and put into this internment camp on the Vltava.

WP: Yes, well the Americans got as far as a southern edge of Czechoslovakia.

DC: Well, he must have got that far. Anyway, he used to cry every time he heard this. He was a huge man and he would bawl and cry. And he had terrible nightmares. And of course, I didn't know anything about these terrible events for the war hadn't touched me at all. And Sax, he was one of the guys my father was trying to kill. It was interesting to talk to him and to know that he didn't have any real choice in the matter at all.

WP: What do you think you might still write, apart from your Rob Donn translations?

DC: I don't know how long it will take me to do that – and it rather depends on my health. If I go into remission, I can stay in remission for twenty years – and finish my Rob Donn.

WP: And what about poems?

DC: I'm not going to say no. It just creeps up on you now and then.

WP: Maybe after a certain time they don't creep up on you and you have to search them out?

DC: On the other hand, Walter, there is another aspect to the Rob Donn thing. You see, the Rob Donn work I do, they are not strictly speaking translations. There are a couple of reasons for that, apart from the fact that my Gaelic is not really very great, there is some doubt about the integrity of the originals themselves. I was just this morning looking at one in which he complains about ministers. And looking at each of the stanzas, I realised very quickly that they were higgledy-piggledy. I don't know how that happened.

WP: They were taken down from memory, presumably.

DC: That's right. It was the daughter of a local minister who wrote them down. She could have got things wrong. He could have said – Oh, I forgot, there's another bit. There's one stanza and, you think, that doesn't belong there at all.

WP: I tried to do something similar with the Gododdin a couple of years ago, which is a complete jumble. I gave up, but such work is never wasted.

DC: Well with Rob Donn sometimes it's quite obvious. You move a stanza and it just falls into place. One that I've done, it's a flyting, called Donald of the Lugs, where it's obvious that the penultimate verse should be the last. So switching them round, the whole thing works. And while I'm doing things like that, and taking the freedom to do that, it's almost like doing your own poems again. But with the big projects, each play would usually take me three months. And probably the last month was the most intensive. And then of course, once you've done it you've got the rehearsals and then you have more work to do. Depending on the director, you'll probably have rewrites.

WP: Is there a terrible anti-climax after that?

DC: Sometimes there is. What is interesting is that once you've got it up and it's going, I lose interest in it. Barrie used to be like that. He used to say he could go to the rehearsal of anything because at the rehearsal people were working. In performance, people were enjoying themselves and he didn't see why he should spend time and money watching people enjoying themselves.

WP: I lose interest once something is published. Until then, it's still alive.

DC: I always tell my students, you can learn so much when the thing is published. You turn around from looking at it as a writer to looking at it as a reader.

JH: Do you have any parental interest in your work, about its survival? Have you any interest in that?

DC: I would like to think it would survive. I put all my plays on to floppy disk and I deposited them with the Scottish Theatre Archive so that anybody that's interested, wanted to do one of the plays, they can go and get it and they can work on it. But sometimes I actually see it happening. If I go and see Blackfrians Wynd – which is often done by amateur groups – I get quite nervous. I see an actor singing a song that Robert Pettigrew and I wrote in 1980 and I remember our experiences as we were writing the song and it just amuses me to see someone approaching it fresh. It is a strange sort of experience.

WP: Are you perhaps more interested in the process than in the final product?

DC: I probably am. I remember one particular occasion. They were doing Widows of Clyth in Dundee. One of the widows, Helen, was being played by Ann Louise Ross, and Markie, who's the character in the play was being played by an actor called Ross Mackay, a very fine actor but he was a bit stiff and we needed to get the tension out of him. We were working on a scene and Ann Louise had this idea, perhaps Helen quite fancies Markie? So she immediately started playing the scene like that and it broke Ross up and from then on he was fine. It was a practical and important thing to do. Also, working with actors, you discover an awful lot of things about your own writing. Roy Hanlon, a fine actor who's dead now, also in The Widows of Clyth, had a scene in which I wanted him to explode into an angry speech. Roy could be quite an angry man, but this time he told me: I'm not going to do it like that. And he did it, quietly, very quietly – and got the effect. He knew what I wanted – and showed me how to get it.

WP: What do you think the theatre is for?

DC: It's to enable people to gather in one place. I think human beings have a need to congregate. Churches used to do it. When our churches were packed, they fulfilled that need. And that's why the state of Scotland is deficient. People will always have that need.

WP: But Scotland is almost entirely now an urban society.

DC: Well, I'm basically an urban writer. One of the things I really loved doing was Glorious Hearts in the King's, which was the first theatre I ever worked in, a stage hand in a 1950s pantomime. It was the first time any of my plays had been done there and as people were coming in they were, quite obviously, relaxed. Brecht used to talk about that. He would call them a cigar-smoking audience. It made a huge difference as far as the performance was concerned.

JH: You have mentioned Brecht a few times. Brecht in his early poetry was very much the performer. He liked to sing his songs to the guitar...

37

DC: Singer song-writer. He was a huge con artist. Most people don't realise that Brecht didn't write his plays. At least, he didn't write plays in the sense that most playwrights do. He didn't write in the sense that I would write a play, he didn't grind out the dialogue and shape the scenes. It was the women he was living with who usually did the hard work. At the same time one of my favourite anecdotes illustrates Brecht's genius. At the time of the first production of The Threepenny Opera, Brecht's girlfriend was a girl called Elizabeth Hauptmann. In fact, there seems to be some evidence to suggest that she had made a modern German translation of Gay's Beggar's Opera before Brecht set up the production. The reason that Brecht's name was given the credit was that he'd recently had a success with a play called Drums in the Night. So the thing was to be done as a play by Bertolt Brecht. They had tremendous difficulty with that production. There was much clashing of egos and they lost two or three of the cast. Then, about the time of the dress rehearsal, the guy who was playing Mackie Meissner – an actor called Harald Paulssen – comes up to the dress rehearsal in a pin-stripe suit, trilby hat, a white shirt, red handkerchief, red gloves and black patent leather shoes. The producer – the moneyman – was furious. He wanted Mackie to look like a criminal, not a city gent. "I have paid good money for your costume. Why aren't you wearing it?" Paulssen said, "This is what I'm wearing in the show. And if you don't want this, I'm gone." And as this argument was going on, Brecht took the producer aside and said: "Look, let him have his costume. Kurt and I will write a song which will make it clear to the audience that he is a gangster." And that very night they wrote Mack the Knife. In the first verse of Mack the Knife.

    Oh, the Shark has pretty teeth dear
    And he keeps them pearly white
    All MacHeath needs is a jack-knife.
    But he keeps it out of sight.

And that song made the show, it made the opera. It made Brecht's whole career. It made him a cult figure.

WP: Do you agree that our individualism is over-played? That we are in fact much more communal creatures than this society allows us to be?

DC: We need to be. An awful lot of the time difficulties are created when people feel excluded from things. I felt excluded for most of my life, in the sense that I felt I had to fight for things. I don't regret having to but things haven't always come easily.

WP: Well, maybe if they came easily you wouldn't value them.

DC: That's absolutely true. People do have to have some sort of sense of belonging.

JH: You are very much an individualist and you have been working primarily in a communal medium. Do you think some of the difficulties you have experienced in the theatre have to do with that tension?

DC: Yes, absolutely. People you think are your friends will sometimes stab you in the back. I often feel pissed off. When I go to the theatre now, I pick up a programme and I see in the cast there are maybe two or three actors all of whom have performed in my plays but none of whom mention it in their blurbs. And I think; ungrateful bastards! Often too, though, this grows from their insecurities. And actors are always nice to you because they think you've got power.

WP: There are different kinds of authority. There is the authority that comes from writing well and knowing it. But many of the jealous people of whom you've spoken in the theatre are not writers. So they don't have to care about that. Poetry's easier because almost no one reads it anyway. But also it is more enduring.

DC: Plays pass. No-one will ever again see Harry Stamper as Spottiswoode or Michael Burrell as Ogilvie. That is gone forever.

JH: You are dealing with a medium in which a lot of other people are involved, a director, actors. And a lot can depend on their conception of your work. Do you ever look back on your poetry and think: Well, in a way this has got a more permanent life than your drama, because although the drama is there on the page, that's not the point of drama. And it may be performed again or it may not. A poem is there, always, and anyone can come to it at any time and create it for themselves?

DC: I do feel that as far as some poems are concerned. Others, I know they're just gone. Some I know, because I know they mean something to somebody, I think, well, they're likely to have a longer life. There are one or two poems in my Selected Poems of which I am particularly fond, but I know that they don't have much more of a life than that. However, people do say to me that they remember particular poems. One that's seemingly very popular is one I wrote for Bold called "Prince Marmaduke", about a cat, a children's poem. Alan was editing a Scottish poetry book for kids and he wanted me to write a poem for it. And I said: "No, I don't think I can do that." And he said: "I bet you can. You've got to write one and I want one." Well, I would do anything for Alan Bold except go for a drink with him – that could prove dangerous – and so I wrote the poem. Now people keep telling me that they remember my poem, "Marmaduke".

JH: I know several poems of yours that I can recite by heart and that must mean something. What do you feel now about the future of poetry in Scots?

DC: Well, it's a bit like folk music; people are always thinking – it's finished, it's died away. But it keeps coming back. Of the younger poets that I know – perhaps not so young now – one who has certainly impressed me is William Hershaw, and there's Matthew

40

Fitt. There's something about this tradition that encourages people to carry on with it. This is like another conversation I had with Jim C. He argues that people often think that when you write in Scots, it gives your poetry much more validity. I could never agree with that but I can understand why people have that idea. It's not just the words, it's the idioms, the Lowland Scots idioms. I can see the attraction that people have to that and I think it will continue. Of course, it's bound to change. I've seen huge differences in the poetry that was being written by poets like Sheena Blackhall and Raymond Vettese as opposed to the kind of Scots verse that I grew up with. There's a big difference there.

WP: Well, Violet Jacob and Marion Angus and those people who were more or less contemporary with Grieve were writing out of what was often a very full canon of Scots. And Scots was still a widely used language.

JH: There continues to be a sense in which the tacit knowledge of Scots allows Scots to read, say, Dunbar, in a way in which the English reader can't.

WP: I think Donald's right to say that what readers recognise in Burns or Dunbar or whoever, are idioms, that is, ways of thinking.

DC: Ways of thinking and feeling, which is a good definition of what a culture is.

2. DUNCAN GLEN

Duncan Glen (1933-2008): Poet, critic and publisher. Founder of Akros Magazine and Publications. Played an important role in re-establishing the reputation of Hugh MacDiarmid in the 1960s and 1970s

This conversation took place at Duncan's home in Kirkcaldy on June 27th. 2006. Present were John Herdman and Walter Perrie.

WALTER PERRIE: Could you say a little, Duncan, about your family background?

DUNCAN GLEN: During my mother's childhood, and until she was married in 1930, she lived on farms owned by my grandfather, George Tennent. Initially in a small farm with a half-thatched roof at East Greenlees on the East Kilbride side of Cambuslang and, from 1920, at Nerston, a hamlet with several dairy farms near East Kilbride. Somewhat unexpectedly, my uncle sold the Nerston property to Robert Wiseman and so now the farmhouse that I knew as a boy is the headquarters of Robert Wiseman Dairies, plc. In my grandfather's day that kitchen was alive each weekend with the buzz of conversation and the smell of good food. There was no drink as my grandfather was a vigorous supporter of the temperance movement. It was a mixed gathering at that large round table. It could include a lawyer, a dentist, at least one minister and farming neighbours, as well as members of the ILP and the Co-operative movement and men who were there because of the daughters of the house; my father was one of these.

WP: This bespeaks a certain prosperity on your grandfather's part.

DG: That's true. And also it bespeaks that, mostly house-bound with arthritis, he liked conversation. He had firm convictions but could see others' points of view. He was not a pacifist, having two sons who volunteered for the First World War, one of whom died on the Somme, but he supported the East Kilbride Free Church minister who preached pacifism. That man left East Kilbride but he came back to perform the marriage ceremony of my parents at Nerston. That was in 1930 so he had continued to come to the Tennent farm kitchen. There wouldn't be what we might call intellectual conversation, but it was that of educated men who liked mixing with a farmer and his dissimilar friends.

WP: Maybe the kind of conversation you would get in some Provençal farmhouses or in north Italy. It's very Scottish but it's Scottish of the eighteenth or nineteenth centuries.

JOHN HERDMAN: It sounds a bit reminiscent of the kind of milieu in which D. H. Lawrence might have moved, with that mixture of industrial, coal-mining and rural life, for he moved in a farming community as well, where there was a lot of informed, intelligent discussion.

DG: So that was my farming background, which gives a knowledge of country ways and language. I know not only the Scots names for birds and beasts but the vocabulary of the tackle of working horses and also riding horses – brechins, rigwuddies etc. I can put the haims and thaits onto a horse as well as on poets that need reining in! My grandfather, like his father before him, who was a coal merchant and contractor and a Baillie in Rutherglen, was vigorously independent; self-made and self-employed, never indebted to anyone outside the extended family. I have had the same attitudes – for better or worse!

WP: The world may have seemed more predictable then. I think a lot of this springs from a kind of optimism, an energy that goes with the belief that, like my grandparents, they saw, they thought, how they could make things better. Hard work and a rationalist view of improvement. Now to many I think the world seems like a lottery.

DG: On my father's side we were straightforward Cambuslang working class. My father's father was one of the first to be able to go into a steelworks rather than going down the pit like his older brothers, and in fact Glens worked in Cambuslang collieries from at least as far back as the 1690s. My grandfather was a moulder and so faced the furnaces and died young from heart disease. My father was a white-collar worker in the same Steel Company of Scotland at Hallside, near Newton Station. He told me, although not fond of looking back or boasting, that he was earning far more than his father by the time he was eighteen! He stayed at Hallside through the stressful war years and, earlier, the pressures of the amalgamation of the steel industry when Sir John Craig headed not only Colvilles in Motherwell and Cambuslang (at Clydebridge works) but also the Steel Company of Scotland at Hallside. My father cracked up and went to work for his in-laws at Nerston; a good healthy outdoor occupation but at first very hard for a man who had spent all his working life in an office. As a small boy I played with his huge bunch of keys. It was through that change of occupation that we ended up first in a cottage in the foothills of the Campsie Fells and then here in Fife. My father came here to run a herd of pedigree Tamworth pigs; going to shows all over the country. He really enjoyed that. So getting out of the steelworks ended up as a good thing for him. It didn't really involve me, any of that. I was semi-detached in many ways. But if we hadn't come to Fife I wouldn't have met Margaret who was born in Mallaig and had also lived in Stirling where she went to the High School, but she took her Highers here in Kirkcaldy. Our golden wedding is due this coming January.

WP: What age were you when you came to Fife?

DG: I would be 16 or 17. I didn't come right away to Fife from the Campsies. I stayed with an aunt in Giffnock. I was working for McCorquodale's, the large Glasgow printers, where I started when I left school. In my day you couldn't take your Highers without Higher Maths as well as Higher English.

WP: And O level Latin.

DG: That had changed for us during the war and I took German and
        not Latin, but you had to take two languages, French and another
        one. So I was taught German by Miss Lucy Dunn, during the
        war! She inducted us into her admiration for pre-Hitler Germany.
        This was at a time when, in the streets, we could pick up shrapnel
        that had been fired from anti-aircaft guns that stood on old
        disused coal bings. The German planes were on their way to blitz
        Clydebank and other towns with shipyards but occasionally they
        dropped bombs near us. There was no way I was going to pass
        Higher Maths at Rutherglen Academy. So, to my mother's anger
        and sorrow, I left school at 16. Our local minister (my father was
        an elder) got me a job in McCorquodale's, who did all the Church
        of Scotland printing. It was good training for me and I enjoyed
        being an office boy, because I was going round central Glasgow
        delivering small parcels. But I got bored with the routine of being
        a junior order clerk and began to ask for work from men who
        were in the same room as me who did estimates and costings.
        When I went into the Reading Room I was a copy holder. We read
        the copy to a reader and these were very good proofreaders. That
        was where I really learned good editorial practices. I enjoyed also
        being an apprentice compositor, but when I moved to work in
        Fife to be with my parents I got very, very bored and rebellious,
        and so I went to Edinburgh College of Art on an Andrew Grant
        Scholarship. That was before I did my National Service.

JH: Were you interested in poetry at that time, in literature at all?

DG: Oh, yes. When I was staying with my parents in Fife, I was
        writing more short stories than poems. I also wrote radio plays. I
        even sent one or two to the BBC but I didn't get anything going,
        but I was keen and interested. My next door neighbour, Eddie
        McGrory, thought I was odd, living in a farm cottage and going
        in for these literary things. His wife was the housekeeper in the

big house and Eddie was not into regular work, then or ever. Strangely Eddie ended up writing poetry for which I wrote Prefaces. He was keen on the Edinburgh literary world of the pubs, knowing Sydney Goodsir Smith; that would be in the 1970s, I think.

WP: How did you see yourself then?

DG: I don't know. I don't think I was sophisticated enough. When I was working in Glasgow, as an office boy, I bought many MacDiarmid first editions. Five shillings, *A Drunk Man Looks at the Thistle*, *Sangschaw*, *Penny Wheep*. So at 16 I was reading MacDiarmid, which was pretty unusual in these days.

WP: That must have been the low point in Chris's career.

DG: I didn't meet him then except briefly when he gave a talk at the Art College. At the College I printed some poems by MacDiarmid and I began to actually write about MacDiarmid just as I started National Service, starting on 9th May 1956. I don't remember dates or numbers but I remember that one as I do my service number – 5019703! I was quite old as a National Serviceman because I had been deferred for years and years. The aim was to be deferred until National Service was abolished. Now I don't know if many people remember this, but the Bibliotheck was first published then. The first issue printed a long checklist by Geoffrey Wagner on Lewis Grassic Gibbon and a lot of the references included MacDiarmid. And I immediately decided I would do a bibliography of MacDiarmid. I was an outsider but, while home on leave, I went along to Glasgow University to see the guy who edited The Bibliotheck and he snubbed me. A senior librarian in the Mitchell Library was very helpful, showing me a card index of a bibliography that he had started to compile. I went back to the RAF and started doing it anyway. When I was stationed at RAF Wyton, near Huntingdon, I got a day off to do educational work and mostly I went to Cambridge Art School, but

I also went to London to the round Reading Room of the British Museum of fond memories and that was when I began to research what became my MacDiarmid and the Scottish Renaissance book. When I got demobbed, we lived in London. So every spare moment I had, even when I was supposed to be working as a graphic designer, I worked on my MacDiarmid researches.

WP: What I would like to know is where all this really came from?

DG: Well I don't know. If you are born with a love of books and have a brain in your head, I think you just do it. When I was a boy in Cambuslang I was mad on football. I was really keen to be in the school football team. I was a bit crude as a football player. I can remember kicking the feet from a centre forward on the miners' pitch at Gateside Colliery, off Hamilton Road. And the miners had come off the back-shift with their black faces and I had just kicked somebody into the air, and they all advanced on me to do me up. So, I don't want to give the impression I was just a bookish boy. I really was keen on football but I was never all that good at it. On the bookish side I was never out of Cambuslang Public Library. Tom Leonard tells how he went to Hillhead and took extra books out. Well I did the same at Cambuslang. It was an absorption in books. It was all Eng.Lit. stuff at that time. It was only later that I learned about Scottish literature – and this is where MacDiarmid was important. It wasn't just the literature, the poetry, it was the rebel side of the man. Having been a left-wing radical, a natural rebel, that side of MacDiarmid appealed to me. From being quite a conventional reader, of literature and stuff that was accepted, I suddenly became interested in Scottish literature. And this is in the forties when it wasn't so much around then.

JH: Were you writing poetry yourself at this time?

DG: No, I didn't write anything really until I came through to Fife, that would be in 1950.

JH: Which is pretty young.

DG: I suppose so. I always thought I was a late starter. When I was
at Art College I set up poems by MacDiarmid, including 'The
Kulturkampf' which no one pays much attention to now but
which in my late teens I thought stirring stuff. It was not long in
print, having been published in the late 1940s by Maclellan in
A Kist of Whistles. A few years later, I went to see Bill Maclellan
in his printing works in Hope Street, Glasgow, and bought a
large quantity of magazines and poetry collections that he had
published in the 1940s and 1950s. Maclellan can be seen as an
example to all of us who have set up as small literary publishers.
Not in his way of working or general business methods, let me
hurriedly add. Whilst at the Art College I went to see Callum
Macdonald, who gave me a copy, I remember, of Jabberwock,
which had a lot of MacDiarmid in it. So by then I was really into
MacDiarmid and I was also writing quite a lot. But before I met
Margaret and before I was in Edinburgh, and when I was here
in Fife, I had a friend who played in dance bands, so, thanks to
his Morris Minor, I was in Bowhill Miners Institute on a Sunday
and in the Bowling Green dance hall in Methil on a Friday. On
Saturdays I was at Cowdenbeath Palais or the Burma Dance
Hall in Kirkcaldy. My friend, Ronnie Mackie, went on to some
considerable success in dance bands in London.

WP: Have you been at the Bowhill Burns Club?

DG: No, but when giving a talk to Japanese visitors to Edinburgh
University, Charles Kennedy, who translated for us, was from
the Club; an ex-miner, who had been president of the World
Federation of Burns Clubs, about 1993, I think. When I went as a
youth to dance in the Miners' Institute on a Sunday it was quite
spooky. You would dance with these good-looking women. Now
a lot of their boyfriends who were miners didn't dance. So you
had to be very careful that you didn't get into bother with any of
them. A funny culture, the dance halls then. I suppose when I

think about it there was a division in my life. When I was a boy I was playing football but I was still a bookish chap and when I was here in Kirkcaldy I was still going to conventional dance halls. But I didn't bring any of these friends into my writing world. And even when I went to Art School, which was really then an educational training place for young men and women who would go to Moray House and do teaching, to have mentioned MacDiarmid to most of them would not have meant anything at all. So there was a kind of division and isolation there. There is also the geographical divide of where I was born, and you, Walter, would come into this too, having been born in a Lanarkshire mining village. Being born in Cambuslang, in fact Westburn near Newton, I was within a ten-minute walk of the Clyde and pasture-lands with cows and farms. Look the other way, and it's coal bings and steelworks. And that division is important. Its where the country meets industry and also, with Rutherglen and Glasgow downriver from us, the city.

WP: People now don't understand that Quarter, the village I was born into, although it was a mining village – there were 18 pits once – looked as rural as Perthshire. There was nothing industrial to be seen, the pitheads were tiny affairs, except as you say, looking over the Clyde Valley to the *Craig* where the furnaces lit up the skies at night.

DG: In Cambuslang it was different, but we were rural enough not to be involved with downtown Cambuslang and slum tenements, And up-the-hill Cambuslang with grand villas.

WP: Not many people would use a phrase like 'downtown Cambuslang'.

DG: Far less, 'up-the-hill Cambuslang'. Some of the grand villas were built on real estate bought, with bank loans, by my great-great-uncle Hugh Glen, who became a coalmaster and who ended his days in the grand Wellshot House but was the son of an illiterate miner who made his mark on many birth certificates.

Cambuslang was a very divided place then. I imagine it still is. The whole of Scotland was like that. And it is still divided about MacDiarmid and the Scots language. For a time MacDiarmid lived in his brother's house in up-the-hill Cambuslang, in a small semi-detached bungalow in Grenville Drive, behind Stewarton Drive, which has grand villas. By the late forties, when I became interested in MacDiarmid, he had quarrelled with his brother and been long gone from Cambuslang.

WP: Was he not at that time up at the Duke of Hamilton's place, at Dungavel?

DG: Yes, he went there about 1950 but soon the Coal Board took it over. They put him out. We live in an age of personalities and celebrities and people don't write anything now without going to see those they are writing about. But in the early 1950s the man didn't interest me, only the writing – and his influence. Even when I was writing my MacDiarmid book in London, and fanatical about it, and spent every hour researching it, it was only after I'd finished it, the first big draft which Margaret had typed, that I then went to Brownsbank to meet him. Valda liked me for having done it that way rather than imposing myself onto Chris.

JH: And when was that?

DG: It would be in the summer of 1962. I'd written to MacDiarmid before that asking him some biographical questions and sending him a copy of my bibliography. He replied at length but not very accurately. I knew at that time more precise details of many aspects of his life and publications than he did. If anyone follows the information given in that long letter of the early 1960s to me they are going to be misled over not a few biographical and bibliographical details. My book came out in 1964. It was finished by 1960, except to find bits and pieces, but basically it was finished by the time we left London for Hemel Hempstead, which was soon after Ian was born in October 1960.

WP: Well, if I'm not mistaken, at that time the only edition of Chris's work which was generally available was the American edition, *The Collected Poems.*

DG: Even that came in 1962 after I'd finished my book. But the round British Museum Reading Room had near enough everything by MacDiarmid. Also there were more MacDiarmid magazines there then than in the Scottish National Library or in the Edinburgh Public Library. Funnily enough, the Edinburgh Public Library at that time had copies of *The Scottish Chapbook* and *The Free Man* that the National Library didn't have. In London I also went out to the Colindale Newspaper Library and got great aggro there because I'd want twenty bound runs of newspapers to compare MacDiarmid's syndicated articles and the porters didn't like that. I was a pushy young man who did not hesitate to ask them: 'what do you think your job is?' But that was a wonderful resource which allowed research that couldn't have been done in Edinburgh at that time. Then the National Library hadn't begun to collect all the twentieth-century material that it now has in abundance. The other thing is, the reason that book took so long to be published, was not because I couldn't find a publisher. I sent it to Faber and they said try someone else, try Chambers. Now Chambers at that time had just published Soutar's *Diaries*, edited by Alex Scott, and also Alex's biography of Soutar, and they had sold well. And so Chambers suddenly had an interest in modern Scottish writing and Mr Collocott, who was then managing director, sent the typescript of my MacDiarmid book to Sydney Goodsir Smith. Sydney read it and he made some suggestions but he highly recommended it to Chambers for publication. But then there was a long gap because Chambers were very strict about copyright and the Macmillan Company in New York, who controlled the MacDiarmid copyright because of the *Collected Poems*, didn't answer for years. That delay cost me four years, which was really quite unlucky because Kenneth Buthlay's book came out quicker and just before mine and they both got reviewed together.

JH: Was that the Oliver and Boyd Writers & Critics book?

DG: Yes, a good series. But that is just publishing chance. But people think my book was 1964, but it was actually finished in 1960.

JH: By then MacDiarmid was becoming more readily available, with the *Collected Poems* having come out in 1962.

DG: Robin Lorimer persuaded Oliver and Boyd to import sheets for about 1,000 copies from New York which were bound up for their edition. It sold out in months, which showed the change in how MacDiarmid was seen in Scotland, but it meant that it was not available to buy for long. The other interesting thing was that by the time my book was accepted, when it came out from Chambers I was working for Robert Gibson's, the educational publishers in Glasgow. They knew that book was coming out. At that time MacDiarmid was still a name that was regarded as taboo and my book and MacDiarmid's name were never once mentioned by anyone in Robert Gibson and Sons. Now people forget that that was so. To mention MacDiarmid in Scotland at that time was risking your career. But Chambers did take my book. That is an aberration you would think, but that was Mr Collocott who was a brilliant and fine gentleman and its editor. He treated me as if I were Maurice Walsh, somebody who had made a fortune for them.

WP: That, I think, was the same year that MacDiarmid stood against Sir Alec Douglas-Home in the constituency in which I now live.

DG: Exactly! When my book was being reviewed, a lot of press cuttings I have of reviews of my book also have stories about that by-election, a set-up election in fact.

JH: It must have been about that time that you started *Akros* as well, wasn't it?

DG: When we left London I went to teach in the Art School and Printing Department of Watford College of Technology. I didn't spend more than one minute in College than I needed to. I taught for a while there just for a job because Ian had been born. And the cost of living in Hampstead in London. Whilst I was teaching in Watford I hand-printed pamphlets for MacDiarmid in limited editions, which sold very well. And it was a disgrace when I think about it. Not that we were putting lost poems back into print but that Chris was so grateful over small sums of money. We would send him thirty pounds or more and that was something that Scottish publishers hadn't done for years, which shows you the state of Scottish publishing. Bill Maclellan did important things for him but he never gave him any money, which caused great aggro with Valda, but I was treated as if I was giving Chris and Valda a fortune. And they were small sums of money.

JH: It is amazing that by that time he still needed that.

DG: Of course, despite the views of those who never knew him and oppose his view of literature and the world, Christopher Grieve was a polite late-Victorian gentleman. He wrote to me as such and so may have exaggerated how grateful he was to get these cheques. So when I got to Glasgow, I did other little pamphlets by MacDiarmid. I bought a small Adana printing press and some type and with that equipment I did the first number of *Akros* magazine in 1965. That was the only one that appeared in Glasgow. I left because I couldn't bear the working conditions I had to endure in Glasgow in Scottish publishing. It wasn't what I was used to in London. So I went south to teach at the Harris College in Preston. It was there that *Akros* magazine and all the other things really got going, at 14 Parklands Avenue, Penwortham, Preston. Well, you know that, John, you came there, as you and Joy did, Walter. Those were the first big productive years, of *Akros* and hardbacks and paperbacks as well as the pamphlets. And your novels, John, were done in hardback and paperback and Alexander Scott's and Maurice Lindsay's collections of poems were done in hardback. So was Alastair Mackie's *Clytach* and my *In Appearances*. And that was thanks to subsidies from the Scottish Arts Council. But also we could sell books then, libraries bought almost automatically. And American libraries were still big buyers of small press publications then. We were lucky with *Akros*. And also, the public libraries in Scotland hadn't started their cutbacks. So even before the Arts Council really got going, we were selling copies without trying too hard. That's one big change. At that time, in the early years of Akros Publications, we didn't really bother about the bookshops too much. We sold to libraries, private individuals and to subscribers. But later on, bookshops became quite important, Waterstone's and a few others took poetry books from small publishers. The other real difference is related to that; we are now in this so-called market economy. So the Arts Council cannot really help publishers who do, not just uneconomic books, but books that sell only in a small quantity. You need to appeal to a wider audience to get Arts Council support.

WP: Which is why, nowadays, you either have to be commercial or simply go it alone and, more or less, give books away. There is no longer room, I think, for a middle-way, for a Callum Macdonald or even Akros Publications.

JH: At the time you started *Akros*, there was a very distinct Scottish literary culture, there was a Scottish literary scene, there were magazines, there were readings, and *Akros* got itself situated publishing Scots language poetry in particular. Later, it all got very polarised. What do you think of that in retrospect?

DG: I think people did see *Akros* as the Scots language magazine while *Lines Review*, particularly with Robin Fulton as editor, was seen as the English language magazine. I think there is some truth in that about *Lines*, but I think if you analyse the content of *Akros* magazine, it's not true. Its stance, my editorial statements, were pro-Scots. As I said at the time, if you have to choose between a minority language which needs help and one that doesn't, you choose the minority language. Now it does not mean you are not publishing good poetry in English. We did, after all, publish a full special number on Norman MacCaig. Alan Jackson was surprised that we published his poems in *Akros*. You, John, took part in a radio discussion with Alan who was opposed to all forms of Scottish nationalism. He assumed that I would be as doctrinaire for cultural nationalism as he was against it and so be unwilling to print his poems. Now people don't even remember these stances but at the time *Akros* was seen in a biased way, and I didn't object to that because I thought that was good PR work for the Scots language. It certainly needed it. But it wasn't actually true on the pages.

WP: Well, you did publish two of my pamphlets in Scots. But the only reason I stopped writing in Scots was because the poems came in English.

DG: That's absolutely right. That's the only way to be.

WP: I think, in part, that was because after my granny died, there was no one to whom I was regularly speaking Scots. In fact, the second of those pamphlets, *Surge Aquilo*, in 1977, was written in my granny's house.

DG: My grandfather, who was the farmer at East Kilbride, was a Scots speaker. William Power, the Glasgow journalist and general man of letters, who went to live in East Kilbride, wrote in his autobiography that the farmers in that area, dairy farmers mostly, spoke a richer Scots than many people in Perthshire. Nowadays that's not often recognised. People say; what is your Scots? And I say, Lanarkshire, and I don't mean urban Lanarkshire, I mean the rural Scots that my grandfather spoke to me. But by that time my grandfather's daughters particularly, rather than his sons who stayed on the farm, had become wary of the Scots language. So typically our generation was not encouraged to speak Scots.

WP: Hamilton Academy and Scots didn't go together either.

DG: No, schools in Cambuslang didn't go for Scots either. But we
        all spoke a mixture of Scots and English outside school. Well, I
        didn't speak so rich a Scots at home as I did to my grandfather
        and to my East Kilbride cousins. But that was a real division, not
        that we were aware of it because you switched between the two
        without thinking. My mother used to say late on that I spoke Scots
        to her father and English to her, but that was an exaggeration.
        Of course, my mother never spoke English English in her life.
        She spoke what she thought was English but it was rich in Scots
        phrases and words. And also constructions. But she had good
        English grammar and could get by in 'polite company' and my
        grandfather could but he saw no reason to do so. But, Robert
        Wiseman, who bought the farm from my uncle a good few years
        after my grandfather's death, could, when he wished, speak as
        good a Scots as my grandfather, so it was still there a generation
        after my grandfather.

WP: Certainly from Lanarkshire and I think from most of Perthshire,
        Scots speakers with anything like the range my grandfather had,
        have just vanished.

DG: One of my aunts in her old age, when I got interested in my
        mother's family history, wrote to me very polished letters – she
        left school at fourteen, but whilst she could write such letters the
        only time they really come alive is when she switches into Scots
        words and phrases that she spoke as a girl in rural Cambuslang
        and East Kilbride.

WP: I do notice some Scots words creeping into what look like my
        English poems – but there is no way I can ever be an English poet.
        And the syntax is always going to be Scottish.

DG: Well, as you know, I have written pieces arguing the Scots case but
        I have always objected to authoritarian purists like David Purves.

Not only to his insistence on a set way of spelling Scots but to a purity of vocabulary …

WP: It never existed anyway.

DG: No, it didn't. Burns didn't have it. Nor MacDiarmid, of course. So my language is always a mixture. Also I was highly influenced by Americans in the seventies. To young people today who say that we are now into a new freer age and so can use a full range of language – Scots, English and American – I say that some of us were doing that in the 1970s. But that amalgamation of language is what Burns did, what MacDiarmid did, and it is what has been done by everyone of note – except the kailyairders or the Doric people. We could use a literary language based on our everyday speech – the mixter-maxter that is our natural spoken Scots language augmented by words and phrases from our readings of literary works. It follows that our literary Scots has always been 'corrupt', in that it is anglicised to some extent. Of course, if a language is a vehicle for good poetry it cannot be corrupt; it is another good literary language. This was expounded by MacDiarmid as long ago as the 1920s.

WP: But the puritans always had a go at MacDiarmid.

DG: There is a nice essay in the latest *Dark Horse* magazine on the poetry of W. S. Graham but the writer ends up, in the final paragraph, riding the old hobby-horse that Scots is dead and that no young writers are interested in it. Now, they were saying that to MacDiarmid in the twenties, they said it to all of us in the sixties and seventies. But when they say it's not of interest to young people, you just need to mention Matthew Fitt, Bill Herbert, James Robertson. Now they are not brand new writers but neither are they old.

WP: Is there a Scottish literary public?

DG: There has been. It must be there lurking in the undergrowth. There are publishers who do still try to reach that public and who don't get the credit. Poets from Faber or Cape or wherever get the reviews, don't they? By the way, I don't think reviews are what makes a reputation.

WP: The kinds of poems, probably not one's most ambitious works, which make reputations are those kinds of anthology-pieces which catch the imaginations of children and women. The first MacDiarmid poem I knew was at school, The Bubblyjock.

DG: I think a lot of reputations have been made recently by poets being willing to endlessly tour the schools.

WP: But these are not reputations in the sense we mean, a couple of reviews, a little money and an ephemeral publicity.

DG: But these reputations based on a few poems that are acceptable in schools are undermining poetry. A poem that is easy for school kids is not necessarily a significant poem. I am not criticising Norman MacCaig or Edwin Morgan for touring the schools if that's what they wanted to do, but to say that the poems recognised by the schools are the major poems by them or anyone else is not what we can accept as critics.

JH: What's your feeling about the academic world in all of this, Duncan? It appears to me that there's a *trahison des clercs,* that instead of forging a canon, in the last twenty to thirty years, they have been following market trends. They've been noticing the writers who are already commercially successful, instead of looking at the whole range of what is produced and deciding priorities for themselves...

DG: I agree. I do think the academic world has always been like that. The difference is that they now take note of contemporary writers much sooner, but only those, as you say, who have been commercially successful. I remember, way back, an American poet saying that his university destroyed creativity. I don't think, even now, that universities see their role as being to encourage radical forms of creativity.

WP: It never was.

DG: But the trouble is, they now give the impression that it's one of their roles. You have all these creative writing courses and they are not, in my opinion, ever going to produce major work, or not major poetry. The other thing is, the academic world, even in my later years in it, followed, as you say, not only market trends but was dominated by market forces, which influenced how research grants were awarded and how many brownie points were given to a department. So if you propose to someone in a Scottish university you want to do a PhD on someone who is not fashionable or recognised by, let's say, London, or the Scottish educational establishment, you can be discouraged from doing it. I know for a fact that a student who much admired the poetry of George Bruce and wanted to do a PhD on his work, was asked: why do you want to do it on that man, who knows or cares about him? But she went ahead and did it. Now Bruce is, by any standard, a poet of interest, a serious poet and to say that he is of no interest to people in the academic world, not worthy of a PhD, is a betrayal of Scottish culture.

WP: Yes.

DG: But that is only one example. It happens every year without its being noticed. What interests them is celebrity, popular status. I don't have any doubt, whatever you might think of it, that Alastair Gray wrote *Lanark*, and spent all these long years working on it, without a thought for the market or PhD futures. He just wrote it because he had to. I was the same working all these years on my MacDiarmid book. And my poems. That wasn't a career. That was just because I wanted to do it. It's the same with Akros

Publications. I know it sounds silly these days to hard-nosed careerists, but we did it, as you both still do, for idealistic reasons.

WP: Because it mattered.

DG: We also thought we could change things. I doubt if the modern academic, even the most scintillating of them, dreams of changing the world. The other trouble I have had in recent years is that if you stand up and make an ideological statement, if you get passionate about anything, show you are committed to something, you encounter the curled lip – seen as indulging in emotionalism. And then I ask, what would have happened without Modernism, without Pound, Eliot, Joyce, on and on. These were committed men who thought they could change the world by their writing. I do think that the language, if you want to create something new – must be made new. Pound's proclamation, 'Make it New' remains unbeatable as a statement. You have to make it new or it's not worth doing. It seems to me that writing soft little poems that get into all the anthologies is not what we've ever been about.

WP: Eliot says something like to retranslate for each generation.

DG: That is true. But the other real thing is that the language you create or try to create for yourself cannot be what is acceptable then. I never thought I could write like MacDiarmid, I was more thrawn and independent than that. Maybe when I was a youth there are poems which people have never seen which are really just regurgitated MacDiarmid, and earlier on they were Yeats or Wordsworth. If you're going to do anything as a poet, you have to create a language that you hear in your own head and that comes from disparate places, as Eliot might have said – and without the rational consciousness being fully in control. As has been said many a time, you know what you're doing but also don't know – Keats's negative capability. I know perfectly well that I wouldn't have written as I have without MacDiarmid, because he showed us that a new non-parochial poetry in Scots was possible. A Scots poetry that aimed to be acceptable to an international readership and not the local couthy world that the kailyard rhymesters inhabited. But I wouldn't have written what I did without William Carlos Williams either, the two came together. As a matter of fact, and strangely enough, there are poems that I wouldn't have written without Robert Graves. I admired the poetry of Frank O'Hara, not just the famous ones involving walks down New York streets but long-lined poems such as that which begins '*My quietness has a man in it, he is transparent*'. I wrote an elegy for O'Hara and all the poets who died too young – Russian as well as American. But earlier I was also influenced by the Black Mountain School – Robert Creeley and Ed Dorn and in a different way Charles Olson. I did research into them, and Black Mountain College was a wild place latterly. It grew partly out of staff from the Bauhaus being transported to America to escape from Hitler's Nazi Germany. It is a complicated situation, not just the Black Mountain Review. The rebellious nature of the Black Mountain people, not just linguistically, but socially. Even at a petty level; when they were so poor in the last years of the Black Mountain, no money and no students paying anything, they were going down, disgracefully you might say, and raiding the village drug store, to get food to survive on. That is not something that's going to be acceptable to Middle England – or Middle America. Or even Middle Duncan Glen. But they were doing that out of an ethos of being radicals not only in their language but in living life. I do think Olson, who was the last rector of Black Mountain College, degenerated into post-Poundian and even post-MacDiarmidian work that was too far removed from the spoken language; or rather from a language that sings.

WP: Too purely cerebral, too far removed from anything anyone might possibly say.

DG: Exactly. The thing about MacDiarmid was that he remained closer to spoken Langholm Scots than is often recognised. I led a seminar of postgraduate students in Edinburgh University, most of whom were Americans by the way, but there were a lot of Scottish academics, lecturers and one or two poets there. And one of the full-time staff teaching at Edinburgh said that MacDiarmid had to go to the dictionary for, for example, *chittering*. When we went bathing my mother would give us *a chittering bite* to stop us *chittering*.

WP: My mother still uses the word, it is hardly obscure.

DG: MacDiarmid went to the dictionary for some words but not for most of them. I stood on a bridge over the Wauchope in Langholm and three boys were guddling in the river below. This was about 1985. I wrote down everything these boys said and that was pure Langholm Scots, which MacDiarmid would have known. So to say that MacDiarmid went to the dictionary is not wrong, but it gives a false impression.

JH: One of the more rare qualities of MacDiarmid's genius was that even when he had gone to the dictionary it sounded so good, it evoked the Scottish landscape, the Scottish way of thinking.

DG: Yes, and even in poems that people sneer at for their vocabulary like *Water Music*, when performed by brilliant people who've got the sounds right, it's as good sound-wise as Sorley Maclean's Gaelic which many listeners respond to without knowing any Gaelic.

WP: Sam said that Chris in the early poems and in the best of the later work had something pathological in its intensity.

DG: Poets are all different and it doesn't really matter how they go about it as long as the words on the page end up right. But the trouble is, most of today's minor poets and safe mainstream poets don't actually write out of their whole being, they construct mechanically, and in terms of what they think will be acceptable.

Many young writers do not do that consciously – but some do formulate a plan of writing verses, or a novel, that will be acceptable to publishers who they think can further their career.

WP: More disastrously, it is often, I think, done on a basis of ignorance.

DG: That is the other development – regression rather – that worries me in recent years. This happens in all generations, but the current generation, who are career-minded, and egocentric in a different way from that in which all poets are egocentric, do not have heroes. They do not look back to someone as I looked to MacDiarmid or William Carlos Williams and that means they do not aim to contribute to the culture, only to their own position.

JH: But heroes are regarded as elitist, aren't they, and many of the present generation are not interested in the past, with no sense of cultural continuity.

DG: Yes, no concept of the tradition. Each generation has to take what it wants from the tradition and develop it. But many of us, really, knew by our twenties a lot about our Scottish tradition from the medieval poets to our immediate predecessors. And we were hardly uneducated in the techniques of European and American poetry. I learned from Miroslav Holub and Zbigniew Herbert. And the 'composition by field' theories of Carlos Williams were important and Olson too for his theories on 'projective verse'. And we could learn from Creeley, who had learned from Olson on the poetic line coming from the breath, from the breathing man who writes within the moment of writing. Not as obvious or as simple as that sounds, as holding that moment is far from easy. Also, revision is usually necessary. But, finally, poetry is of physical aspects of our bodies, of dance and song, the beat of the heart and the intake of breath. But then I have to quickly say that that is not to reject our educated intellects.

WP: Then these people of whom you speak, who are they writing for
      if they are not writing for the tribe? Their best motive might be to
      make money to feed families, but many are not even doing that,
      they are writing out of egotism.

DG: This egocentricity can mean that many young poets do not
      seem to be interested in actually reading the work of their
      contemporaries. Of course poets have never been good at
      buying poetry books. That has long been so, but generally it
      has gradually become more difficult for a small publisher to
      sell books, at least Scottish poetry books. But a bigger change is
      the attitude of young poets to how they earn a living. In my day,
      and I am not saying this was a good thing, you accepted, unless
      you were lucky with money, that you had to get a job and work.
      Now that could be very bad. It wasn't good for Robert Garioch
      or Iain Crichton Smith to have to work as teachers. The trouble
      now is, there's a certain tendency for young writers to think that
      the world owes them something, that they should be given Arts
      Council grants and residencies and so on. That is good, but they
      can devote too much time to pleasing the people who will give
      them these jobs.

WP: What, now, about contemporary Scotland? You've been back
      here now, for what, twenty years? We were saying last week
      to Donald that the failure of the 1979 Referendum made an
      enormous difference to the way things were. It was a sudden shift
      in direction. Now we have a parliament which I find profoundly
      disappointing. I don't know anyone who doesn't – I am curious to
      know what you think of Scotland now.

DG: I have got pessimistic about what politicians have the courage to
      do, but I do think that finally it isn't about a Scottish parliament
      or an English parliament. I actually believe we should aim for a
      federal government of the United Kingdoms which recognises
      the historic equality of the three nations of the United Kingdom.

That will be difficult for so-called Middle England. I think the core problem is not the administrative quality of the Scottish Executive or of members of the Scottish parliament, but the lack of real powers to tax, and therefore be in charge not only of putting out a little bit of money, but of deciding how it's brought in. Scotland's parliament will never really be seen as working well until it has more tax-raising powers and also a direct influence on the UK's foreign policy. There is no way that a Scottish parliament would have indulged in grandiose military involvements in the Middle East. We do not suffer from England's failure to accept that Britain's days as a world superpower are ended. But I think it's far more world-wide than our relationship with England. I think of the Berlin Wall coming down, of right-wing America sweeping in Reagan, and then Thatcher in this country. The whole cultural infrastructure has been changed, not only in Scotland but everywhere. Now the real structure, political, economic, education, even the health service, is market-driven. The populist wave that the Thatcher years brought in sees the market as more important than the creative artist. That is what undermines not just the ethos of the Scottish parliament but our way of life generally. But I think, as both of you do, that that is seeping away. I spoke earlier about National Service. After Korea and after Suez, there was just no political will in the British people to have their young men conscripted to National Service and be killed. And I think something similar is happening now culturally even if it can as yet be seen only in the undergrowth. I think the work that both of you are now doing is a symptom of that change. Perhaps soon we won't be sneered at for having idealistic aims. And I do think people will get braver again. Perhaps it is necessary to be a knowledgeable outsider to say what Anne Stevenson said in a review of the recent large Edinburgh anthology of twentieth-century Scottish poetry. She wrote that if amateur poets want to publish poems they should first master poetry's disciplines. She also said that publishing work by the lazy and the ignorant will pull down the level of poetry. And for good measure Anne criticised the politically acceptable tendency to give equal representation to women poets, although the twentieth century did produce more outstanding male poets. I am not advocating a narrow elitism but the setting of critical standards. Not the standards of mainstream or established writers. There is growing ill feeling about the influence of what I hear described as the St Andrews Gang which is centred on the University where Douglas Dunn, Robert Crawford, John Burnside, Kathleen Jamie and other writers lecture. Has anyone counted the number of anthologies that have involved either Douglas Dunn or Robert Crawford as editors? Am I the only one to note that there are no poems by George Bruce in anthologies edited by Dunn or Crawford? A spread of editorial opinion is important. We cannot know who's going to be the next important writer, so a wide spread of encouragement is needed. You don't say: we must anticipate selling 1,000 copies of your book before we'll publish it – or subsidise it.

WP: But all this is attacking the problem from one end. The other approach is to say: well, who is your audience. If you have a Duncan Ban or a Roderick Morrison, you have people writing for very particular, small audiences – as Sam Maclean was writing for – as in a sense MacDiarmid was writing for. He had no illusions that he was writing for masses. But we are stuck in this horrible position that, not being court or tribal poets, there being no such thing as a mass poet, we have, by and large, no one to write for. You cannot elect your audience, remembering Brecht's satirical poem on the East German government saying: *This is not a satisfactory election result, we need a new people.* Poets have to write for some community.

DG: Well I do think poets have to have somewhere at the back of their brain that they are writing, not to please people, but for someone. I write because I think that in my own way, I am writing for 'the Scottish people' No doubt I have an idealised view of Scotland where there are people who, as MacDiarmid said, will be going to a great lecture in Ibrox Park. Such ideas can be laughed at as over-idealistic. MacDiarmid's political ideas were sneered at, but without him and other creative people there would have been no great surge forward in the national movement We needed the Billy Wolfes and all those who gave us our political movement ...

WP: The mechanics, not the designers ...

DG: How a nation sees itself and the world sees it is changed only by an artist: by a Shakespeare, a Robert Burns, a Yeats, a James Joyce or a MacDiarmid.

WP: All this suggests to me that you are not in any ordinary sense a religious man. Because the alternative view is the Yeatsian one, which says: *here is the secret truth of the universe – I am going to tell you how it is and this is right*. And that gives Yeats a kind of authority and energy which you just can't imitate.

DG: Well, I was brought up in a church-going family. My father was an elder. My mother was a very active Church member. But I never joined the Church and I don't like organised religion. But I do think there are mystical understandings which we can all get, less so as you get older, but you suddenly have them.

WP: That's very Wordsworthian.

DG: Yes, I think Wordsworth got it right as a young man. The famous,

> *A motion and a spirit, that impels*
> *All thinking things, all objects of all thought,*
> *And rolls through all things*

Wordsworth's had his 'visionary moments', or 'spots of time', and in *The Prelude* there is a passage in which he writes of how, following such an elevated moment, he retained an obscure sense of possible sublimity which as we mature we can aspire to, whilst still being aware that there is no final understanding as there is always something more to reach for – 'And something evermore about to be'. I am not accepting the religious aspect of Wordsworth's understandings: his sense of religious immanence, whether God in Nature or Nature in God. I am not signing up to a branch of Christian mysticism which starts with a submission to a Divine Order. Blake's apparent mysticism is of another order and very complex, as everything involving him is, but I like his well known,

> To see a World in a Grain of Sand
> And Heaven in a wild Flower,
> Hold Infinity in the palm of your hand
> And Eternity in an hour.

For me more like eternity in a brief moment, but to see that wild flower in a certain state of awareness, can seem to suddenly answer the whole world for you. And you don't have any doubt about it, you have understood the whole world. Of course when you come round, blink, it's gone. But after that, you think you can say that statement.

WP: And you have a confidence, an assurance that that is not wrong.

DG: That's right. Now that is not to say that that is not 'religious' even if not what is generally understood by that term. But I cannot accept that only conventional religious faith allows believers to understand the nature of the world. I am a humanist. I think my human brain is what's working in contact with other people and the world around me. That confidence is fainter in me now but it's still there. I don't really like to call it mystical experience but what else can we term it?

WP: But a proper self-assurance, all that you have done with *Akros* and your writing could not have happened without it.

DG: You may laugh at this, but I am not by nature nakedly ambitious or arrogant, but I do know what I want and what I believe to be important. The man knows what he likes! Seriously, I can drive forward – haud furrit as MacDiarmid put it – to achieve what I believe in. I have recovered from spinal injury, resulting in paralysis. Now you don't recover that without being thrawn and I have been the same way with *Akros* and my poetry. I must admit, in the last few years, less so. Not because I am older but because the cultural situation has depressed me and I don't feel like fighting it and being put down. .

WP: Are you saying that there has been some conservation of the core?

DG: I suppose so. I do retain my core beliefs. Also, although older, I don't think I have got more conservative in the way the unique Wordsworth did. But I do think I am aware that things won't change as easily as I once thought they would. At one time I thought that great poets, important poets, only had real powers when they were young. And later on, I thought, it wasn't age. It's just that usually it's a certain span; that Burns had so long and MacDiarmid had so long, much shorter than maybe people would recognise. I thought that creative span was short.

WP: I have never believed that.

DC I don't believe it now. I think Yeats proves it completely.... But you need to be in the right situation and you need to have the courage ...

WP: And a wee bit of luck.

DG: Definitely. It's like Colin Montgomerie never winning a major; he could have won three majors. At least two of them just needed a bit of luck. And MacDiarmid was lucky to be in the right position after World War I to be innovative but, that said, he needed great courage.

WP: But of course, he couldn't have known that.

DG: Yes, he was being brave without knowing the future and only too well aware of the kailyaird past. And with Sydney Goodsir Smith and others it was the same after the Second World War. If I was not a modest man, I might say that some of us did something similar in the early 1960s although we did not form a movement to proclaim that we were doing something new; to show that we had moved on from not only MacDiarmid but Goodsir Smith, Garioch, the two Scotts and all those who were writing in traditional Scots forms. And then I think in the last ten, fifteen years, post Thatcherism, post-Reaganism, we have lost that opportunity, the chance hasn't been there. Or there was no one with the courage to go against the prevailing mood. But it can come if the will is in an individual or two to make it happen. But I do think the cultural background important. If Christopher Murray Grieve had emerged as a poet in 1890 I don't think the Scottish literary renaissance would have taken the forms that it did. I think Grieve would have written great poetry but quite different, we might not have had 'Hugh MacDiarmid'. Of course this indulging in the world of 'if' is a waste of the space on your recording machine. What I'm really saying is that I think the First World War and the Second World War changed how people saw the world and gave writers new opportunities. I think Thatcherism, commercialism, market-forces changed it again. These materialistic extremisms must in time, surely, cause a balancing reaction and then even people like me, who are somewhat old, can see new opportunities and become brave again. And go back to writing works that aim to make it new.

WP: That's what has to happen.

DG: If careerism is rejected who knows what that change can encourage. I didn't have much confidence until recently that much would change in the next decade. But now things are on the move.

WP: But the cycles of change seem so slow.

JH: I think we can never get away from this idea that in culture, bigger is better; again it's market forces. You as editor of *Akros* and as a poet represented important cultural developments but they were on a comparatively small, intimate scale. Now it seems that if anything is started, it has to get bigger and better the next year. Why should this be so?

WP: There's a Northern Irish poet called John Hewitt, who said something like: if you cannot get a civilisation which is rooted in the local and in the parochial, you don't have a civilisation. What he meant was: if you don't know your neighbours, the people you are addressing, whatever technology does is just debasing. So the technology has to be there to draw on, to make the parish work, that we have to get back to some kind of human closeness and away from a world in which we are not talking to anybody. I wonder what you think of that?

DG: Yes, I agree. There has been a breakdown in localness and a sense of varied communities within a larger local community. The world of TV or the internet can be more real than the family four doors down the street. In a recent poem I wrote of 'my very own global community network in my chosen fireside chair' and asked 'Tomorrow out on the street, / can you see the child crossing the street to school / touch the old lady?'

WP: But this is why I think, at moments of crisis, people often turn to poetry. People do recognise very often that there is something fundamentally wrong with the lives they are living. They are unhappy and poetry offers some kind of meaning.

DG: The first time I went to Langholm to find out first-hand about where MacDiarmid had lived, I went to research the book called *Out of Langholm and Into the World*, which was based on a diary I kept whilst in Langholm. Seeing me walking about the town with large red notebook and camera, many people spoke to me and I would ask them questions on Langholm and MacDiarmid. For a few days I was a feature in the town. I met many knowledgeable and kind Langholmites. Willie Graham, who had worked as a joiner on the Buccleuch estate, drove me to see Tarras Bog, Baggara, Scrog-nit Wood, Warblaw, the Whitsheil woods and the Curly Snake below the Langfall. Whilst we do not wish MacDiarmid to dominate Scottish poetry as Burns did, he has given us emotive names that are part of the Scottish scene, the Scottish landscape, the Scottish way of thinking that you mentioned, John. After my book was published, I went back to Langholm to give a party for anybody who would come, upstairs in a pub on Langholm High Street. Jean White, MacDiarmid's second cousin who had lived in Langholm all her life, was there and a lot of the people who had spoken to me months earlier, including Willie Graham. They came to that party, at which I read some poems by MacDiarmid and so did Jean White. Then I handed the book, MacDiarmid's *Selected Poems*, to this man who I knew had not read MacDiarmid until I spoke to him about the poet, although he was Langholm born. And immediately he said; 'Oh, I can't do that.' And I said, 'Of course you can, you know the language as well as anyone else.' And he read it. I'm not saying he read it well, but he knew it. That was a convert, made by his having met me and being encouraged to read the poems. Not just in that room in a pub but in the few months since he had first spoken to me.

WP: One of my observations about the Scottish working-class tradition is the way in which Burns used to be used almost as a kind of church, the poems were somewhere to go for special occasions.

DG: The trouble with Scottish education, certainly in my generation, and I think still, is respectability, a fanatical concern with bits of paper that say – you are qualified. But it's worse than that. When I was teaching in Preston, by then a principal lecturer and course leader, they put up an exhibition of my books, open with my poems on view. And there was a man there, a Glasgow engineer, and he had been very friendly to me, always chatting to me in corridors as a fellow-Scot. He saw that work on the wall and he came up to me and said; 'You've disgraced us, that gutter language!' And he never spoke to me again.

JH: Was living in England whilst you were editing *Akros* an advantage or a disadvantage?

DG: When I was working in England I didn't really think about that. When I came back to Edinburgh I thought about it. I think I was very innocent in England about what is was like to work in Scotland. When I came north for meetings with you and Walter and others of the literary world I was only in Edinburgh for two days. It seemed ideal to me, coming home for two days. I didn't really know the backbiting and the aggressions that were going on. I got it second-hand but I wasn't really aware because I wasn't living it. And I was receiving dozens of letters every month and there wasn't too much nastiness in them. Almost unbelievably, one post brought a threat by Tom Scott to sue me for a libel by Alexander Scott and a threat from Alex threatening to sue for a libel by Tom. Only in real life do such events occur! But in a way I was detached and innocent. When I did think about editing *Akros* outside Scotland I quite convinced myself that if I had been editing *Akros* in Edinburgh, instead of Preston, I would have met with the sneering abuse or silence which would have upset my ability to make independent editorial decisions. The downside is that you can lose touch with the roots of what's going on. I don't mean politically. I don't think it was too important that I didn't really realise what had happened at the first Referendum. I didn't think that was too important to me as a literary man. But maybe it was. I think being outside it, I wasn't hemmed in by the narrowness of what was happening in Scotland. People with generous attitudes in some ways, like Alex Scott, didn't really want to know about America, didn't want to know about certain European poets. Eddie Morgan is a notable exception. When I introduced the work of Ian Hamilton Finlay in a special visual number of *Akros* I immediately met silence from the Edinburgh literati, who didn't want to know. If they had listened to me they would have learned that I did not fully approve of the aesthetics of Ian Hamilton Finlay's work and the concrete poetry movement in general. I got a similar Scottish reaction when I issued a large American number, which sold exceptionally well outside its normal circulation area. In Scotland it was ignored.

WP: But it can be the same living in Scotland. In Dunning, I am as far removed from Edinburgh literary life as you probably were in Preston – and John in Blair Atholl. I have said several times that, as writers, we need somewhere else to stand.

DG: But John has always stood somewhere else. The reason John wasn't a mainstream novelist in the eyes of the academic writers of Edinburgh University Press is because he has stood on his own ground, which was not their ground and therefore they didn't recognise it. Eventually they did of course. John is on his own ground, simply because he writes out of his own impulses. John is independent because he has an independent mind.

WP: Thrawn.

DG: As well! I don't think any of us here was ever not thrawn and independent. But I like to think that we had a sense of humour and could see that in some respects we could absorb ideas that once seemed wrongheaded or just plain foreign to us. I mean I can almost see some good in Larkin's poetry! The word thrawn always reminds me of the superb first line of MacDiarmid's 'By Wauchopeside': 'Thrawn Water? Aye, owre thrawn to be aye thrawn!'

WP: MacDiarmid aside, you have met at least two generations of writers now. Who has impressed you?

DG: In the generation after MacDiarmid I think first of Goodsir Smith and Robert Garioch and then of George Bruce, W S Graham and then Alexander Scott and then Edwin Morgan. There may be a critical judgment behind that ordering in my memory and of some obvious omissions. I do not know enough Gaelic to properly respond to Sorley MacLean's work but I accept the view of those who do know Gaelic that this is major poetry. I am suspicious of those who know no Gaelic yet swooned over it at a reading by Maclean. The less sonorous stanzas of Derick Thomson get underestimated by such sound worshippers. As you know, Sydney Goodsir Smith, like MacDiarmid, could charm anybody but he is not getting his due now. I'm not sure that Garioch deserved the quite exceptional praise he had during his later years. But I think Goodsir Smith really did produce important work.

WP: I have always thought the best thing that Sydney produced was that sequence of love elegies, *Under the Eildon Tree*.

DG: Yes. I think that's a poem that is good enough to be mentioned in the same breath as *A Drunk Man*. Not that it is anything like as great as MacDiarmid's long masterpiece which is unique in Scottish literature. After that generation, not thinking so much of the English-writing poets, I don't come up with too many. But when Bill Herbert appeared – and I published his *Dundee Doldrums* – I thought that he was a significant poet and I have yet to revise that opinion. I think David Black, when I first read his poems in the 1960s, was quite a poet.

WP: It was an impressive voice.

DG: Exactly. And so was Alan Jackson's. He was influenced by the Americans as I was. Writing some years after my *In Appearances* was published, Ken Smith wrote that it still had the 'shock of the new'. As I have said, I had moved away from the traditional forms used by Goodsir Smith, Garioch and the two Scotts and, with hindsight, it seems that I could have aligned myself with David

Black, Alan Jackson and Roderick Watson, who had learned from the American poets, rather than these Scots-writing poets who used traditional forms. The forms and aesthetics were more important than whether we used Scots or English, but that was not seen clearly in the 1970s and 1980s. George Philp did not include me in his Scotsoun series of tape recordings and my guess is that that was because both my verse forms and the mix of my language did not conform to what was expected of a poet writing in Scots. I suffered by not being fully acceptable to Scots-writing traditionalists, yet by being grouped with them I was not seen as belonging with other writers who, like me, used new verse forms and constructions. I could align myself with the more innovative poems by Alistair Mackie that were included in his *Clytach*, which I encouraged him to write and which were published under the *Akros* imprint. And when Tom Leonard's six *Glasgow Poems* were first published they were something strikingly new. They appeared in a wee pamphlet in Glasgow University and then I quickly published them in *Akros*. It is now difficult to see these as we first read them. Of that generation, you, Walter, and Donald Campbell also feature in my memory. You were wide-ranging, unlike Donald who used what was essentially a traditional and conversational style. He didn't build, as you and I did, an intellectual structure behind his poetry. I'm not saying that's necessary to all poetry, but I think it enables the poetry, gives it a greater width. I also think that poets can be aided as poets by building supporting theoretical structures for themselves. It can be seen as nonsense by hard-headed critics but so what; if it facilitates genuine poetry it is good and worthwhile for the poet who believes in it.

WP: Yeats says you cannot separate poetry and philosophy. Donald was saying to us last week that he never had wanted that kind of poetry. That he wrote poems because they gave him pleasure.

DG: Well, that comes through. His writing has vitality.

WP: And we asked which of the senses was fundamental to him and he said, sound.

DG: That's clear from his plays. He is a natural dramatist. He knows the craft of theatre and the history of the theatre, he can speak with authority about J.M. Barrie, who I just think of as a maker of West-end pot boilers, but Donald sees Barrie differently.

WP: He sees the technical side of it, which I don't.

DG: Exactly. So Donald is a professional playwright. And although his plays are not produced the way they were initially, they will come back.

WP: He was for a decade at least the most important dramatist writing in Scotland. And that is a very substantial, if unacknowledged, achievement.

DG: Exactly. As for creative prose writers, the only one I published was John. I did two novels and that wasn't out of kindness. I don't set up to know novels, though in my youthful days I read many great American and English novels and many others in translation. But John's works have a depth and an imaginative range that I can recognise. Most contemporary novels bore me and most of them seem to me to be simplistic. I was pleased, through John editing them so well, to publish Robert McLellan's Linmill stories although now I see them as almost lightweight.

WP: There cannot be many poets of that generation who you were not among the first to publish in the sixties and seventies.

DG: Yes. But if I were publishing now I might be more judicious, not that I would rely on the literary judgment of many judges, legal or, indeed, literary!

WP: Seventy-three is a reasonable age or, some would say, far too old.

DG: I would. You know Groucho Marx said, when asked what it was like to be old: It's not good but it's better than the alternative.

WP: Looking over what has been an enormously energetic output, and which isn't by any means finished, are you reassured or disappointed – or don't you think about it in that way any longer? The impression you give today is of a fundamentally confident and contented man, sitting in a sunlit garden on a lovely afternoon.

DG: I am comfortable and I am pleased with what I have done. I can't say, as MacDiarmid did on his deathbed, that I have achieved everything I wanted to do. I'd like to have written a long poem or sequence that could be placed with *A Drunk Man Looks at the Thistle* but having published this year my *Collected Poems*, which was a selection I made over many years, I am pleased with it. There's no point saying I'm not pleased with it when I am.

WP: Better than a lifetime in the pits.

DG: Yes, or than the steelworks or even on the farm. I wouldn't have minded being a gentleman farmer, not doing the work.

WP: You would have become bored.

DG: Oh, I would have done. That is one of my problems; I do get bored. When I was working, after two or three years in a job, I was bored. The last job I had in Nottingham was at first so interesting that I stopped doing so much literary work. It was a big challenge to head the department and there was trouble there when I went – real failure. I was appointed to sort the department out and to devise and get approval for new BAHons courses in Graphic Design and Fine Art Photography. I needed to be involved in that academic world as a member of the Council for Academic Awards and to go into Whitehall, which was interesting. But before long, the work was routine and going to these academic meetings became boring. I get really bored with jobs but, apart from a brief spell of nervous exhaustion in the late 1960s which resulted in an attack of depression, I have been very healthy until two years ago. You printed, Walter, in an early issue of *Chapman* a small sequence of poems that came from my limited experience of depression. For several years I wrote every other week to Alastair Mackie in Anstruther and he suffered dreadfully from clinical depression, undergoing electric shock treatment and much else that made his life very difficult.

WP: I only knew him through Schiltrom, a writers' group of which we were both members and which met once a month in the late sixties in Edinburgh. He became Andrew Greig's mentor for a time.

DG: That's right. And Christopher Rush too and Andrew Lloyd. Alastair was a fine poet. He wasn't a fighter of course. He was too fragile. I don't think he knew that I had briefly suffered from some depression whilst I was writing to him.

WP: There are often very good reasons to be depressed.

JH: David Black once said to me, people always speak about depression as if it was necessarily a disease. But many people have very good, objective reasons to be depressed.

DG: Apart from this recent trouble with my infected and broken vertebra which resulted in my being paralysed, I have never really been ill in my life. I had never been in a hospital. To suddenly end up with what I had was a new Hell, but you just do it.

WP: Often people who have always been healthy take it very badly.

DG: Well I thought I would. And on my back with a tube carrying antibiotics into me for six weeks and not actually knowing whether I would ever walk again. But in a funny way, that's what makes it easier to cope with. You put up with the six weeks day by day with some objective to be reached each week. And the months of rehab with physiotherapists – these were certainly a challenge and hard going but always with an end in sight; learning to use a wheelchair, crutches, a zimmer and then two sticks; learning to walk again.

WP: I was very often ill in my younger years, and now, I think, that gives me a kind of resilience.

DG: I think that's partly why you see me the way I am. And I like to get out, having got through this spell. But I don't feel I have to be driven to do literary things. I just do them all the time, but I like to go up the coast, and sitting by the seaside or in a nice village with Margaret is good. But I have always been like that, taking time out after a time of intense concentration. Margaret can concentrate when proofreading and remember back references and previous forms of spelling and punctuation, an interesting form of intense concentration.

WP: I try to persuade students that almost everything about writing is finding some way of cranking up that intensity of attention. It's all in the quality of attention. I'm told it's he same in sport.

DG: Yes, in the zone, and we all know it, don't we? Shelley said that he could only write poetry when he was happy. Clearly Shelley did not write the stanzas of 'To a Skylark', 'The Cloud' or 'Ode to the West Wind' in dejection. By 'happy' he could have meant that relaxed concentration that we're talking about. Shelley's cloud brought, 'Fresh showers for the thirsting flowers, From the seas and the streams' and his skylark, as well as being a blithe spirit, also gave the world 'profuse strains of unpremeditated art'. Perhaps it was in the zone, on the golden spot. Perhaps it was singing with Pope, 'Oh happiness! Our being's end and aim!'

DG: Somewhere, John, you suggested rightly that my poetry was least successful when I got too involved in philosophical ideas. But there are also poems that came from my knowing the realities of life on a farm. And there are my many short elegies and even more love poems for Margaret without whom I would not be sitting here with you enjoying the sunshine. She made *Akros* possible through many a day of hard slog on typescripts, and printing using a Gestetner, and invoicing and packaging. Margaret also guided me out of my sillier ideas and wilder or sillier words. Still, I think she likes the last words in my *Collected Poems*, 'here come the dreamers, full of joy and laughter.' Perhaps the joy and laughter more than the dreamers. Recently an American friend's wife got bitten in her South Carolina garden by a poisonous snake and had to be rushed to hospital. There, when out of danger, she was told by her husband, 'You have been in the garden of Eden and didn't even get an apple!' Now, there's a thought for *The Drunk Man Looks at the Apple*. Or a novel to continue *The Justified Sinner*, or *Pagan's Pilgrimage*, John, or *From Milady's Wood*, Walter, or my 'John Atman' which was printed early in my *In Appearances*. That was just like yesterday: 1971.

3. TESSA RANSFORD

Tessa Ransford (1938-2015): Poet and a key figure in the founding of the
Scottish Poetry Library

*This conversation took place at Tessa's home in Edinburgh on 13th. December,
2006. Present were John Herdman and Walter Perrie.*

JOHN HERDMAN: A few things about your background, Tessa, to begin
with: I believe you were born in India?

TESSA RANSFORD: That's right, in Bombay, now called Mumbai.

JH: You came to Scotland when you were about ten years old?

WALTER PERRIE: What were your family doing in India?

TR: My father was in the First World War. He was the youngest of
     six children, four girls and two boys. His father, my grandfather,
     was the surviving child of eleven, born in India to my great-
     grandfather, John Ransford, Surgeon General of Bengal. My
     grandfather became a physician at the Mineral Water Hospital
     in Bath. He had studied medicine in Liverpool where he met my
     grandmother, Florence Macalister, daughter of William Boyd
     Macalister, who had moved to Liverpool from Clydeside to work
     in the new Steam Navigation Company. All six of her children
     were sent to boarding schools in Scotland. My father could not
     study medicine, as he wanted, because it could not be afforded.
     His elder brother had the chance but the war intervened. My
     father was in the Royal Engineers, Sappers, went into the First
     World War in 1914 aged nineteen. He survived, perhaps because
     he was laying cables and telephones and not having to go 'over
     the top' but many of his friends and his horses were killed. After
     the war he took a course in radio, which was new then, and was

sent to India where he was assigned to work in the Mint, first
in Calcutta and then for sixteen years as Master of the Mint in
Bombay.

WP: A very senior post.

TR: It was a very senior post because during the Second World War
they minted all the coinage for the forces east of Suez. This was
without supplies from Britain. They had to design their own tools.
The Mint worked twenty-four hour shifts with every possible kind
of religion represented among the workers and they never had
any riots, even during the Partition troubles. The staff and the
workers were treated well.

WP: Do you still have clear memories of India?

TR: Not clear, but some.

WP: Do you speak any of the languages?

TR: As a kid I could speak the language. And then I went back to
Pakistan and became fluent in Urdu and Punjabi, although I have
forgotten them mostly now.

JH: And you brought up your family there for some years?

TR: My first three children were born there. The eldest was eight
when we came back.

WP: So you have spent something like a quarter of your life in the sub-
continent?

TR: Fourteen years. But I didn't come straight to Scotland. There
wasn't any leave home during the war. Eventually in 1944 my
father got six months leave. We were delayed landing after a long
voyage in convoy, because of D-Day, although Suez was open by

then. My father went back to India and my mother stayed with me and my brother. We were with relatives and from pillar to post really.

WP: That must have been a fairly common experience then.

TR: We stayed in boarding houses, or as paying guests with relatives until we came to Scotland in 1948 when my father got a job as Bursar at Loretto School, Musselburgh. He was 53, had a knighthood and quite young children. That was because three of my siblings had died as infants. My brother and I were the fourth and fifth.

JH: Then all your education after that was in Scotland, at St. Leonard's School and then Edinburgh University?

TR: Yes, at St. Leonard's but it was not really by choice.

WP: Why not?

TR: There were no places at any of the Merchant Company schools in Edinburgh and we didn't have connections.

WP: Why were there no places, was it a sort of general rush after demob?

TR: Perhaps. I don't know. But my father's eldest sister had been head girl at St Leonard's in 1902. In those days it was a liberal school giving an education to girls. By the time I got there it was still Victorian. We were physically, emotionally and intellectually deprived. The school motto was *Ad Vitam* and we used to joke about what this life might be to which we were destined. I eventually married a missionary, while my best friend, who joined the Foreign Office and became a secretary to ambassadors, told me that wherever she went the ambassador's wife was from St Leonard's!

JH: My great aunt was the first head girl at St. Leonard's. My mother was there too and it was a terrible experience for her. What did you do at Edinburgh University, modern languages, is that right?

TR: I did an ordinary degree which included languages and geology with archaeology cognate.

JH: A very unusual structure.

TR: We had to do a Science subject and I was absolutely fascinated by Geology. In your second year you continue at a higher level in two subjects, and for me those were German and the archaeology, following on from the geology.

JH: Were you interested in poetry or in writing poetry by this time?

TR: At school I wrote poetry unofficially all the time. When I was a teenager I was allowed into the Queen Mary Library which belonged to the school, where I found the poems of Rabindranath Tagore. As I see it now, it was the Indian and Scottish, the hot and cold meeting and issuing in a new synthesis. Tagore's poems put me in touch with what I now call 'my Indian self', which had been suppressed by the trauma of returning from India and the boarding school in St Andrews. I loved the poems so much that I didn't tell my friends about them. They were too precious. This was before the hippy revival and renewal of interest in Tagore. When I was at home in Edinburgh I bought copies in second hand shops in Edinburgh with the help of my parents.

WP: It sounds as though you had very understanding and sympathetic parents.

TR: Yes, They were fantastic. I was very lucky. My mother was courageous, capable and beautiful. I don't know what they thought of this ugly little thing that was me. They were both so good looking.

WP: Were they intimidating because of that?

TR: No, no. I think it was entirely me; I felt I was not nearly as good-looking and not nearly as clever as they were, so perhaps I compensated by working hard at school.

WP: Is it the case that the attitudes you grew up with, familial attitudes, were actually – perhaps because of the colonial connection – more Edwardian and Victorian than were typical of, say, post World War Two Britain?

TR: No, my parents were very enlightened.

JH: In a social sense, that segment of society, particularly in Edinburgh perhaps, was further back in history than you might think.

TR: They found the perspective fairly narrow when they came here. They didn't fit in to some extent in Edinburgh, but they did find friends and were quite gregarious. My mother was an artist and had artistic friends. She made friends with Patrick Geddes' daughter, Norah Mears. My father, a very courteous man with a delightful wit and charming presence, was liked and respected always.

WP: I have always been curious, Tessa, about what it is that precipitates in a certain individual that particular passion for verse, for poetry. And very often poets turn out to have been, in some sense, linguistic outsiders.

JH: You were aware of other languages, from the beginning, which may perhaps have made you more linguistically aware.

TR: And I was good at French and German when I was at university and always enjoyed words, books. I worked for OUP for a year after graduating.

JH: When you went back to Pakistan, were you pursuing poetry at that time? Or did you have other preoccupations?

TR: In Pakistan I did write poems. Some I sent back to my former professor of German, Eudo C. Mason, who encouraged me. I know when I went to university I was writing poetry, although not showing it to anybody. I had one published in *The Student* in my last year. I think I was mostly influenced by the German poetry I was studying: the tradition of *dichten und denken*, poetry and thought, which meant that I assumed poetry was a way of thinking. This is what Heidegger says, that the nature of thought is poetic. Perhaps I did my thinking through poetry.

WP: I saw recently that Bishop Holloway of Edinburgh said something very similar of religion, to the effect that religion is like poetry, a way of assimilating the world, a set of institutions through which we can think about the world. He seems to have, more or less, assimilated religion to aesthetics.

TR: He has changed his bishopric to the arts!

JH: You were married to a missionary?

TR: That meant welfare work for me among women and children, among Christians who were three percent in Pakistan at that time, mainly third generation converts from Hindu outcasts. My husband's father had been the minister at St Michael's Inveresk. (He subsequently went to be minister for the Ross of Mull and Iona). They held a series of 'get to know your neighbours' parties We were 'piscie' so didn't attend St Michael's, but that was how we met. My parents didn't worry about church beyond duty occasions, such as the Loretto School Chapel. They tended to play golf or we would go out into the country on Sundays. When I said I was going to marry a missionary they were horrified. They didn't let on but I overheard them once assuring a friend that we were quite normal really!

JH: Was religion an important thing in your life at any stage?

TR: Well, not really. I don't think so except that at school I loved the poetry of the Bible, which was emotionally sustaining, and we had to learn passages by heart.

WP: Yes, so did we, sometimes a chapter a week.

TR: Later I came to accept the idea of Bonhoeffer's 'religionless Christianity', but yes, I did want to believe something and that there is a power of goodness at work in the world. At university I had this wonderful professor, John MacMurray, and I discovered that he joined the Society of Friends after he retired. When I was in London I attended Quaker meetings there and learned about their pacifism, and their history of social and political engagement. They were still much involved with displaced people and refugees after the war, some of whom I met in London at that time. I decided that I could be a Christian as a Quaker because I hated hierarchies and couldn't take on board the whole priest thing. I didn't like being told what to think. I had to work things out for myself. Then this very handsome young man wanted to marry me. He needed a wife and a tin trunk in order to be a missionary and I came with an inherited tin trunk!

WP: You then went out to Pakistan?

TR: My poor parents didn't want me to go. It was a five-year tour. My mother was terrified that my babies would die and all this kind of thing.

JH: But you stayed for eight years?

TR: Yes, we had a furlough in between.

JH: And when you came back to Edinburgh, you were then what, about thirty I suppose? Did you get involved in the literary scene quickly when you came back home?

WP: When are we talking about now?

TR: Sixty-eight.

WP: Well, this was round about the time we all began to be active in Edinburgh. You had what, three children?

TR: My third child was about to go to school and my friends were getting training and jobs, when I had a fourth baby. I found myself needing to keep my mind alive. I joined the Teilhard de Chardin Society and attended various evening classes.

WP: That's a name I haven't heard in a while. I remember in the mid-sixties that de Chardin was immensely influential.

TR: He wasn't a dualist and that was what attracted me to him.

WP: That was what attracted most people. He was one of those rare creatures with a coherently articulated view of the whole of existence.

TR: Yes, coherent is a good word there; or co-inherent, a word of Charles Williams' that I really like, to describe the way everything is always interdependent.

WP: You read him originally in French?

TR: Yes, while still at university. He fitted in with the geology and archaeology. In the Teilhard de Chardin Society we were a lively inter-denominational group of people, discussing not only Teilhard but other thinkers and ideas that spin off from his thesis of spiritual evolution within the material and increasing complexity-consciousness. But I also attended evening classes in Scottish literature run by the Council, first with Charles King and then with Bob Tait and at Bob Tait's evening class, Norman MacCaig came along.

WP: And this encounter got you involved in the Scottish literary scene?

TR: Norman that evening gave what I later discovered was his usual spiel and said "When the urge comes upon me I light a cigarette and write a poem..." And I put my hand up and asked: "How do you account for the urge? And he gave me, you know, that baleful look he could give and he said, "How like a woman!"

WP: You had caught him out.

TR: He had also gone on about: "I don't believe in philosophy with a capital P. I don't believe in poetry with a capital P. It's all rubbish."

WP: He did, however, believe in Poseur with a capital P. (laughter).

TR: So I went home and wrote a poem about Norman MacCaig and Gerard Manley Hopkins, suggesting that Norman would have treated GMH the way Robert Bridges did, with misunderstanding. I gave the poem to Robert Tait who, at the next class, said "Would Mrs Stiven please wait behind", so I waited behind and he said "Come along to The Golf" (the pub on the edge of the Bruntsfield Links.) Garioch was at the pub and was sweet and said it was a very interesting poem.

WP: Interesting also the connection with Garioch.

TR: This was my first break because Bob Tait asked me for more poems. Later, when I was editor of *Lines Review* and people would send huge batches of poems, I always remembered Bob saying,

"Do you know how many poems you gave me? Forty! I'll take two." He published two in *Scottish International* and I was very happy.

JH: That was your first break. So the sequence of events was what?

TR: Then I won first prize in the jubilee competition for the *Scottish Association for the Speaking of Verse* (now the Poetry Association Scotland) of which John MacQueen was the president at that time (1974). Alexander Scott was the judge. That led to Norman Wilson of *The Ramsay Head Press* offering to publish a book of my poems. It didn't happen until 1980 because his wife died. Before that I had two pamphlets published through Gordon Strachan at the Netherbow where I had a part-time job helping with photographs for *Life and Work* and slides of the oil industry for the use of the Kirk's Science, Religion and Technology division. I just kept on writing, including a long poem on the Peace People of Northern Ireland, for which I went over there to meet them and experience the situation. I also wrote a verse play about Teilhard de Chardin and a book, *Towards a Theology of Art*. I was back with the Quakers in Edinburgh by then. None of these was published apart from a section of the 'epic' in *Chapman*; although the play was performed at one of Dr. Winifred Rushworth's Jungian 'Easter Schools'.

WP: I first met you in, I think, the very early seventies at one of those Irish events.

TR: I think it was probably at The Heretics. I also went to the launch of SCAMP, the Scottish Association of Magazine Publishers and I listened to everybody speaking and of those speaking, you most impressed me, talking about Rilke and *Chapman*. And the internationalism and the intellectualism you promoted. All that appealed to me because I was unashamedly intellectual.

WP: I hope I still am. So does that make three of us in Scotland? The difficulty is that the expression carries such terrible overtones. In Scotland to be an intellectual is to be a poseur, a fraud, a snob. All those thing go with it.

TR: But a woman intellectual seems to be rather threatening. Generally speaking women are expected to choose between their head and their body and not to live equally in both or in both simultaneously.

WP: Really?

TR: Yes, well Mary Queen of Scots got her head chopped off. That's symbolic of the whole thing. Medusa got her head chopped off because her head, full of snake wisdom, petrified men. I think to combine the two is difficult in our society for a woman.

JH: And was there some further development which led you to found the Poetry Library and to engage in all those other activities in which you have been so prominent?

TR: I went to America in 1981 to visit a poet called Julia Budenz, who was a friend of Bill Montgomerie's (then editor of *Lines Review*) and also of Emily Lyle. Emily edited the Greig–Duncan Ballad volumes at the School of Scottish Studies. I stayed with Julia in Cambridge, Massachussetts for a month. She had a research job at Harvard and a card for the Harvard library which had a poetry library, where I was made welcome and a recording was made of me reading some poems. I was also made welcome by Julia's intellectual women friends, who seemed to think I was on a par with them and wanted to know about my poetry. It was a creatively liberating experience for me. I hadn't had that sort of stimulus in Scotland, when I'd been at home with the children. When I came back I thought, "I shall die, I can't breathe, I'll have to change my environment if I'm to survive."

WP: Perhaps as a species that's our defining characteristic, our willingness and ability to change our environment...

TR: And that's why I started the Poetry Library, for myself, I wanted it for myself ...

JH: Interesting that you should give such a personal answer to that question, and a very honest one. And what did you hope from it?

TR: A milieu and an environment in which people like me could breathe and live and discuss poetry without apologising and share our intellectual ideas and get an energy field going to sustain us.

JH: So that it should be more than simply a library, was always, right from the very beginning in your conception.

TR: Yes, absolutely. It was to be a milieu: a centre and an environment for poetry, for all Scotland's varied poetries, a focus and a manifestation, a 'field' or a base-camp for the poetic expedition, as Tom Hubbard used to call it. Obviously there was a need for poetry to be given visibility; the material had to be gathered from all the airts, heaps of it out of print and virtually nothing in the way of cataloguing, indexing or bibliographies.

WP: And there was no money to be had for it.

TR: Scottish poets, who cared about them? They weren't in the university libraries; they weren't in any libraries except perhaps the historical ones in the Mitchell. But our aim was to begin with the contemporary and work backwards.

WP: Back in the seventies I suggested doing an M. Litt in compiling a bibliography of the Scottish periodicals from 1920–1940 but no-one was interested in it as a topic for academic research.

TR: Well, you couldn't even look up author catalogues or indexes.

WP: Yes, unless you were going to look at Gavin Douglas or Dunbar or Henryson.

TR: That's why Tom Hubbard was so good. He had a first class honours degree from Aberdeen and had worked on the MacDiarmid archive in Edinburgh University Library. He used to help students who came in and was passionate about it. We were very lucky with him because, although an excellent librarian, he was much more; he was a scholar and teacher and understood the interconnections.

WP: Writers, major writers like MacDiarmid, need not just to generate interest from readers but, specifically from those with the skills to do something about it. If you don't have the devotees in the generation immediately successive to your work, then nothing happens and then it's too late. So often, there's an enormous element of fortuitousness in literary reputation.

TR: We set out to be international, although we said our first duty was to look after our own health, as it were, and then the world. Why try to replicate the Poetry Library in London? So we ended up, for example, the best library of European poetry, with more of a selection of European poetry in one place than any other in Europe.

JH: Was it a struggle getting it off the ground or did you find that people were helpful? Were funding bodies helpful?

TR: Both. It was a hell of a struggle to begin with to get a grant from the Scottish Arts Council. We put in five applications within eighteen months.

WP: That would be Walter Cairns by that time.

TR: Yes, but he wasn't the worst of them.

WP: Who was?

TR: There was a woman called Janice Fox. Generally they were against the idea of the library because they said it would take money from the poets themselves.

JH: So these problems were overcome.

TR: In the end they gave us £10,000 for the first year, but not until I had already won £9,000 from the Calouste Gulbenkian foundation as 'pump-priming'. By the end of the 1980s we were still receiving only £20,000 a year from the Scottish Arts Council. I remember this because Magnus Linklater became chair of the SAC and demanded £20,000 expenses for loss of earnings as a journalist. I sent a copy of John M. Caie's poem 'The Puddock', to the Literature committee. This is about the puddock who is puffing himself up and boasting, when a heron gulps him down with the reflection, *puddocks are nae whit they yased to be*. I knew I was running the whole library: book buying, staff, insurance, overheads, the van service, taxes, international events, on a basic £20,000 annual grant. But I took the attitude: with the amount of money that I have, what can I do? Rather than: I want to do this but haven't got the money to do it, so I can't do anything. What I had was a huge number of volunteers and terrific support from the Scottish literary world.

WP: From the point of view of bureaucrats and administrators you can see their logic when they say: Well, we'll give it to some kind of answerable, established organisation, we'll give it to publishers and book distributors and cultural promoters. Actually to give it to anyone new on the scene, far less to individual writers, is more difficult, for that requires a different, more difficult kind of judgement.

TR: Ideas inherent in George Davie's 'democratic intellect' were important, showing how poetry infuses the life and thought of a society in every aspect. Patrick Geddes too was an inspiration, with his ecological understanding (I like the term 'cultural husbandry') his advocacy of a folk-work-place balance and his motto 'creando pensamus'. This last is engraved on the inside of the frontage glass of the SPL and is probably a good summing up of my own credo: *by creating we think*. There is also a Gaelic verse from a 17th. century MacEwan bard: "It is not gold nor other treasure/ that you will get from me in special/ It is not tribute nor gift of cattle/ but the choicest of our hard-wrought poems." The last line says it all: *poems are ours, the communities'; there are plenty of them to choose from; they require real work.*

JH: You have been involved in the Scottish literary world in a number of different ways: you have been editor of *Lines Review,* you have also, I think, founded a School of Poets. You have also been president of Scottish PEN recently. I think MacDiarmid held the same position.

TR: He was honorary president. He founded Scottish PEN in 1927 and made a niche for Scottish literature on the world literary stage.

JH: Can you say a bit about how all these things have worked together? That's probably a difficult question – too comprehensive.

TR: A comprehensive answer would be to say that they are all integrated in the sense of cultural activism. When I had a fellowship at the Centre for Human Ecology recently, I was in a community of social and environmental activists, so I decided that I was probably a cultural activist! I have wanted to make conditions which are more positive and encouraging for poets and for more poets, men and women, in the various languages and regions of Scotland.

JH: And you were also active as an editor of *Lines Review*. When did that happen?

TR: I think Callum asked me to be editor of *Lines Review* in 1988.

WP: Why don't you tell us a bit about Callum? He's a character who hasn't yet figured much in accounts of our period. I do remember saying to Duncan that but for Bill MacLellan, Callum and Duncan himself, and a very small number of other people in the forties, fifties and sixties, there would have been no Scottish literature to speak of, because everything through those early days was published by one or other of those people.

JH: Yes, quite right.

TR: Yes. Callum has been a terrific support to me. He brought every book he had published, armfuls of them, all the way up Tweeddale Court in a blizzard to the library on the night of the opening party on 23rd January, 1984. It was Trevor Royle who recommended me as editor, when he was retiring, on becoming literary editor of *Scotland on Sunday*. I think there was a lot I couldn't have done without Trevor. Anyway Callum wrote a beautiful letter asking me to edit *Lines Review*.

JH: There was a series of quite short-lived editors after Robin Fulton finished.

TR: Yes, there was Bill Montgomerie...

JH: And Robert Calder did a couple I think.

WP: I guest-edited the Canadian double-issue but that was under Trevor's aegis.

TR: That was number 95 and I took over at number 107. I was very excited at having this to do. Callum was so charming and sweet and kind to me that it seemed we had better get married. It was always understood that my work would come first. Callum was the ideal husband. *Husband* means someone who cares for and nourishes you. And he taught me a lot too.

WP: He was an immensely knowledgeable man.

TR: He taught me about politics, about history and how to edit. I wrote a book of poems inspired by Callum's life story called *Seven Valleys*, taking that title from the Sufi classic, *The Conference of the Birds*. Callum was desperate to escape from Lewis after leaving school and his ambition was to make his way in the wider world. He was immensely proud of his Hebridean ancestry and heritage and he loved the Gaelic language, and was an excellent editor for Gaelic.

WP: I had always found Callum to be somewhat ambiguous about his Gaelic and Island background.

TR: He didn't want to be trapped within Gaeldom and most particularly not to be trapped within the religion. He detested churches to the extent that he even hated setting foot in them. His youngest brother, who was killed in the RAF, had been studying in the department of Celtic at Edinburgh at the time he joined up. John MacInnes was a good friend of Callum's, as was Sorley, and Callum was one of the first encouragers and publishers of Iain Crichton Smith, even paying his train fares so that he could come from Oban to Edinburgh to meet other poets.

WP: *Lines Review* always had rather a classical look to it, which is one of the things we try to achieve in *Fras*.

JH: That was always a feature of Callum's printing, wasn't it?

TR: Yes, the printing was designed to be for the poem's sake. And Callum loved poetry. In fact I used to tease him and say: you love my poems better than me. And he would say: yes, I do really because they're not so argumentative. (*laughter*)

WP: Callum produced one of my early books, *Poem on a Winter Night*, in 1976, and at a time that no-one else would have looked at it.

TR: He was devoted to literature. I think it was friendship with Sydney Goodsir Smith which gave him the impetus to do so much and made him want to publish.

WP: There was a sort of bubbling energy which made Sydney so attractive a character to everyone.

JH: You have been also quite a nurturer of other poets; you founded the School of Poets. What was your intention in that? And do you want to say a bit about creative writing, about how you write poetry?

TR: I had had *Light of the Mind* published by The Ramsay Head in 1980 and I changed back to my maiden name then. There was plenty of reviewing going on then, but I had no-one to talk to and therefore decided to start a group of poets to discuss their poems, discussing the poetry as poets, not as friends, but as professionals.I asked Trevor to recommend people (he was editing *Lines Review*) and he sent me six people and I found six others. I had found this cottage to rent down at Dunsyre. We held the first school of poets there over a weekend in February 1981. I thought of 'school' in the sense of an artist's 'scuola.' I didn't want to use the word *workshop*.

WP: I remember MacDiarmid saying: There are all these young poets appearing every year, but within a short time most of them disappear. It's a lucky country to have *one*. He meant himself, of course.

TR: I remember I walked along the road and up the cart track through three gates to knock on the door of Ian Hamilton Finlay. He welcomed me very kindly, took an interest in the School of Poets and allowed us to use his poem *Sail Plan* as our emblem. This was a clipper with its various sails named after poetic forms with 'free verse' the flag flying in the wind. (In those days we could use the appropriate word *emblem* and the inappropriate use and worship of *logo* had not taken over.) Ian inducted me into his garden and the ideas realised through it. His was a kind of angelic playfulness – that is, a playfulness imbued with meaning/message, which is perhaps certainly one definition of poetry in general. I once, memorably, collected a crate of large white geese from Waverley Station and took them down to Little Sparta, where they were installed to protect it, as the sacred geese of Rome had defended the Capitoline. Malcolm Fraser, who became the architect for the SPL, built a goose house for them. Ian's tapestry for the new Scottish Poetry Library is stunningly beautiful, being a white foamy list of fishing boat names on a sea-green background. After the new building opened, in May 1999, I must have written to thank him because he replied in a letter I rediscovered recently, referring to my recent bereavement – Callum had died in February : "When he was last here with you (we went to see him about the tapestry) he smiled a most astonishingly sweet smile, which I have often pictured to myself since and have wondered about. It was the sort of smile a happy child might give in their sleep. I hope you are not too lonely, but I know you must be, and that there is no cure for it. Thank you so much, from the bottom of my heart, for taking the trouble to write to me about the tapestry." Ian was definitely someone who practised 'creando pensamus'.

WP: And was there any programme for the School of Poets?

TR: To begin with we met in people's homes. The idea was that we would learn from one another by discussing each other's poems and incidentally discovering what we individually needed to learn.

WP: What do you make of the notion that poetry has lost much of its force and place, as a living thing, because it has been overtaken by writing, which was, to begin with perhaps, a record of the spoken poem. Poetry if it is about anything is about voice and, of course, it cannot adequately develop that voice if you have no-one to talk to, no-one to listen to you, answer you back and where you can see the responses in a face, whether they are pleased or bored. What is more important to poetry than anything else, is its sound. And if that is so, then who are we doing it for in the modern world?

TR: Absolutely. It's from your breathing, it's from your chest, it's from your feet, it's your body.

WP: So what makes it poetry, rather than music, is, if you like, its thought, its semantic content, and without both, it's nothing.

TR: I once had a submission to *Lines Review* and I wrote back saying it would be better written as prose because it didn't breathe. The poet wrote back saying he had written it first as prose and he'd never heard of poetry breathing. That is what I would say of many of these 'language poets'. OK you don't necessarily want to have nothing but 'performance poetry' but I wouldn't write any poem without hearing it myself, without reading it aloud to myself.

JH: Can you say something, Tessa, about how you write and what keeps you writing?

TR: Poetry is my practice in the community of the human. Poetry is what I keep practising and in all these senses I call myself a practising poet. Robert Louis Stevenson writes in his essays *The Art of Writing* that "intellectual courage is required" and "the first duty of any man who is to write is intellectual" but also that ultimately the author's own attitude to life will be implied in all they write. My life has been a continuing attempt to discover and understand, often unlearning and uneducating myself in order to do so. My poems are built on thought, pattern and gestic rhythms in varying proportions to one another, depending on the poem in question. I am often inspired most when ideas and experiences throw light on one another. Sometimes I have written in advance of something happening. In the creative sphere we are out of chronological time; perhaps operating in what Teilhard de Chardin called the noosphere, co-inherent with the biosphere and the lithosphere. Many others, Coleridge, Keats, Blake, Rilke, Ted Hughes, Elizabeth Jennings, for instance, have been here before me. Ted Hughes refers to it as "The elemental power circuit of the universe".

JH: Would you like to say a bit, Tessa, about your current views on the condition of literature in Scotland in particular. I know that you are, much as I am, against the commodification of literature and also the perpetual festival syndrome in Edinburgh and elsewhere.

TR: Right, I agree on both those things. I dislike the festival mania. I feel there's a miasma of festival which prevents the light. It settles like a fog around us and nothing can be done unless under the banner of some festival, for which you need sponsorship and thence the whole commercial tyranny under which we suffer.

JH: It's one part of the commodification of the whole of cultural life, and we get told *ad nauseam* how important it is and what a good thing it is and how many things are happening. In fact, you said, I think in a letter to the *Herald*, that Edinburgh was far more culturally alive forty years ago, in the sixties, when things really were happening on the ground, not under the aegis of a huge festival umbrella.

TR: And there were bookshops round every corner and music everywhere. When I was a student there were marvellous events going on, including in the Festival, and again when we

returned from Pakistan at the end of the sixties we came back
to a completely new world, absolutely buzzing with people like
Alan Jackson and the Heretics; and Bob Tait organised big poetry
festivals, which were real festivals, because a festival should be a
harvesting of what is naturally growing, a bringing of it together
and celebrating it. Things are not allowed to grow naturally now.
If they don't have a subsidy from the Arts Council they don't
exist. Therefore anything that grows wild, as it were, doesn't
exist. Everything has to be limited and controlled by the Arts
Council and grants are then given and a prize and another award
and another fellowship, whereas the things that are wild are
neglected. I call them the red squirrels of Scottish literature.

JH: That's absolutely right and I think there's a danger that such
native activity completely disappears in this potted plant setting.

WP: But is any of this a novelty?

JH: I think it's more extreme than it ever was before.

TR: I think people like Tom Scott with his long discursive poems felt
discriminated against, but to apply for a grant now you have to
have a course in...

JH: Well, you have to have taken a course in form-filling for one thing.

WP: In communist eastern Europe official writing was always a state-
funded enterprise and lots of money was poured into official
writers' unions and eastern European literature was disseminated
all over the world in lavish publishing networks. The moment
the system collapsed, almost every writer within the system
disappeared. There was hardly one worth a penny. Whereas the
ones who were on the outside, like Havel, suddenly achieved
recognition. This kind of state-promotion, like commodity
promotion, cannot work to produce real literature because the

springs of literature cannot be encompassed in administrative requirements. The administrators always want to take over because they have to control the flow of funds.

TR: You have to have some clear streams running, if there is to be fertile ground. The pamphlet campaign is a stream. The Poetry Library was a stream. My last book was published in 1998 without an SAC grant because The Ramsay Head didn't have a sufficiently good marketing policy, so Callum subsidised it.

JH: What this means is that unless you are taken on by a publisher that they approve, you're not going to get support, which makes it a self-fulfilling prophecy of course; that the book will be unsuccessful.

TR: The energy systems are killed off or move elsewhere. James Robertson started Kettillonia pamphlet publishing because he was fed up waiting for magazines to print his poetry and he wanted to publish stuff quickly, say for Hitchcock's anniversary. He received a little award with which he started Kettillonia. Others have now started publishing pamphlets. Duncan Glen had always done it of course; and he has been publishing some pamphlets for me after The Ramsay Head went into decline and then folded up. He saved my poetic life.

WP: Technology: when we published the first one and sixpenny number of *The Chapman,* it was printed by a local letterpress printer. That was expensive. There were no options. So much more is possible now.

TR: The thing is to change the mindset. With computers and the web itself the technology has changed and made pamphlets much more possible. The aim of our campaign was to change attitudes towards them. We're now in the seventh year of the Callum Macdonald Memorial Award and people don't talk about self-publishing but about independent publishing. We have forty stall holders at our Christmas fair this year, 2006, and at the first fair in 2003 we had four.

JH: In a very short space of time.

TR: Actually it's the only way of being published now unless you're a prize-winning poet. There's no normal literary publishing now. You're asking me what my view is. It is that Edinburgh, city of literary publishing is....(*pause*)

JH: Edinburgh as a city of literature is a joke.

TR: Let's say it's a virtual reality. It does have some advantages.

WP: What about the fact that Scotland in the time since we first met has undergone enormous changes, not just in its literary life but politically. How has that affected you, do you feel that that matters to you at all?

TR: I think that people are more at ease with the concept of poetry now. You don't have to apologise now for poetry in general and sort of keep it under your hat and not mention that you write it. It was always suspect unless you were talking about poets of the past in an academic context or were yourself very well known. So in that sense things are better. But Carcanet, Cape, Faber and Bloodaxe are still the arbiters of Scotlit.

WP: Have you been affected by the political changes, the establishment of the Scottish Parliament, for example?

TR: I'm very much in favour of Scottish independence. I can't understand why anyone or any country wouldn't want to take responsibility for their own decisions. My parents had served in the Empire and subscribed to King and Country. They were of their day. But if they were here now, I'm sure they would agree with me. They loved Scotland and thought of it as their home.

JH: It seems to me that the balance has been completely lost between indigenous Scottish culture as exemplified, say, by the poets of the sixties, and the international, that there is now no distinctive Scottish literary culture.

WP: Americanisation?

JH: Americanisation and globalisation. Do you think that that would change to some extent with an independent Scotland? Could a healthy balance between the distinctly national and the international be rediscovered?

TR: I agree with you entirely about a distinctive national context. When I set up an Edinburgh Book Festival fringe in 2004, the criteria were that you had to live in Scotland and not be appearing in the Book Festival. We had seventy applications for fifteen slots. It was to be like the fringe, self selecting, but we had to select fifteen from the seventy on the basis of range and language and area and genre. But we did not get general or financial support from the literary world and people complained about the criteria. I said: this is the Edinburgh Festival where people come from all over the world and they see almost nothing of Scottish literature and certainly not a representative range of it.

WP: Imagine going to Barcelona and not seeing anything distinctive of Catalonia?

TR: There was no platform for the Scottish literary field, what I call the *tilth*. I love the word tilth, if you are talking about cultural husbandry or cultural ecology, understanding the interactions, something quite different in concept from 'the market' or the subsidised charade.

WP: Even someone as supposedly extreme in his views as MacDiarmid would agree with you there, for he said: I may be a volcano, but we need all the foothills as well.

TR: You cannot have things growing in a culture without that tilth. There are hundreds of people in a multi-cultural contemporary Scotland, writing and writing well, and they should have opportunities to publish, translate each other, and be heard and read.

WP: Speaking of that tilth, there did use to be a plethora of women poets, not just Violet Jacob and Marion Angus but many others and then people like Helen Cruickshank who helped Grieve and Leslie Mitchell and many others with money and hospitality and encouragement.

TR: Yes, she was a real handmaiden. We need a publisher with the standing of Cambridge or Oxford University Press for Scotland.

JH: Whoever was running it, though, would almost certainly be from Oxbridge anyway, or at any rate from England.

WP: I think there is a terrible dilemma, and it's one I was struck by very powerfully quite recently. It is this; in regard to one's own work, the writing, one cannot allow oneself to be too upset by pity or by the selfishness, the ignorance, the unfairness, the injustices and all the rest of it within the literary world, although one ought to be upset. Because if you do, it will keep you from what you really need to do, with the freedom and the exuberance and *joie de vivre* you need to do it. To achieve *that* balance at all, you need friends, one or two, a handful, audience enough.

TR: Well this is perhaps what you're doing in these interviews. It is a readership we need as writers, not a market.

WP: We have been astonished at how welcome our overtures have been, for example, to Donald and to Duncan.

TR: The National Library has supported the pamphlet efforts. Well you see, they receive the pamphlets for their archives and see them as future jewels, and they are.

WP: What motivates you?

TR: The love of Life: what Blake called the golden thread: poetry, which for me gives some meaning to life, to my life anyway. I don't separate matter from spirit.

WP: I often wonder whether those who create our literature don't inherit some extra measure of appetite for life.

TR: I don't know. I've wanted to end it at times. When I feel down I think how one of my Scottish ancestors sailed a Clyde paddle-steamer to Australia in the 1850s. If he could do that, I think, well, I can carry on with what I have to do. I believe there has to be darkness as well as light. I don't believe that everything can ever be wonderful. There will always be the shadow which is created by the light. We should dwell on the light, on the joy, on the life that is always emerging, the energy, what Joseph Campbell called "following your bliss."

WP: And the ordering of words in a given sequence? For they are magic, they are action at a distance.

JH: And Yeats of course says: *Words alone are certain good.*

TR: I made the following note from the Reith lectures this year by Daniel Barenboim: *Music does not communicate: it is the communication. Notes are bound to each other; they are physical as well as invisible; they are Becoming rather than Being; the sound ultimately dies. In these ways they constitute life.* So it is with poetry, my life.

4. TREVOR ROYLE

Trevor Royle, 1945: Historian, editor and broadcaster. A key figure in the Scottish literature in the 1970s as Literature Director of theScottish Arts Council

This conversation took place at Trevor's home in Portobello on the fourteenth of March, 2007. Present were John Herdman and Walter Perrie.

JOHN HERDMAN: Trevor, you were born in India, I think.

TREVOR ROYLE: I was indeed. I was born on the 26th of January 1945, in a place called Kolar Goldfields. It's in modern Karnataka but, of course, in those days it was Mysore. And the reason I was born there in KGF, had nothing whatsoever to do with silver spoons in mouths or anything like that. My father's brigade, was training up for Operation Zipper, which was the invasion of Malaya, and at that stage in my father's army career he was senior enough to have his wife with him. My mother being pregnant with me, the army doctors thought that pregnancy was far too dangerous a thing for them to deal with, so my mother was sent off to the local civilian hospital, which happened to be in this Goldfields.

JH: At what age did you come to Scotland, Trevor, and what brought you to St. Andrews, where you grew up?

TR: Well, what happened after was India became independent in 1947 and my father was offered a transfer to the British Army but he didn't really want to go and spend his life in post-war Germany, because that's where the bulk of the British army was. So he resigned from the Indian army and we went to live in Malaya, present-day, Malaysia, and later we came back to live in Britain.

WALTER PERRIE: So you spent what, two or three years in Malaya?

TR: We were in Malaya until the early 1950s and then my parents'
      marriage broke up and we went to live in Britain, first of all in
      England and then in Wales. My mother's sister meanwhile, who
      had married a Scot, had retired from India and had gone to live
      in St Andrews. And the two of them being very close my mother
      then took us up north and we pitched up in St. Andrews. If my
      mother's sister had married someone from the north of England,
      we would have lived in the north of England. Pure luck.

WP: And what age were you at this point?

TR: When we came up to Scotland I was eight.

JH: So did you begin to feel that you had a certain Scottish identity
      after a time?

TR: No, to begin with, on the contrary, I clung desperately to my
      English identity. This itself was not a difficult thing to do because
      St Andrews, as you probably know, is a very anglicised town. I
      went to the local school, to Madras College, a lot of the pupils
      were the sons of academics and also, of course, from the base at
      RAF Leuchars, so there were a fair number of English people
      there in St Andrews. If anything, I exaggerated my English
      identity and indeed on several occasions got punched in the face
      for it.

JH: Which changed your mind very quickly!

TR: But the other thing too is that although Madras College was
      a Scottish school, you would never have known that from the
      education we received. I mean, when you did history, it was
      British history, and I'm not sure that even in English literature one
      knew much about other than Scott or, to a certain extent Burns.
      But no, the education was pretty anglicised.

JH: That was a very general experience, I think, for people having a Scottish education in the fifties and sixties.

WP: And in almost any kind of school.

TR: It wasn't until I left school that I knew the Clearances had taken place.

JH: I didn't either, no.

TR: It was a very solid education, very heavily biased towards the classics. The rector was John Thomson, and, incidentally, the other contender for the rectorship of Madras College was none other than Sorley Maclean.

JH: Oh, really. That's very interesting.

TR: But I didn't find that out until later. And I wouldn't have known who Sorley Maclean was in 1963, when I left school. I'm not even certain that I knew who Hugh MacDiarmid was.

JH: That was the case with me as well.

WP: It wasn't in my case because, although I knew nothing to speak of about Scottish literature from my secondary education, I did from my primary education. We knew MacDiarmid poems and the main Scottish dates – Bannockburn. I suspect our headmaster, Mr. Wilson, was both a socialist and a nationalist.

TR: Well, our reading for English was dominated by Dickens, Scott, Trollope and later of course we were introduced to Buchan and Kipling. And that had a profound effect on me because it taught me the value of story-telling. I enjoyed reading Buchan and especially Kipling – and it wasn't just because of Kipling's Indian background – it was just the fact that I responded to him as a story teller.

JH: So you were obviously interested in literature at that time and you went on to read English at Aberdeen, is that right?

TR: Well, come 1963 when I left school I was in a bit of a quandary. I was involved in outdoor sports and did a lot of hill-walking and adventurous things like that. I was very keen to go into the army. Now there had been a corps at Madras College but that was no longer the case by the time I was there. And part of the problem was that there was no infra-structure to give you any support. I suspect that, if my father had still been around, he would have encouraged me and I would probably have gone into the army and my life would have been very different. It would have been very difficult for me to have been commissioned into a Scottish regiment, the infantry, which is what I wanted to do, because without family connections to a particular regiment, it would have been very, very awkward. National Service had just come to an end. If National Service had continued, then I would have embraced it, it would have been much easier, and probably have ended up doing what I always wanted to do. But the other thing too was that in those days, you had to choose between army and university, because the course at Sandhurst was two years long and, although you could do a degree beforehand, by the time you got to Sandhurst you were hopelessly behind everybody else. I didn't want to commit myself in any sort of way and so I went to Aberdeen.

WP: Am I right in thinking that the military connection goes back a long way in your family?

TR: Oh, on both sides, yes. On my mother's side of the family they'd been in the army for several generations. And my father had gone into the Indian Army. His family comes from Lancashire. He'd gone into the Indian Army for the simple reason that it was a highly contested commission, because in the Indian Army your expenses were lower but your pay was higher. That was an important consideration, especially in an age when an officer was supposed to have a private income.

WP: And it was infantry?

TR: My father was a military engineer.

WP: Take us to Aberdeen then and your career there.

TR: I went there originally to read German and History. I was dissuaded from doing German because I remember my Regent said to me when we were discussing what course I should be doing: Why do you want to do German? And I said, because I love the country and I speak the language reasonably fluently and she said, in which case don't study it, because you'll grow to do the opposite.

WP: Good advice!

TR: So in my first year I did modern history, moral philosophy and English literature, a general course. At the end of the year I decided to switch completely to language and literature.

WP: So they were still teaching Anglo-Saxon at that time.

TR: We did Anglo-Saxon and Middle English and literature; again, it was a very broad, general education. I was fortunate in my last year: you had to do a special subject for your finals and I did The Literature of Imperialism under Andrew Rutherford, who shortly thereafter went to Goldsmith's College in London. Andrew Rutherford was a very fascinating man. He had been a National Service officer in the King's African Rifles and was a great expert on Kipling, which suited me down to the ground. And I found this course was one of the invigorating things I did at university. But I have to say, and I am sure the people who taught me would agree with this, that I was lazy, refused to do the course work, was late with my essays, spent more time doing other things than going to lectures and tutorials. Aberdeen nonetheless changed my life, because my tutor in my second year at university was Walter Keir.

JH: Oh, a famous man.

TR: Now Walter had a very straightforward but for me disastrous attitude towards teaching, he said: 'Now look here, you are nineteen. I am not particularly interested in you regurgitating other peoples' thoughts in your essays. You have no thoughts of your own at this age, so don't write me any essays but come and have a drink and a discussion with me once a week'. I followed that advice, didn't write any essays. But he put in marks anyway. Walter Keir was a great friend of Chris Grieve's, MacDiarmid, and it was through him that I first met Grieve when he came up to Aberdeen.

WP: In the mid-sixties...

TR: This was about '64, '65 – and Walter encouraged one or two of us to restart the poetry society, which we did, and that was all very liberating.

WP: Was it to Walter Keir you addressed yourself after Winston's funeral?

TR: No, what I did, I went to Winston Churchill's funeral in 1965. And I did this because I thought it was the end of an era, the end of something, and I just felt that I should be there. So I went with a great friend of mine called Alastair Smith and we hitched down to Edinburgh and got a standby flight to London. Of course, I was missing from university for a week. And I was immediately grabbed, not by Walter Keir but my language tutor. She was furious and said that she was going to report me to the professor and I put on a very sad face and said: Look, you've got to excuse me, I had to go south for a funeral. And she immediately commiserated. I felt an absolute bastard that I hadn't told her the truth.

WP: You said you met Grieve, did that leave an impression?

TR: No, none at all. But what did happen was this: one of the reasons people wanted me to join the poetry society was that I actually knew a published poet, D.M. Black, David Black. He had published his first couple of pamphlets through Outpost Publications I think. It was called *From the Mountain*, the first one.

JH: And there was one called *Rocklestrakes*.

TR: And David came up to Aberdeen to read to the poetry society and of course this added considerably to my credentials and he enjoyed himself. He was promptly seduced by one of the committee members, a very attractive girl. In fact, she is probably the legendary blonde in The Black Judge Debonair.

JH: Really? I must tell him that he's been discovered. Had you known him in St Andrews?

TR: His brother, John, was a good friend of mine. John and David Black lived in St Andrews, their father was an academic. They went to Glenalmond but I got to know John through the local tennis club and we played tennis together and I was hugely impressed that he had this brother who was a published poet. You know, when you are eighteen, these things can take on a certain importance.

WP: You left Aberdeen when?

TR: I left in 1967. I got a very bad degree because I had done no work. I didn't know what I wanted to do and thought about teaching but I had no aptitude. I did in fact work for Aberdeen City Council as a gravedigger for a bit *(laughter)*, which, again, was a fascinating experience. I think my fellow workmen were quite nonplussed by me. I liked them immensely. One of the things I found when digging graves: six feet under is absolutely literally true. Of course, there would often be coffins in the same lair and you'd have to drag the coffins up and then smash them down and then dig down a bit more and then throw the coffins back in again with the bones and everything.

JH: Alas, poor Yorrick.

TR: I'll never forget: a child had died and been cremated and they were burying the urn in the family lair and, of course, it was obviously a very tragic occasion. And as we were standing there with our caps off, it started raining and the foreman turned to me and he said: "*Ah, fit a life, first burnt an then drookit.*" That introduced me that wonderful reductive idiom in Scottish humour.

   I then wanted to go into publishing but, again, very difficult to get into publishing in London unless you knew people. So there was a job advertised with the venerable Edinburgh firm of William Blackwood, publishers of *Blackwood's Magazine* and I applied for it and was given it, largely on the basis of my Indian background and because my father had been an army officer. The head of the firm, Douglas Blackwood, a very interesting man, no interest whatsoever in literary matters, had been a wing commander in the Royal Air Force during the Second World War and, indeed, commanded the Czech fighter wing during the Battle of Britain. And because the firm had moved sideways, he found himself having to take over the firm. He wasn't really a publisher at all. He was a very decent man. I remember being given a copy of Orwell's Collected Essays, and I took this home and when I read it I was absolutely dumbfounded to find that Blackwood had been at St. Cyprian's, the prep school, and at Eton at the same time as Orwell. So, on the Monday I said to him: You know, that's really astonishing. I was reading this work and I found you were at school with Orwell. And he looked at me rather surprised, and said, Orwell? I said, Yes, George Orwell. He said, No, there were no Orwells at Eton. I said: Well, perhaps you might have known him as Eric Blair, and he said, Oh, I remember Blair. He had a motorbike.

WP: You were there for what, just over a year?

TR: Eighteen months.

WP: And you had various literary discoveries while you were there, did you not?

TR: I did indeed: the Blackwood's firm lived in a wonderful office in 45 George Street in Edinburgh, and had the original saloon where the Blackwood group had met in the nineteenth century: Hogg, Scott, de Quincey. And there was a library behind it and one day when I was going through the library looking for something, I found these flat sheets and they were the flat sheets of MacDiarmid's *A Drunk Man Looks at the Thistle*. Of course, Blackwood's had published MacDiarmid in the 1920s, through the influence of John Buchan. But, alas, a lot of the sheets had been used for wrapping up books.

JH: How extraordinary.

TR: And the other thing I discovered was there were all the corrected proofs of George Eliot's novels, which were sold for a huge amount of money. And the interesting thing about that was that most of the proofs had been corrected by her partner.

JH: Yes, G. H. Lewes.

TR: Yes. The tragedy for Blackwood's was that by the time I was working there, it was a shadow of its former self, and unfashionable and its backlist was made up of work that had been published in the 1930s, mainly tales of imperial derring-do and generals' memoirs and they didn't really have any opportunity of competing with other publishers. On the other hand, because they had their own printing works in Thistle Street, at the back, I was given a very solid grounding in book production: how printing worked, proof correction. And also, I went out with the firm's reps.

WP: What was your job there, Trevor?

TR: Oh, I was called an editorial assistant, I did most things from reading manuscripts, correcting proofs, marking up for press. And also helping to publicise the books. But the main emphasis was the magazine, which was published every month.

WP: By this stage, had you any active writing interests?

TR: Yes, I had. I had written quite a lot for the university newspaper when I was at university. I reviewed for *Blackwood's Magazine* and as it was always done anonymously, I didn't have the satisfaction of seeing my name against any of them, but this was a good grounding because learning to write a thousand word review was a very good discipline in getting your point of view across and being as comprehensive as possible.

WP: So that takes us up until when?

TR: 1970.

WP: How does the Arts Council happen?

TR: By this time I didn't want to stay with Blackwood's any more.

WP: You were preceded by Douglas Eadie and Bingo Mavor, who was the son of O.H. Mavor, 'James Bridie'.

TR: No, the way the Arts Council existed when I joined it, was that Bingo Mavor was the overall director. There were four separate departments; there was touring, which dealt with small theatre groups; there was the drama department, there was an art department, a music department and then something called drama and literature. It was a man called Alastair Skinner who ran that and Alastair went on to become a distinguished playwright and he became a teacher as well, a drama lecturer. Alastair's main interest was drama and to be honest, it was a big job because you had to deal with all the principal rep theatres in Scotland and also with the vexed question of whether we should have a national theatre. And literature was sort of tagged on to it. He had an assistant, called Douglas Eadie and Douglas wasn't made out for this kind of work, on his own admission, although he did a lot of good things when he was there. He left to pursue an independent career as a writer and film maker and so the job of drama and literature assistant became available. I applied for it and was interviewed by Bingo Mavor. Funnily enough, when I turned up for the interview there was somebody else there and she went on to become director of the Edinburgh Film Festival –

JH: Linda Myles?

TR: Yes, Linda Myles was also waiting to be interviewed. So, being a gentleman, I said, well, you go in first. Anyway, she went in and I didn't hear from the Arts Council for some time afterwards so I phoned them up to ask them what was happening and they said: Haven't you had our offer letter? They had forgotten to post it to me. Anyway, I got the job and Linda Myles went on to much greater things and subsequently became a very well known and highly respected producer in California. So, I got the job and I began on the first of February, 1971. Well I'd never done a job like this before in my life. I didn't know anything about how an administration worked. Within two days I had to take a literature committee, and I had to take a meeting, do the minutes and all the rest of it and this was a very steep learning curve. The chairman of the literature committee, a very good man called Neil Paterson, a novelist who'd got an Oscar in Hollywood for writing the screen play of John Braine's *Room at the Top*. He was a prince among chairmen. He had a very sound philosophy; he said: If it's got talent, reward it, if it's got promise, encourage it. So that was a very enlightened guiding principle. He was very keen that drama and literature should be divided, because I had to deal with drama as well to begin with. By the end of 1971 the two departments were divided and literature then became a separate department within the Arts Council. Because I had such an ambitious chairman, we pushed very hard for a rapid increase in the literature budget but that meant you can't just throw money and hope for a solution; you have to have a policy which was workable and there was an awful lot to be done. Because Scottish literature and the literary scene in Scotland in the early 1970s was in a very parlous position.

JH: It was a very vibrant time, but, as you say, very dangerous as well. The thing was, there were a lot of factions, a lot of cross-currents, the Bob Tait, *Scottish International* scene was seen to be at odds with the Scots language lobby. There was a lot of altercation, really a lot of aggro going on.

TR: Yes, there was. I mean from that point of view, it was very dynamic. But what I would want to say is that although the Arts Council did a tremendous amount in stimulating the growth of the literary scene in Scotland, it couldn't have done it had there not been people out there writing and producing and editing and publishing. So whenever people want to put the credit solely on the Arts Council, I always say: no, I demur from that completely.

JH: But I think what immediately struck, at least all the younger writers in Scotland at that time, about yourself, was that you seemed very quickly to become an integral part of the Scottish literary scene in a way that's perhaps never happened before and has never happened since – that you were extremely approachable and no-one was afraid to talk to you and socialise with you and that kind of thing. Was that a conscious decision on your part or was it just part of your personality, was that the way you decided to approach things?

TR: Well, I thought that the first thing that I had to do was to get to know every writer who was worthwhile in Scotland and to get their point of view. I'll never forget going across to Glasgow University to see Alexander Scott, a great poet and a great facilitator as well, through his editing work. But Alec was a touchy man and he didn't know who I was when I went to see him in his department in Glasgow University. He'd finished doing a tutorial and he sat me down in a chair in the tutorial room and I felt that I was back at university, which was entirely the impression that he wanted to give. And his first words to me were: Well, Mr. Royle, what university did you go to, was it Oxbridge or red brick? And I looked at him and I thought, this is great, fantastic, and I said: Well, in fact, grey stone. And he said: Och, St Andrews. And I said: no, Aberdeen. And of course, from that point, I couldn't put a foot wrong, because he too was an Aberdeen graduate. This was the beginning of a very rapid and very exciting expansion in government expenditure in the arts, which had been instigated by Jennie Lee, the great Labour arts minister. And money was available, but of course we had to have policies as well. And we quickly identified that one thing we had to do was to try and provide additional funds for writers, through bursaries and also through writer's fellowships, we had to fund the literary magazines and we had to establish a grants-to-publishers scheme to help publishers bring books into print which would otherwise remain unpublished. And then, finally, we thought, well, there's a public aspect to it and we started the Writers in Schools scheme and funded lots of literary events so that writers could gain a greater audience.

WP: And this was established with whom, with Alexander Scott and your committee?

TR: I had a literature committee and I had lots of advisory committees, which changed all the time, so lots of people were able to be part of the decision-making process. For example, on our advisory committees, nobody ever served more than two years so that you had a change of emphasis. Anyway, I saw it as my job to go out and about and meet people and to be encouraging. I like to think that from early on I could tell whether a scheme was going to get support or not, because I knew my committee well, and if I thought it was going to succeed, then obviously I would encourage it. The other thing is, it was great fun; I'm a sociable person, I like parties, I like meeting people. And one has to say too that it was a very companionable time when there were certain pubs you could go into in Edinburgh, the Abbotsford, Café Royal, Milne's, where you would be certain of meeting people.

        But the other thing that I liked about it as well is that there still was the older generation: MacCaig, Garioch, Sydney Goodsir Smith, Callum MacDonald in the early part of the 1970s and Alexander Scott and Edwin Morgan in Glasgow. They were social animals as well, who liked a good chat and liked to have a drink and enjoyed each other's company. Mind you, that being said, there were also great enmities, tremendous quarrels and massive feuds which took place. But that too was part of it.

WP: Would you agree that what you did then was very much a young man's job and it was fortunate that you were that?

TR: Yes, I was lucky. I was twenty-six when I got the job. It was a hopelessly young age.

JH: Well it was probably the fact that you were young that allowed you to push through these things; you came in with a completely fresh view of things, you weren't partisan and you just stood a little apart, because of your cultural background, from the background of most Scottish writers and yet you were fully committed and enthusiastic.

TR: Yes, I could see that there was a huge problem, that writers
        weren't getting published, either because they lived in Scotland or
        because they wrote in Scots or they wrote in Gaelic or their work
        was unfashionable or else they had grown into middle age and
        were unknown. And I felt that this was challenging and so I set
        about trying to make sure that we encouraged writers to apply. I
        mean, I could see no point in having schemes unless people were
        able to benefit from it.

JH: All of these schemes have endured, or many of them.

TR: Some have, some have disappeared, some have changed. I think
        the very big thing that the Arts Council has done and the right
        thing to do, as the literature budget has grown, it has devolved a
        lot of its activities to the Scottish Book Trust, which I think was
        a very sensible way to do it. You can't be both the administrative
        body and the executive body, you can't do the two things together
        so that's the big criticism I would have about what we were trying
        to do. Too often we tried to do things ourselves.

WP: Yes, but it was all very innovative.

TR: Well, it had never been done before, so, to a certain extent,
        nobody said: oh, that's the wrong thing to do, because it hadn't
        been done. We tried to make it work and if it didn't work, we
        refined it.

WP: And you haven't touched on your efforts in the direction of
        internationalising Scottish literature, with the various exchanges,
        for most of which you were, at least in some degree, responsible;
        the Irish exchange, the Canadian fellowship and so on.

TR: One of the first tasks that was given to me in 1973, Neil Gunn had
        his eightieth birthday...

WP: He died in 1973.

TR: Yes. So the task I was given was to look into how the Arts Council might commemorate Neil Gunn's eightieth birthday and I came up with a couple of ideas: one was a collection of essays in his honour, which was duly done; a second was a film about Neil Gunn, which got the Arts Council into making films about Scottish writers; and the third one was that I felt that there should be a fellowship named after Neil Gunn. And I thought that rather than have just a fellowship at a Scottish university, we should make this an international fellowship. I got fantastic support from Neil Paterson on this because Neil Paterson greatly admired Neil Gunn, they were very good friends and, to a certain extent I think Neil Gunn had influenced the young Neil Paterson. Neil was a wonderful man who, if you had lunch, believed in a couple of dry martinis beforehand and at least one bottle of claret...

WP: Sensible fellow.

TR: So it was lunch lunch

WP: Alas, those days have gone.

TR: And we were having lunch and we were kicking around the notion of the fellowship about and the idea of an international fellowship came up and we put this up to the Arts Council and they accepted it and then we thought, it should be in the sense of a prize ... the Fellow would be given an honorarium and they would be given two weeks in Scotland and shown around the country...

WP: As a punishment...

TR: No... and given a jolly good time while he or she was there. And all this was accepted by the Arts Council and then we had to choose a Fellow and, it was a very enlightened choice, Heinrich Böll...

WP: He was the first, then.

TR: Yes, a great German novelist. I remember, I flew to see him in
       Cologne, where he lived, and to my great surprise and pleasure it
       turned out that while he was a prisoner of war in British hands, at
       the end of the Second World War, he had read Neil Gunn while in
       a British prisoner-of-war camp.

JH: How extraordinary.

TR: So there was a connection there and then to our complete
       astonishment, in 1972, before Böll came across to Scotland, he was
       awarded the Nobel Prize for Literature.

WP: Which also happened to your subsequent choice...

TR: Saul Bellow, yes, the third one. Chinua Achebe was the second.
       It was awarded every two years, so Achebe came in 1975 and then
       Saul Bellow in 1977. We set a pretty high standard. By that time,
       by the mid 1970s, Neil Paterson had retired as literature chairman
       and was succeeded by Derry Jeffares, a great Yeats expert, he
       had been given a chair at Stirling University. Well, he was just a
       wonderful man to work with. He seemed to know everybody.

WP: The fixer's fixer!

TR: The fixer's fixer; he knew everybody in every country in the world
       and could arrange anything and he wanted us to expand the
       international side of the Arts Council's work, and so we fixed up
       with the Canada Council to have a Scottish-Canadian writer's
       fellowship, whereby a Scottish writer could go to Canada and
       a Canadian writer could come to Scotland. It was incredibly
       successful. It happened after I left, because that was one of the last
       things I did. And we also set up a Scottish-Australian fellowship,
       which was less successful. It didn't last. There may have just been
       the one. One of the reasons why the Canadians liked it was, they

felt … the proportions are different but the problem is the same; that you have a southern neighbour, which speaks the same language and is much more influential and more powerful.

JH: And also of course, you've got a strong Scottish heritage in Canada as well, which must have appealed to many.

TR: Yes, it did, although my opposite number in the Canada Council, was of Iranian origin, Naim Kattan. But I think by the 1970s and 80s the Scottish influence wasn't as dominating in Canadian life. It was becoming much more a polyglot society and with influences especially from other parts of Europe and from, indeed, south-east Asia.

WP: You have spoken of both Neil Paterson and Derry Jeffares and of how well you got on with them, but that not everyone could have done that job.

TR: They were men who were prepared to encourage younger people; both of them liked, above all else, encouraging young people and those whom they felt had something to offer. I remember James Kelman came to see me and said: Oh, I'm not going to put in an application, because they won't like my work. And I said: Look, I can't decide that, but you've got a very good chance of getting a Writer's Bursary. So he gave a portfolio of his work; it was read by the committee which dealt with this and I remember there was one very po-faced member of the committee who took huge exception to Kelman's use of the f-word and thought that this was a very good reason for not giving him a bursary. And Derry just leant back in his chair and said: Yes, I think he probably does over-use it a bit, but, let's be honest about it, it's only a vulgar word for sexual intercourse, isn't it? And Kelman got the bursary.

JH: And went on from there. Another of your pet projects which endured for a very long time was, of course, the exchange of Scottish and Irish Gaelic poets.

TR: Yes, the first steps had been taken by the time I joined the Arts Council, because the approach had originally been made by the Department of External Affairs in Dublin. You say I like meeting people, well it was also that very agreeable things happened to me. I had to go to Dublin and I met lots of people, including Gareth Brown, who ran Claddagh Records and he immediately set about recording a lot of the Scottish poets and making long-playing records of them. But the chap I had to deal with in Dublin was a most remarkable man called colonel Eoghan O'Neill, who'd been a regular officer in the Irish army and was the director of an organisation, Comhdháil Náisiúnte Na Gaeilge, which was an umbrella group for various cultural bodies which dealt with the Gaelic language. And he was a fantastic man, because he knew an awful lot about Gaelic culture and literature and especially music, pipe music. He also knew a lot about Scottish Gaelic culture as well, unusual in some respects. And the original idea was that in spring three Scottish Gaelic-speaking poets would go to Ireland, where they'd tour round the country for a week and give readings. And in the autumn three similar Irish Gaelic-speaking poets would come to Scotland. The tours began in 1971 and I'm afraid to say that we sent our heavy brigade: Sorley Maclean, Derick Thomson and Iain Crichton Smith, very difficult to beat that. But during the course of the tours we suddenly realised that because music is such an integral part of Gaelic and Gaelic cultural life, musicians and singers should be added. And of course this changed the complexion of the exchange. And of course, John, you will remember I asked you to be a roadie in the very first one.

JH: A wonderful experience.

TR: Because the Colonel was very keen that we should do everything by road and we went by car so that we could talk with people and get on with it. But to my great chagrin, the tours were always much better supported in Ireland than they ever were in Scotland.

JH: That was symptomatic, wasn't it.

TR: There was a lot of suspicion about the exchange. And we have to remember in the early 1970s this was the beginnings of the Troubles in Northern Ireland and it had a knock-on effect. I was under a lot of pressure from various people at the Arts Council to stop these tours; one, from the security point of view, because we always used to go up to Donegal. And then there was a feeling that perhaps we shouldn't be giving encouragement to a cultural background which seemed somehow to be tied up with the Troubles.

JH: Isn't that revealing.

TR: There was a lot of residual dislike about it and we didn't get large crowds, people didn't turn up, although those who came across from Ireland were first-rate poets and terrific singers and musicians.

WP: There was no tradition of it here.

TR: Probably not, no. And it was also one of mass as well, I mean the smaller population in what we would call the Gaidhealtachd.

JH: Nonetheless, I think these exchanges did help to raise the profile of Scottish Gaelic.

TR: Yes. I was astonished to see the extremely high regard in which Sorley Maclean was held in Ireland, it was really quite something.

JH: You left the Arts Council in about 1979, which seemed to be a time when things were changing; it was a time of the failure of the first devolution bill and then Thatcher got into power, becoming prime minister and introduced a completely new era really in Scottish politics.

TR: Yes, things changed very rapidly then. I'd just like to say something about devolution because we wondered at the Arts

Council how devolution would affect us. The Scottish Arts Council was in fact only the Scottish Arts Council in name, it was a committee of the Arts Council of Great Britain and we got our money from London, which meant there was a certain feeling of, well, just give the money to the Scots and let them get on with it. They didn't want to be bothered thinking about it, which allowed us to have policies which were separate and much more radical than were ever carried out in England. Now what worried us more than anything else was that, come devolution, a devolved Scottish assembly or parliament, call it what you will, would want to take over responsibility for the funding of the arts. But we thought this would be utterly disastrous for the arts in Scotland, if we were to become responsible to a devolved assembly, which we feared was going to be dominated by Strathclyde 'cooncillors'. This was our great concern. One of the great things about the Arts Council in those days was the arm's-length policy which guided it. When it was established at the end of the Second World War, because the world had had experience both of Nazi control of cultural funding in Germany and Stalinist control in the Soviet Union, it was felt that any funding organisation set up in Britain should be completely independent of government and that government should not have any capacity whatsoever to influence it. Obviously, of course, the government funds it but there should be no government interference and we felt that this was entirely right and proper for any cultural administration. Now we see under the latest culture bill which is being considered by the Executive, the precise opposite is going to happen. The Arts Council is going to disappear, to be merged with Screen Scotland to become something called Creative Scotland and ministers are going to reserve the right to interfere in its decision-making.

WP: And the funding to be provided by?

TR: By the Executive, as indeed it is now. That I think is a great pity but I know that steps are being taken to try and contest this, because once you have politicians sticking their nebs into cultural policy, you're finished.

WP: Cultural life is reduced to television-level. But if memory serves, by the time seventy-nine came along, you were wearying of that role.

TR: O, yes. It wasn't a political consideration which forced me to leave. I'd been there for eight years and I'd enjoyed most of them. By the end, I was getting wearied by it, as you say. It's a bit like pushing a snowball; I'd pushed the snowball along until it was a certain size and I felt it was time for someone else to come along and put their shoulder to it and also, I think I'd gone about as far as I could in terms of suggesting innovations, producing policies, and I felt it was time really for somebody to come along and to consolidate. And they chose the perfect candidate in Walter Cairns. Because he made a lot of things work better than they had done before. He stopped doing one or two things which weren't working properly and he proved to be the ideal successor.

WP: A good administrator, though I would say his grasp of literature was uneven. But that, perhaps, did not matter.

TR: I was getting bored by it as well; I didn't want to do it any more.

WP: And in any case, in terms of initiating change, you had already achieved an enormous amount.

TR: Yes, there had been fantastic changes and, I'll be honest about it, I was very proud of what we achieved in those years. The Arts Council was very central to what was happening, made some wrong moves but most of the moves it made were the right ones and did help facilitate things.

WP: I have a very ambiguous view of what John just called the 'failure' of the seventy-nine referendum. Because, had we ended up with that seventy-nine settlement, things would have been astonishingly different from how they are presumed to be now. How do you look back on that? The other observation we have come across in these conversations is that that 'failure' led to a period of retrenchment and fragmentation in Scottish cultural life; people went their own way and lost heart.

JH: There was a loss of that sense of artistic community, I think, which had been so strong in the sixties and seventies.

TR: Well, and there was a sense of high expectation about the 1970s' devolution movement. And, of course, people had come back to Scotland. Neil Ascherson, for example, came back to Scotland, worked for *The Scotsman,* and we have to remember that *The Scotsman* in those days was a great newspaper, very true to its Whig background. It made a momentous decision to support the move towards devolution and there was this great feeling of expectation. So you had a cultural explosion and a very high level of creativity, not just in literature; look at theatre, in terms of the 7-84 theatre group and in the visual arts John Bellany and others and in music... There was a huge amount of creativity and a lot of this was allied to a terrific burgeoning of self-confidence in Scotland.

WP: 7-84, The Heretics, all these things were going on.

TR: And the Traverse Theatre and the way in which the Edinburgh Festival and its associated Film Festival was gaining a huge international reputation. And there was the feeling that Scotland was becoming an independent country.

WP: There was a shift in the credibility of Scotland round about the mid-sixties and it showed itself initially in the election of Mrs Ewing in Hamilton. People hadn't believed it had been possible until then.

JH: Yes.

WP: I can just remember the 1959 election in Hamilton, when the man who later became Mrs. Ewing's election agent, John MacAteer, stood for the SNP and lost his deposit, attracting only a few hundred votes.

JH: Yes, after Mrs. Ewing's victory a lot of people who had been romantic nationalists, like myself, but never thought it was anything to do with a possible reality, realised that it could be and threw themselves into the general maelstrom of activity, cultural and political, that was going on at that time.

WP: You haven't said much, Trevor about the stick you must have got during those years.

JH: From people like Tom Scott, for instance.

TR: He was a particular bugbear because he believed that he was being personally put down at my instigation and he wrote me a wonderful letter at one point, saying that in the last analysis it didn't matter, because there would just be himself with Hamish Henderson, like Horatio at the bridge.

WP: Hamish would have fallen off.

TR: He saw it in those heroic terms. But his grudge was that he'd written a history of Scottish literature, which couldn't find a publisher and he wanted to be given money so that he could publish it. And he was very angry when I told him that he had to find a publisher. He said that he had too many enemies, that he would never get his work published. The point is, that was part of the problem. Yes, he was awkward and was a thoroughly disagreeable man in many respects, but he summed up the predicament; here was a man in his late fifties, early sixties, as old as I am now, who had been bypassed, simply because there was no means of getting his work published. He would not fit into academe, he wouldn't apply for any of the fellowships and he probably wouldn't have gotten them because he had the wrong kind of personality for that kind of thing. And yet, the man was talented.

WP: By the same token, in his early years, he had had the encouragement of T.S. Eliot, Edwin Muir and others but had alienated most of the people he came into contact with.

TR: Yes, and Scotland being a small country, there were various cliques, that's certainly true and, John, you mentioned *Scottish International*, which was a particular problem.

JH: There was a feeling among certain people on what you might call the Tom Scott side of the nationalist front, who felt that *Scottish International* had been singled out for special treatment in getting a larger grant than the existing magazines and so forth.

TR: Well, looking back on it, those critics were absolutely right. Because *Scottish International* exemplified what was wrong about some Arts Council initiatives. I should say that I had no responsibility for its creation because it was in being when I joined. But looking back at it, this was a magazine which had been created by the Scottish Arts Council. And although it had an independent existence, in that it was run by a board of directors, the fact remained that it was SAC-funded. And in the early 1970s we backed it to go monthly and Bob Tait had very ambitious plans for it to become more the *New Statesman* than a literary magazine. So I found myself having to defend it all the time in the Council because people were critical of it because they thought it was becoming increasingly politicised and they thought it had a nationalistic slant to it.

JH: The nationalists thought otherwise.

TR: Yes. And eventually Bob Tait resigned and Tom Buchan took it over and that was the end of it. By that time it was just finished.

WP: And shortly after that, no-one cared. That all suddenly became history.

TR: Yes.

WP: So then you turned elsewhere, Trevor.

TR: Well I had started writing when I was still in the Arts Council and I realised that I could write, which I hadn't really realised before. I should say that none of this would have been possible without the support of my wife, Hannah, a very gifted and strong-minded doctor.

JH: Your first book was a biography of James Kennaway?

TR: No, I left the Arts Council in '79 and I had two commissions because I didn't just leave, hoping that things would work out. I'd got two contracts; one was to write a Companion to Scottish Literature, which was part of the series of companions to world literatures which never took off. I think one or two appeared but I did the one on Scottish literature. The other one was a book called *Precipitous City*, which was a history of literary Edinburgh.

WP: You had written assorted essays before that, though.

TR: I'd written various pieces. But Kennaway was my first biography and it was an interesting book to write because Kennaway was a fascinating character, who made his name as a scriptwriter in Hollywood, like Neil Paterson, but also his fame had been established by writing *Tunes of Glory*...

JH: Which, of course, became a famous film.

TR: And this was wonderful for Kennaway because he got famous at an extremely young age, but it also dogged him, because everybody wanted him to write more books like *Tunes of Glory*.But he was much more interested in writing a different kind of fiction and subsequently did write a number of very highly regarded novels but never had the same kind of popular acclaim, although he had the literary success. And we'll never know whether he was a really great writer or not because he died at the early age of forty.

WP: What took you to Kennaway, what was the connection?

TR: The connection was that Mainstream, Bill Campbell and Pete MacKenzie who had started up Mainstream Publishing, as one of their first publishing initiatives was to republish all Kennaway's novels, the eight surviving novels, and they also found that Kennaway had also written a long short story, called *The Dollar Bottom*, which was made into a film in 1980. It was his very first published piece in a magazine called *Lilliput*. Now, there was a fragment of another story, which is a sequel to it, and I edited that and put it together and the Kennaway family liked it and, as the novels were being republished, the idea came about that a biography should be written and I was fortunate enough to be asked to write it. By this time, this is in the early 1980s, I wasn't just writing these books, because I did a lot of work for BBC radio and I found radio one of the most enjoyable mediums in which to work. I wrote a number of plays for radio drama and I adapted books, for Book at Bedtime. And I did a lot of on-air work behind the microphone.

WP: Which you must have found to be wonderful training ground for narration.

TR: Indeed, yes, because if anything has guided my development, it's been an absolute insistence that you must have a strong narrative line, tell a story. And that's why all the books that I've written, I've always tried to make them readable, because all that you're doing is telling a story.

JH: And of course now you have very successfully brought together your military family background and also your early desire to be in the army, with writing, as a military historian.

WP: Your first military book was *Fighting Mac*, why don't you tell us a little about that, because you didn't elaborate earlier on the German connection.

TR: *Fighting Mac* was a very personal book: it tells the story of a man, major general Sir Hector MacDonald, who had the distinction of starting as a private soldier in Queen Victoria's army, being commissioned from the ranks, a most unusual achievement, and ending up as a major general, only to lose everything when he was involved in a sex scandal in 1903 and chose to commit suicide in a Paris hotel rather than face court martial. I think the army was saying to him; having turned you into a gentleman, we expect you to behave like one. I didn't know anything about Hector MacDonald until the Summer of 1962; I'd spent some time at a school in Germany, the Kieler Gelehrtenschule, where the family I'd stayed with was the von Mackensen family. Knut, the Field Marshal's great-nephew, was a great friend of mine, and still is, we still see a lot of each other. Now, as I was making my way back to St Andrews, I found a copy of the Sunday Express, and this headline jumped out at me; *Did a crofter's son lead the Kaiser's army?*, written by a man called Edgar Lustgarten, in his day a trained barrister, who became a very popular journalist, and whose specialty was writing about unsolved mysteries. The story that he told was a fantastic one: Lustgarten postulated that instead of committing suicide in 1903, Hector MacDonald had faked his suicide and gone across to the German army where he'd taken the place of a cavalry officer, August von Mackensen, who then went on to become a field marshal in the German army. I thought this was absolute rubbish and wrote, probably very intemperately, to Edgar Lustgarten pointing out the impossibility of this happening. And I got a very polite letter back saying: Well, I know what you're saying, but of course the facts are by no means easy to prove. It remains a possibility. And so I just left it at that and thought nothing of it. It wasn't until twenty years later that I found myself in a train from Glasgow and I told the story to an executive with Scottish Television and he said: Well, we must make this into a television film, which we did and Bill Campbell getting to hear about this said: Trevor, you must write the book at the same time. Now I wrote that book in about eight weeks. It shows. But the important thing was that both book and film were very successful and it introduced me to the fact that there was a huge audience out there – and a very voracious audience – for military history. That made me change direction.

WP: In our recent interview, Tessa Ransford suggested, very tellingly, that one of the problems with the Arts Council now and with the whole festival syndrome, is that they think that writers only want money, whereas primarily, they want readers.

JH: Yes.

TR: Yes, and that's why I outlined the way our policy worked at the Arts Council, encouragement of writers, production of work, promotion of work.

WP: Yes. But you had several activities underway at this time, 1983. Round about then you were also editing *Lines Review*.

TR: I was asked to edit *Lines Review* by Callum MacDonald and I felt very privileged to be able to do that because there had been a number of very distinguished editors before me, and the other thing too was that I personally liked Callum MacDonald. He was a man I took to.

WP: Did you take over from Robin Fulton?

TR: No, from Bill Montgomerie.

Editing *Lines Review* was wonderful because it meant spending a lot of time in the company of Callum MacDonald and his stories about literary life in the 1950s and 1960s were fascinating. I wish I'd recorded them. One of the reasons why I warmed to him was that this was a man who had put his money where his mouth was. He believed it was necessary to promote and publish Scottish writing at a time when it was unfashionable to do so. He did it against the odds. It was hard graft.

WP: Again, Tessa was telling us that there was also quite a lot of internal opposition to Callum's publishing, from within his own company.

TR: Yes, indeed. The other thing too which was a distinct pleasure of working with Callum was that *Lines Review* was a purely literary magazine, it wasn't anything else and he encouraged me to do one or two special issues as well, which opened it up. We did a Canadian issue.

JH: So he did take an active interest in the editorial policy?

TR: Yes. Everything went to the editorial office in Loanhead and then once a week a big parcel would arrive *[for me]* full of submissions or the latest proofs and I could always tell it was from Callum because Callum was an unreconstructed smoker and you could always smell it in the package. In fact, when I gave the oration at his funeral, I mentioned that and there were one or two nods of recognition.

JH: Yes, I remember that.

TR: Again, Callum had exceptionally high standards, of editing, proof reading, typography and he would tell me if I was encouraging someone whose work he didn't think was up to the mark. He could be very firm about that.

WP: And by this point, the high point of the Thatcher years in the mid-eighties, Scotland is beginning to change again: massive unemployment, a lot of discontent, the Old Guard, as it were: MacDiarmid, Muir, Sydney Goodsir Smith, Alex Scott, Neil Gunn, Robert Garioch are all dead. So there is a whole generational shift.

JH: And also there has been a shift from Edinburgh towards Glasgow.

TR: Well, the 1980s saw the revival of a great deal of literary energy in Glasgow: Alastair Gray, James Kelman, Tom Leonard, Liz Lochhead, all of whom of course had been around in the seventies but it seems that they came to the fore in the 1980s. Jim Kelman won the Booker Prize. The thing about them too, is that they were able to have a readership outside Scotland in a way that hadn't always happened before.

JH: That's right.

TR: Other perhaps than someone like MacCaig. You must remember that earlier there had been writers like Eric Linklater and Neil Gunn and they'd had audiences outside Scotland.

JH: But the world of the 60s and 70s was very much orientated towards poetry. Again, with Gray and Kelman, the Scottish novel began to expand outside the bounds of Scotland.

WP: And then, Trevor, you begin to become known I suppose primarily as a military historian.

TR: Yes, by the late 80s the subject matter of my books was either military history or imperial history. I was fortunate enough that a number of these books achieved very high sales and that gave me financial security, which I might not otherwise have had.

WP: The book on National Service attracted an enormous amount of attention.

TR: *The Best Years of Their Lives,* which appeared in 1986, sold thousands of copies, it was serialised by the *Sunday Times* and was made into a very successful *Channel 4* film and in fact is still in print, astonishingly, twenty-one years later.

WP: There must now be a generation younger than ours who think of you entirely as a military historian.

TR: Military historian or journalist, all of which were late-life developments really. The journalism is quite interesting because although I'd written book reviews and the occasional literary feature for *The Scotsman*, especially when Harry Reid was there – he was a great encourager of my work – I would never have counted myself as a journalist. I still don't. But what happened was that in 1990 I was writing a book about John Bagot Glubb, Glubb Pasha, who was a great British soldier and diplomat in the Middle East and he'd also worked in Iraq. I was doing a lot of work in London at that time in the National Archives on British policy in the Middle East and when Saddam Hussein invaded Kuwait, in August 1990, I was one of the few writers who could actually explain why this was a problem. I was also asked to be a commentator by the BBC and by that time I had a lot of close links with the British Army. I was forty-five at the time, which meant that a lot of the people who were my sort of age in the army, were a new generation of army officers who didn't mind giving out information, discreetly. So I knew a lot of what was happening about the government's defence policy and I was taken out to Saudi Arabia on the eve of the military operations and spent time with senior commanders, air, land and sea commanders, and so I had a pretty good idea about what tactics were going to be used when the attack began. Unlike many other people who were talking doom and gloom about chemical and nuclear and biological weapons being used, I could see that the sheer weight of the American, British, French allied army, which had been training to fight the Red Army, was not going to be defeated by a second-division army run by the Iraqis. And so it proved. As a result of this, I was asked to have a deeper involvement in journalism and Andrew Jaspan, who was the editor of *Scotland on Sunday* at the time, another man who influenced my life, gave me a high-falutin' title as an associate editor, which is totally meaningless but it sounds good, and he got me to write on defence and international matters and I travelled a lot during the nineties as well. And of course had a lot of close connections with the armed forces. So you can teach an old dog new tricks and I found myself becoming more deeply involved in journalism.

WP: Which must also feed your historical writings.

TR: Yes, it does and I had to learn how to write concisely because a newspaper article is doing well if it's eighteen hundred words; more often than not it's a thousand, twelve hundred words. And it's very difficult honing your work down for that. Then I left *Scotland on Sunday,* shortly after Andrew Jaspan went off to *The Observer* in the mid-1990s, and also Andrew Neil came in and I left because I couldn't work with a barbarian like that. Even if I hadn't left, I would have been pushed. But when the *Sunday Herald* started up in 1999, again, another Andrew Jaspan initiative, he got me on the team but this time he wanted me to be more involved in the editorial side of the papers and I'm still there and of course, things are changing in Scotland too, and we felt we had to respond to that, following the success of the devolution bill.

WP: You have established a reputation as, at the least, a serious military historian. Did you have difficulties at first because you didn't have an academic background?

TR: Not particularly, no. I think there's a very good tradition of independent historians in Britain anyway. And my subject matter by 1983 was mainly British military history. I realised that there was no point in ploughing a Scottish furrow. I suppose if I did find a difficulty, it was getting research facilities. I was helped in the late nineties when Professor Peter Jones invited me to become a Fellow of the International Institute for Advanced Studies in the Humanities at Edinburgh University. This was a very stimulating academic and intellectual background to be in, because you were given an office in the Institute and, more importantly, you had a handle to your jug and people overseas, especially Russia – I was writing a book about the Crimea at the time – didn't understand an individual, but they could understand somebody who was a Fellow of an Institute. But also, it was a very stimulating environment to be in.

JH: Do you find any conflict between the much faster pace of journalism and the presumably slower pace that you have to work at on serious historical work? Can you move from one to the other?

TR: Relatively easily. It's helped by the fact that I only have to devote a day and a half to two days to journalism, so the other days I'm writing.

WP: The kind of career you have outlined is itself extraordinary enough, but doesn't account for the sheer quantity of your labours. I have almost all of your books and they occupy a large bookshelf if I put them together. That's a tremendous amount of work. How do you account for that productivity?

TR: Well, you see, unlike an academic, I don't do the research and
      then write the book. I'm writing and researching at the same
      time. And what has helped me – and has helped every writer –
      has been the advent of the computer. I wrote my last book on a
      typewriter in 1992 and since then everything else has been on the
      computer.

WP: And your writing has allowed you to re-establish ancestral and
      other ties, by going back to India, for example, and out to Africa.

TR: Well, two books which gave me particular pleasure to write: the
      first one was *The Last Days of the Raj*, which is a history of the end
      of empire in India. And funnily enough, Walter, you helped the
      spark, because we had a lunch party for my mother's seventieth
      birthday and you were there and I heard my mother telling a
      story to you which I'd never heard her tell before. And I suddenly
      realised that a lot of these people who had lived through the
      period of the end of empire in India, were into their seventies
      and eighties and that unless you recorded their memories, it
      would have disappeared. So I began with my mother and then
      got handed on and eventually found myself interviewing a large
      number of people who had lived through that experience in
      Britain. But I thought: there's something wrong here, because it
      wasn't just a British experience, it was also an Indian experience.
      So I wanted to interview people in India, Pakistan and Bangladesh
      and that was done for me by a researcher called Gillian Wright.
      She was an associate of Mark Tully's, famous journalist and writer
      about India and the India correspondent for the BBC for many
      years. I was doing a programme with Mark Tully and I asked
      him if he could help in any way and he said, no, he couldn't,
      but he had this associate who would. So she did all the Indian
      interviewing for me, which was terrifically helpful. I just couldn't
      have spent several months in India to do those interviews, so she
      did them for me under my direction. And *The Last Days of the Raj*
      was the first British history, which also included an Indian aspect.

JH: Yes, quite ground-breaking.

TR: And in fact, *Last Days of the Raj* is still in print in India. The rights were bought by Rupa Books. It was published in India as well as in Britain and I was very proud of that. And when I started going to India a lot in the 1990s, I got a great kick from seeing it on sale in various places. Quite ridiculous really but it is very important to me. And I wrote a companion about the end of empire in Africa, which was less successful, probably because Africa was less coherent. But that did take me to Africa for, again, I felt I wasn't going to make any sense of it unless I travelled there.

WP: And you still maintain your ties with Scottish writing?

TR: Yes, I do. It's never really gone away. I know a lot of people look on me just as a journalist and a military historian, but throughout that time I was still producing Scottish literary books, a collection of Scottish war stories, an anthology of poetry and prose of the First World War and in fact, now, of course, I have managed to marry the two in a book which Hugh Andrew encouraged me to write on Scotland in the First World War.

JH: Are you working on something at the moment?

TR: I am finishing off a book on the Plantagenet wars. I was given a three-book contract to write; the first book was the Crimean War, the second one was the Civil War, the Wars of the Three Kingdoms, which, the English Civil War was in a British context, and the Plantagenet wars. Again it's about the development of warfare but seeing it not just in terms of the Wars of the Roses, by which name they're better known, but there was also a lot of fighting against Scotland, a lot of fighting in Ireland and of course the tail-end of what is also wrongly known as the Hundred Years War.

WP: Will you at some moment turn to fiction?

TR: I have tried my hand at the short story and plays but I think it's too late to turn to fiction. They say that writing history is the new fiction but writing history you have to stick to the facts. But I just have so much on my plate. Going back to the Arts Council, we often gave money to writers who were in positions like myself so that they could stop doing what they were doing and concentrate on something else.

JH: You're very fortunate in having reached the position in which that's not necessary.

TR: Well no, it is because I earn my living from journalism and writing military history. If I wanted to switch to fiction, I'd need the space to do it. My publisher isn't going to suddenly fund me to write fiction when I've never written any.

WP: People may forget or never have known that Churchill made his living from journalism, not from his politics, from journalism and his historical works.

TR: We should also not forget the tradition within Scottish literature of Scottish writers writing military history. In the nineteenth century James Grant kept himself alive by writing military fiction but in our own century John Buchan wrote the history of the Royal Scots Fusiliers as well as a voluminous history of the First World War, Eric Linklater, historian of the Black Watch, George Blake on the Lowland Division.

WP: And you wrote the official history of the Welsh Guards. Is there any one piece of work you are especially proud of?

TR: One's books are like one's children, you don't have any favourite. But the books I feel that have been ground-breaking, I suppose have been The Crimean War and Civil War, simply because with Crimea up till now it's always been seen as a series of disasters and it's always been seen more or less completely from a British point of view. Yes, the French were there, but very few people understand that the Sardinians were there. I tried to see it from the Russian perspective as well, using Russian diplomatic correspondence and Russian diplomatic papers, because the war was in the Black Sea area and there was also a huge naval war in the Baltic but everybody forgets about that. And I felt that made people sit up and take notice. And the Civil War, which was subtitled War of the Three Kingdoms, I put the history of the English civil war into a Scottish and Irish context.

WP: I know your children think of themselves as Scots. Do you think about your own nationality? You obviously don't really think of yourself now as English.

TR: No, I can't think of myself as being English. There's only English blood in me, but on the other hand, yes, I think of myself as a Scot.

WP: Would you have said that thirty years ago?

TR: No, I had mixed feelings. It is such a long time now and Scotland has been so central to my development. And I have such a genuine love for the country, an exasperated love of course.

WP: Well, in Scotland if it's not exasperated, it's probably not love, it's probably sentiment.

TR: I have great attachment to the Scottish countryside, especially Angus, where I've spent a lot of my life over the last fifteen years. And the Scottish people, Scottish literature, Scottish music. I like dancing Scottish reels.

WP: This is clearly your home.

TR: Yes and it could be nothing else.

WP: Are you a member of the Church of Scotland?

TR: I am a member of the Church of Scotland. I returned to the Church of Scotland when I went up to Angus.

WP: Returned?

TR: Aye, well I was a member of the Church when I was a boy, in Martyrs Church in St. Andrews. And I returned to the Church about ten years ago in Glen Prosen. The minister at that time was a remarkable man called James Leadbeater, whom I liked immensely, a terrific man. Alas, he's dead now but he gave sermons which tickled the upper brain cells and he encouraged me back into the Church. I don't worship on a regular basis. It is important to me.

WP: Would you say you were a religious man?

TR: No, not at all, but until my beloved youngest son Patrick died of heat exhaustion in Oxford last year, while taking part in a charity cycle run, I would have said that I put my trust in my faith. Can't say that now. I'm not asking, where was God on the road to Oxford? It doesn't work like that. But I was dismayed by the Kirk's response, which was indifferent to say the least. What kept us going through those dark and terrible days was the love and support of many loyal friends. That counted and meant much to all of us. If there is any glimmer left, it's the strength I get from being in the hills and wild lonely places, the sense of God reduced to the pure breath of reason. Yes, God in natural things.

JH: A Wordsworthian vision.

TR: Perhaps.

WP: Are there any other issues you want to comment on which we haven't already touched?

TR: Yes. I supported the devolution movement in both the eighties and nineties. I was delighted that devolution came to pass. In the early days I supported the Scottish Parliament. I thought it was a fine thing. But like many others I've become very disillusioned by what's happened. I think that the calibre of a lot of the parliamentarians is very low indeed. I feel that there's been no leadership from the Executive and what many of us feared originally in the 1970s has come to pass, that we have an Executive dominated by people who were probably doing very well as local councillors but really don't have the same capacity as parliamentarians.

JH: The trouble is this half-way house. I see now some movement among certain people who at one time saw continuing strength in the Union. I think that some of those people are now beginning to see that this half-way house isn't any use whatsoever and that the only way forward is full independence. Only then will you get people of stature offering themselves for a real parliament.

TR: Well you see the only person of any stature in Scottish politics is Alec Salmond. It's going to be interesting to see what happens at the May election. But all that's happened is that the Executive is just a local council writ large.

JH: Yes.

TR: With more money, more power and with more capacity to make a fool of themselves.

WP: We have to hope that they are kept at arms' length from the arts. Otherwise, they will be a catastrophe.

TR: I had a good example of this: one of the things that I became involved in in the 1990s was the Airborne Initiative. This is a ground-breaking organisation which provided alternatives to sentencing for high-tariff young offenders, young thugs who were going to spend the rest of their life in prison. By offering them an alternative, based very largely on outdoor recreation but also on making them face up to the reasons why they committed crime in the first place, they would be dissuaded from spending the rest of their lives in prison. And it worked. But the problem about it was that we were dealing with very damaged young people who were hardened criminals. These were really tough guys, very difficult to turn round and also they came from the most desperate backgrounds. It was an eye-opener for me quite honestly. They came from what I would almost term was an under-class. We raised twenty-five percent of our funds, the executive funded us by giving us the £6,000 per skull for the nine-week course, which otherwise would be spent on keeping these young men in prison. But the executive could not stand the notion that here was an independent body doing something which they ought to be doing. And in 2004 they withdrew funding from us. I had to deal with the Justice Department and it was a very unhappy experience because it was clear to me that they had this Stalinist need to control everything and didn't like the idea of an independent group. It didn't help also that we were establishment and also because of the army link to it. There were a number of ex-army people on the Board. Well, the chap chairing us resigned precipitately, leaving me as deputy chairman to close down the organisation. It was a desperate and unhappy period. Also, I'm afraid to say, made me antagonistic towards the Scottish Executive.

WP: The buffooneries of the present Executive, notwithstanding, I think it's become clear that there's no going back to a previous dispensation.

TR: To a certain extent, one has to take the long view. As an historian it would be absurd to be judgemental about the possibilities this early in its existence.

JH: It was always going to be like this.

TR: Yes and no, because in the original discussions, they hoped that they would be able to encourage people into politics who were talented but weren't part of the political set-up. And this has proved to be utterly impossible, because of the domination of the party system.

WP: That may change shortly.

TR: It may. It could change at local level. Originally it was hoped that independent candidates would be able to stand. You've got someone like, say, Iain Noble, who is a gifted chap who has done a tremendous amount for Scottish life, the establishment of *Sabhal Mor at Ostaig* on Skye, who might want to stand as an independent but would never have any chance of being elected. And there are countless other examples, of talented people in Scotland who could make a substantial contribution to Scotland by being independent members on the Executive.

WP: There is also the question that, who would want to stand when the name of politician probably has a less agreeable odour now than at any time in the past century?

TR: That's probably true. You also have the strength of the Labour Party, a more or less non-existent Tory Party, an SNP which really can't make up its mind whether it wants to go for independence or not, and a Lib-Dem Party which nobody knows what it stands for. So it's a very confusing situation and it remains to be seen whether the large exodus from the Labour Party and the breaking down of support for it, largely as a result of the disastrous decision to go into the war against Iraq in 2003, and the way in which British foreign policy is being wrapped up with American foreign policy and the unhappiness many people feel with Iraq, whether this will translate into not voting for Labour. You just don't know. Traditionally, foreign policy hasn't guided people's voting.

JH: Perhaps Joseph Devine, the Bishop of Motherwell, will, having asked his flock not to vote Labour.

TR: But then he did that over Section 28 and did that translate into anything? No, I don't think so.

WP: Do you feel optimistic about the Scottish future?

TR: A number of things make me feel very pessimistic, the failure of the Executive over a decade really to get any sort of grip. Sooner or later, Scotland's going to have to face up to the question, does it want independence or does it want to continue in this twilit way. The bulk of our family lives in England and I find myself spending increasingly more time there at the moment, with the boys' families growing up and being a grandfather myself now. There's no knowledge of and little interest in what happens in Scotland. Scottish affairs are not reported in the British press. They are reported in the British press in Scotland but that's for Scottish eyes only. People in England aren't terribly interested about what happens in Scotland. There's a growing irritation with Scots taking a major part in British life, the West Lothian Question, as formulated by Tam Dalyell. At Christmas I said, We've got the anniversary of the Act of Union coming up next year, and a relation responded: Yes, let's celebrate it by repealing it. (*laughter*)

JH: That's the way it'll probably happen.

Trevor Royle has added the following postscript:

"In the May 2007 election TR voted SNP. Within weeks of forming a minority government the new Justice Minister, Kenny McAskill, wrote to TR promising that the party would keep its election manifesto pledge to restore the Airborne Initiative."

5. WILLIAM HERSHAW

William Hershaw, 1957: Poet, playwright and musician

*This conversation took place at Wullie's home in Lochgelly on 28th. July, 2009.
Present were John Herdman and Walter Perrie.*

JOHN HERDMAN: Willie, you must be one of the most prominent of
the younger generation of poets. Duncan Glen always used to
talk about being among the younger generation of Scottish poets
when he was about fifty, and you are just around fifty now. Would
you regard Scots as your native tongue?

WILLIAM HERSHAW: Yes I would. I think I've come to realise that as
I've got older. The other day when I was teaching, I was teaching a
George Mackay Brown poem...

WALTER PERRIE: Which one?

WH: It was *Peerie Mansie's Boat,* because I really like George Mackay
Brown, a fantastic poet, and one of the pupils said to me *What does
peerie mean, Sir*? And I said, Oh, it means *wee, smaa.* So I translated
a Scots word into Scots. I guess that is my natural default mode,
if you like. I know we were talking about George Philp earlier;
George referred to me as a native Scots-speaker. I don't think of
myself like that. I think of it as more of a kind of hybrid thing,
which I think causes problems at times for me. I have different
modes of speaking.

JH: Most Scots do.

WP: Could you elaborate on that a bit? Is it about English as a class
language?

WH: Yes, I think class comes into it. I was very interested to hear about Matthew Fitt when he was at university, because I believe that Matthew insisted on speaking in Scots and also writing his essays in Scots when he was a student.

JH: That is interesting.

WH: Now back in the seventies I would quite like to have been able to accomplish that. I guess I didn't have the confidence and the bollocks to do that kind of thing. But that's interesting. On the other hand I am always very conscious of what I would refer to as the kind of style of speaking Scots, which strikes me as a wee bit... artificial, literary, self-conscious?

JH: I would agree.

WH: So I guess I've felt often just caught in the middle a bit. But when it came to writing poetry, that was a different matter. I think when I was a young poet, like most young poets I was looking for a voice, because you want to write with authority, above all. So the early poems were in English.

JH: Oh were they? Was that when you were at university?

WH: No. Actually, well, it might be a good idea just to go back to the beginning.

When I was at St. Andrews' High School in Kirkcaldy – this would be in the early seventies – I was very interested in writing songs, singer-songwriter stuff, because at that time there was Bob Dylan and Neil Young. There were also local people; there was a guy called Rab Noakes who came from Fife.

JH: Indeed.

WH: And I was very influenced by Alan Hull, *Lindisfarne*, he was a Geordie songwriter. These guys were all around. I guess it was the tail end of the folk revival. There is always a folk revival going on at any given time. We all had guitars and were forming bands and stuff like that. I was writing about twelve songs every day.

WP: Twelve songs a day?

WH: I was very prolific – all rubbish. But what I discovered was that the lyrics were coming, they were flowing along more freely than the music because I wasn't very musically accomplished at all.

WP: But you could write a score?

WH: No, I could bash oot some chords and I could write words and make up a tune. Anyway, at that particular time Carl MacDougall came to Fife and he was Writer in Residence with the Arts in Fife. And I think a big bit of their budget went into a magazine called *Words*, which was quite a good magazine.

JH: Yes it was, a very important magazine.

WH: Because you had all these people, Hugh MacDiarmid appeared in it, George Mackay Brown, Norman MacCaig, all the kind of literary giants of the day. But he also published a lot of new writing and that was the very first time I read stuff by James Kelman, Alastair Gray, and yourself and Alan Spence because there they were, all these young writers coming through at that time. And he had a section for Fife writers as well. I think that's how he had to justify it as "Arts in Fife".

I had a great English teacher, a guy called Dennis MacNamara, and when I think back and compare my own job as an English teacher now, Dennis was great. We never saw a past paper, he never spoke about examinations. What he did was, he gave us literature the whole time. He would tell you to read that, and then he would discuss it and talk about it and ask your opinions about it.

WP: And that must have been with a certain enthusiasm.

WH: Oh, aye, it was a time when I think schools and English departments were not accountable in the way that they are now.

WP: Can you put a date on it?

WH: Well, I was lucky to have him in fourth year, fifth year, sixth year, so that would be '73, '74, '75. And he taught a wide range of literature and he said, why don't you have a go? I know you write a lot of songs, why don't you have a go at doing poetry? About that time I can remember we were studying John Donne, the *Holy Sonnets*. So I thought, Oh, great! and I wrote a sonnet and that was easy, a piece of cake: fourteen lines, ten syllables. So I actually wrote a sonnet sequence, gave it to my teacher. It disappeared and then I forgot all about it. Then one day this magazine appeared through the post and I had a cheque for ten bob or whatever. So I was right in there with George Mackay Brown and John Herdman and all these guys and I felt this was great. I thought "this is easy! I will make a career out of this." First time lucky! So I decided I would be a writer. It changed my whole view of things, because I didn't intend to study English at university. But I thought; I'll go to study English at Edinburgh and the great secrets will be unlocked to me.

WP: Had you had any intention of reading English before that?

WH: No. I think I was going to do something like science, like my pals. Anyway, so there was this kind of kudos of being a published writer while I was still at school. But I do think that is a great thing, that kind of encouragement, because it keeps you going.

JH: It's absolutely vital isn't it, to get some kind of feedback when you're a young writer?

WP: Yes, you are in the process of forming an identity.

WH: Yes, but these were poems in English, because I really felt that Scots was the language of an older generation, much as I admired it. Dennis MacNamara had introduced us to MacDiarmid and to Burns and to Robert Henryson, among other writers.

JH: That's very good.

WH: So what I did was I started writing every form and genre of poetry known to man: elegies, odes, villanelles, stuffing them into envelopes and sending them away, and looking up *Catalyst* or *Gairm, Lines Review, Chapman, The Scotsman* or whatever, the whole lot. And I was very naïve, I mean I didn't even put in a stamped addressed envelope, the poems were hand-written, and I waited. I think about three years later I was still thinking they were going to get published. Because there was no reply. I was questioning the silence! So I began to realise that it was not as easy as I thought it might be. In fact, it has been down hill all the way since then. (*laughter*)

WP: Tell us a bit about your family background.

WH: Well, I came from a mining background, my mum was one of eight and my dad was one of twelve.

WP: That's twenty!

JH: A lot of first cousins, second cousins.

WH: That's handy when you bring a book out. My dad's background was Kelty and in those days it was called a mixed marriage because there was a lot of sectarianism around here. My mum was Catholic and I think there were a couple of my dad's brothers refused to have anything to do with them.

WP: Was that Scottish Catholic or Irish?

WH: A bit of both.

WP: Interesting, because where I came from in Scotland, people usually made that distinction.

WH: Aye. My mum's family came from Lanarkshire, they came from a wee village caa'd The Forth and they moved through to Ballingry I think in the thirties or thereabouts.

WP: On the way here I was telling John that my grandfather came to work in the pits here briefly in the thirties. There was no work in Lanarkshire.

WH: Yes, a job and a new house, and it was a big deal. I remember being very influenced by both my grandfathers, but particularly my maternal grandfather. He was called Comp; it was a nickname he had picked up in the Pit. But round about the early eighties when he had retired, a few years before he died, I think he had a notion to revisit a lot of the places he had known. And I remember we went down to High Valleyfield, to the Miners' Institute there, and when you go in the door there's a big plaque like a war memorial, for a pit disaster in 1931 I think; there were about thirty five people killed. And you could see from the names that a lot of them were related to each other. And I remember we had a few pints that night and a game of dominoes and there was a guy speaking to me and to my grandad. He was a retired miner; he had been on that shift that night in the thirties but he had had the flu' or some such thing and he didn't fancy it either because they all knew it was dangerous. The atmosphere was full of dust and whatever and they knew that something could kick off. So he didnae go down and he just sat and told me all about it and there was this kind of guilt coming through that his mates had been killed.

JH: Survivor guilt.

WH: He spoke about them as if they were still alive and still down there, in their youth and he had got old and had bad lungs. And when I came home I just wrote it all down because I had always assumed that Scots was the language of my grandfathers and Hugh MacDiarmid and old people. But I was really delighted to be able to write a poem in Scots because it was perfect, I think, from a poetic point of view, because you're writing in a language that you half-know.

WP: Why do you say half-know?

WH: I would say a language of bairnhood.

JH: I think there is this, that most Scots, even if they're not in any sense Scots-speakers have got a tacit knowledge of Scots.

WP: It is why so many can still make sense of *hearing* a Burns poem.

JH: I was always able to read Scots without any difficulty, although I don't have any Scots-speaking background apart from a few words which my parents would use that were Scots.

WH: I think the reason I say 'half-know' is probably because I felt I didn't have the range of vocabulary but what I had kind of hard-wired in there was the kind of, I don't know, syntax?

I was initially put off because I would pick up these words when I was reading Soutar or MacDiarmid or whoever, and think: I don't know what that means, but the rhythm was there.

JH: That's right.

WP: It's the rhythm that carries the emotion and fixes our feelings to the language, our identification with it, it's the sound, the pacing.

WH: Aye. My attraction to it was also the strange words though, because you would have to choose your word carefully, more carefully than in English, where you might get sloppy.

WP: So was English debased for you?

WH: I wouldnae say debased, I mean all poetry is artificial language, it's contrived.

Whether it's Tom Leonard spelling *the* as *thi* or whatever, it's a contrivance. So I was really pleased that I could write in Scots. But then again, it was a big challenge in the wake of the people who had gone before.

WP: Can I put the matter the other way round and ask whether your espousal of Scots and the way you have taken it on from your background, as the language you identify with, excludes anything in English?

WH: No. The title poem of *The Cowdenbeath Man* is in English. It is an elegy for the mining community of Cowdenbeath.

WP: You don't feel any dichotomy?

WH: I don't. I remember one of the very early *Stanza* poetry festivals; we had brought out *Four Fife Poets*: Harvey Holton and Tom Hubbard, John Brewster, myself, and we were invited up there to do a reading and it was being recorded for a programme, *Time for Verse,* and it was Carol Ann Duffy interviewed us all. Her very first question was: You write in Scots, obviously this is a political statement? What a loaded question!

I'd never ever thought of it like that. And I said: Well, no, I write in Scots because I'm Scottish. You wouldn't ask someone French why they were writing in French?

WP: Well you might actually, say in Provence or Brittany. Most people in France didn't speak French until after about 1800.

WH: That is very interesting. Just the same point though?

JH: That's something I didn't know until fairly recently when I read a book about nineteenth century France. The number of different dialects there were in France is quite extraordinary.

WP: They weren't for the most part dialects, they were distinct languages.

WH: I didn't know that. Getting back to the *Stanza* event, that threw me a wee bit. But it made me think about it. I write poetry because that's what I can do. I can make a decent fist of it – sometimes.

WP: There has to be more to it than that; it's not much of an answer as to why you write poetry.

JH: Can I bring in something here; your forthcoming book *Johnny Aathin* has got a very original technique of combining a prose commentary, offsetting on one page the prose and on the other facing page, the poetry. That is one of the most interesting uses of Scots prose that I've seen in a long time. And actually, this kind of commentary-chorus has not been used very often in poetry. One example that springs to mind is *The Ancient Mariner*

WP: Explain!

JH: Well, in *The Ancient Mariner*, the final edition anyway, there is a prose gloss alongside the poetry which gives the narrative in a different way. I think in Willie's poem the narrative burden is really carried by the prose and then the poetry elaborates on it lyrically.

WH: Well I am very conscious of the fact that there is an awful lot of very turgid poetry in Scots, including my own. The first volume, the Aberdeen University Press volume, *Fower Brigs tae a Kinrick*, festooned with footnotes, these kind of poems where you are determined to prove some kind of philosophical or political point and all that really happens is that the lyric magic evaporates, and I have written a lot of bad poems like that, that don't flow, that just don't work as poetry. You could call it polemical poetry.

WP: MacDiarmid never seems to have suffered from that lack of confidence which reassures itself with footnotes. In the early work in Scots, the poetry is completely confident. Later on, writing in English, he does show a sort of deference towards erudition and the erudite and Chris thought there was nothing better than a professor.

JH: That's right.

WH: I think originally with *Johnny Aathin* the publisher was thinking that there should maybe be a glossary, but I thought the prose commentary would suffice.

JH: That's a very good way of looking at it because it perhaps explains a lot that wouldn't be obvious to anyone who wasn't a Scots speaker.

WH: Also, it was fun to write the prose.

JH: It's also important because Scots prose has been so relatively undeveloped. I thought you used it in a very easy, natural way there, whereas very often when people have tried to write Scots prose in the past, there's been a kind of arch, couthy quality to it.

WP: What do you say to this, Willie: that we lose the Court in 1603, so we lose the greatest centre of patronage; we have already lost with the Reformation the patronage of monasteries and the great Prelates, which supported the Makars, as the French Court supported Ronsard, who, incidentally, came to Scotland in the entourage of Mary Queen of Scots, almost certainly to Fife and to Perth and Stirling. So it's no longer possible to have a Dunbar, a Henryson, a Gavin Douglas. Then you have a century and a half when nothing much is allowed to happen in poetry and there's no drama, because the Kirk dominates everything. Then along comes 1707 and you lose the other main centre of patronage and, crucially, when that happens Scots ceases to be the language of authority. Where then does the authority of Scots and what you have to say in it come from if it no longer has any purchase on authority, on the state, on the centres of power? I remember once hearing that a language was a dialect with an army and a navy.

WH: But that's fine though. That's where a poet should be. If it's an outlaw attitude that's fine. I am quite comfortable with that.

WP: Yes, that's fine for the writer, but what about an audience? One consequence further down the road of that loss of linguistic authority is the Kailyaird.

WH: Well it depends who you think your audience is. I go back to the fact that I do write for myself. It's a compulsion. As I said before, it's a bad habit I should have given up in my adolescence. But you do need an audience.

WP: Why do you need an audience if you are writing for yourself?

JH: Because language is communication. Even if you are writing for yourself there is always an assumed audience, if only notionally.

WP: Is language not quintessentially a public instrument? Can it exist without an Other?

WH: I don't know the answers to these questions. Part of the problem for me and always will be for anyone writing in Scots, is Hugh MacDiarmid, for anybody   who comes after him. I have to make myself really clear here because what Hugh MacDiarmid achieved, the accomplishment of what he did is so huge, but there is also a negative side to it too, for anyone writing now in Scots is compared to him. The other thing was that he was a bit of an intellectual snob.

WP: In part he may have been an intellectual snob because he had no very extended schooling, because he was an auto-didact.

WH: Yes, but possibly poets don't follow him so much now: Don Paterson, John Burnside, Robert Crawford, Herbert, the people who have made a reputation for themselves – the successful poets – have eschewed the MacDiarmid thing but what they have picked out of it obviously is that MacDiarmid is reacting to the Kailyaird. What we've got now is a real fear of expressing anything that could be labelled as 'sentimental'.

JH: Yes, that's right.

WH: It's gone too far the other way so you get all this clever post-modernist, ironic poetry. I wrote a poem satirising that:

> *Turner Prize;*
> *A cou and a cauf,*
> *cut in hauf.*

JH: Yes, there's nothing from the heart.

WH: There are bits of *Johnny Aathin* which are quite sentimental and nostalgic and that's deliberate because it's the mind of an old miner who's cracking up, so he will deteriorate into sentiment and bathos and so on.

JH: It's feeling.

WH: Aye, he's looking back at his life but, as I say, in modern Scottish
       poetry there is this real fear, it's almost like exposing yourself
       emotionally. Because MacDiarmid, great as he was and a fantastic
       poet, was relentlessly name-checking and name-dropping, and all
       the rest of it. You know, Russian poets and novelists...

JH: (*in Grieve's voice*) My friend, the great Azerbaijani poet Kaikhosru
       Shapurji Sorabji....

       (*own voice*) well he was a composer actually. He was Persian,
       Iranian.

WH: I just want to free myself from all that because that's no me.

WP: Yes, but perhaps you have a kind of intellectual confidence Chris
       didn't have. You don't speak the way Grieve spoke, at all. Your
       speech is more relaxed. His spoken Scots was in the context of a
       cultivated and, I suppose, early twentieth century, rather formal
       English. You have been to a university. And although he could
       seem deferential, there were moments when, if you touched
       another nerve, you were no longer talking to an agreeable wee
       man, but to a persona which claimed a place in history. Sam
       Maclean said to me that Chris's early lyrics and the best of the
       Drunk Man were not normal, he called it a pathology; he meant
       a match between language, insight and sensibility which just
       happens, you can't contrive it. And that I think must also be true
       of the greatest of Sam's poems.

WH: All I'm saying is you have to make your own road. If Scots is
       going to continue, if people are going to continue to write it, as
       hopefully they will, there has to be room for lots of different
       things. We were talking earlier about the ayatollahs of Scots,
       laying down the law about orthography and so on.

JH: Well Duncan Glen was one of the people who was more forthright about that really, he said that he spoke the language that was in his head. He wrote the language that was in his head and that was it basically, but that attitude was liberating to a lot of Scots poets...

WH: Definitely.

JH: ...who had felt before that the artificial language of, say, Sydney Goodsir Smith, who wasn't a Scots-speaker, not remotely at all, who wasn't even a Scots-born writer, that they had to aim for this kind of synthetic highly-literate Scots and Duncan did say, No, you don't have to do that, you speak the language which is in your head.

WP: That doesn't work in every genre.

JH: No, nor for every person.

WP: You can't write philosophy in that vein.

JH: No-one's going to write philosophy in Scots anyway.

WP: Precisely, the registers of learning and authority have gone.

JH: The language of philosophy: I've just been reading a philosophy book which made me aware that the language of philosophy itself is a sub-language, it's full of technical terms which I as a fairly literate person just didn't understand.

WH: You spoke about university earlier. I didn't enjoy my time at Edinburgh.

WP: Of course John might have been your teacher, being writer in residence there at that time.

WH: I'll tell you what I did. I had a sheaf of poems and you (John) had a wee office in the David Hume Tower and I pushed them under the door and I ran away. But you gave me some really good feedback on them.

JH: Did I? I'm glad I did.

WH: What John said, I think there was one poem, I had written about six verses and he said: you could have had the same poem in three verses. Great advice!

WP: You were talking earlier about admiring Mackay Brown. He I think is an underestimated poet. He may yet end up being thought of as one of our great poets. The poem of his I have taught most often is *Hamnavoe Market*, which is wonderful.

WH: Yes, the one about all those characters coming to the fair.

WP: Yes, and all that subtle religious imagery buried in innocent-looking description.

JH: In prose, I think, he tended towards self-parody a bit.

WH: I think what I like about Mackay Brown is that for me he links in with the ballads.

JH: That's very interesting.

WH: And I think I called them the DNA of Scottish literature, the ballads.

JH: Well, here's an interesting thing because you have pursued your interest in music and in writing songs, and, as you know, I have written this book about Bob Dylan. I got extremely interested in the way in which Dylan had been influenced by Scots ballads, I think possibly through Joan Baez originally, who introduced them to him.

WP: And how would she have come by them?

JH: Well her mother was Scottish. And the elliptical methods of the ballads where something is left out, often the crucial point is left out, unstated, understood. Have you found that useful for writing both poetry and your own songs?

WH: I would love to be able to write poems like that, like the dry stane dyke with so many stones removed there's almost nothing left of it, which leaves a lot out, leaves the reader to work it out, you know, really spare and pared down and you just have the bare bones there.

JH: It sometimes goes with the laconic nature of Scots, pithy but laconic.

WP: Not just Scots, all classical traditions are by definition laconic, because the tradition itself provides the framework of missing elements, there is no need to state what everyone knows.

WH: But inevitably, once you start to write a story, you get carried away. The one which *Fras* published, *The Ballant o The Sovereign Power*, it goes on and on.

WP: Something your work has, if I may say so, which most of what we receive is lacking in, is energy.

JH: Well, the *Caedmon* poem particularly had tremendous energy in it and it was quite interesting that you turned towards an Old English poet.

WH: He probably spoke a dialect of that language spoken from York up to Edinburgh, it was probably a kind of Inglis, a proto-Scots derived from Friesian. He has this reputation as the father of English poetry, thanks to Bede. I took it that he probably spoke a form of Scots.

JH: I think you're probably right there.

WH: What we know about him is probably all derived from Bede, more than a hundred years later and who was writing a propaganda job as well. So we don't know a lot about him. That poem might have worked better as a short story, because there is a kind of narrative in it.

JH: I don't think so.

WH: And you have different perspectives on the guy, what he thinks about what he's doing, what people who know him think of him.

JH: Well, narrative poetry is something that has almost disappeared in the last generations.

WP: Willie and I are both writing work with narrative elements. And why is narrative poetry important?

WH: Well, for anyone reading it there's a bit of story to interest them.

WP: Don't you think that all the worthwhile poems are stories. Unlike those of, say, the French Surrealists, where there is *no* narrative content, where the language itself *is* the content, which means that it can only be enjoyed by an elite for whom poetry is an aesthetic dilettantism, décor. Any classical tradition must have content, because the form, rhyme or rhythm, was mainly there to help with memory, for purposes of recitation: Homer, the Old Irish. Hardy is a poet who always has a wee story buried there in the lyric. Do you like Hardy?

WH: I do. Yes, very much. I think he's a great poet.

WP: Who of the living writers you may have met has influenced you?

WH: I mentioned George Mackay Brown, though I didn't meet him. We were up in Orkney just after he died and there was a real sense of loss there. Across the road from his house there's a lovely museum and we spoke to the curator. He had gone in there every day I think.

JH: A man of regular habits.

WP: He reviewed *Lamentation* generously many years ago. I passed up on the chance to meet him not long before he died and I regret that.

JH: One of the few writers of that generation I never met. He was so reclusive.

WP: Was it you, John, who told the story of the Somerset Maugham, award?

JH: Yes, the award is for travel, you are supposed to go away and have to spend a year out of the country. He went to Ireland.

WH: "Travel flattens the mind." Send a turnip round the world, it comes back a turnip. Send a neep round the world, it comes back a Swede... Getting back to influences, I think Bob Dylan said: never steal off anybody who is contemporary with yourself or younger than yourself.

JH: Quite a good rule of thumb.

WP: Did you ever meet the Fife poet, Alastair Mackie?

WH: No, though he was a teacher, at Anstruther. I know that he taught Christopher Rush and Andrew Greig. I think he could be quite an irascible man. Typical English teacher!

JH: He was very depressive.

WH: But he was appearing in the *Words* magazine and *Akros*. And that was the kind of thing I was reading at that time, reading everything I could, and trying to soak it all in. I really liked his poetry.

JH: Well he was an interesting character because he'd rather broken away – he was a very erudite poet – but he wasn't in the same mould as the previous generation of makars, his Scots wasn't out of the head like theirs. Some of them were genuine poets.

WP: You know, many of the great classicists were Scots, like Gilbert Murray, and the man who translated Aeschylus into Scots, Douglas Young.

JH: And George Buchanan.

WP: Just so. In the modern period it maybe says something about Scots and the alienations of language. One thing I'm not clear about, Willie, you talked about your poetry being of yourself and from yourself. I cannot conceive poetry without an audience; someone like Chris Grieve could hardly conceive his poetry without a sense of a national destiny, nor could Yeats. Auden saw his poetry as having a moral or quasi-religious, a truth-telling function: you must see some role for your poems in relation to the body politic from where you are, and what your poems would ideally do.

JH: Their public role.

WH: Well I've always been interested in politics and I've been
      a member of the SNP, because for me that moment of
      independence is the starting point, where we actually start to put
      things right properly, from the moment we get independence.
      And that's an idealistic view. Like most people, as I've got older my
      idealism has diminished. When I was younger I was very much
      involved with the SNP.

JH: Same as me.

WP: Well I was living in Winnie Ewing's constituency, Hamilton, and
      worked in the campaign office and later stood in the rain outside
      the count that famous night in 1967.

WH: But as I've got older I've become more cynical about politicians
      and politics. There's nothing new there.

WP: But they still control all the levers, the money, the authority and
      you can't get round that.

JH: Have you been disappointed by what devolution has done so far?

WH: No.

JH: I haven't either.

WH: No, although I wanted to be. I have friends in the SNP who would
      have nothing to do with the Holyrood Parliament and who see it
      as a watered-down version of independence, a half-way house.
      From a personal point of view, because my wife works there,
      I've been in the building, I've seen what goes on. I've got a great
      admiration for Alec Salmond.

WP: I think we all do.

WH: He's a conniving politician but he's very good at it.

JH: I think his heart and head work together.

WP: Donald Dewar could never have done what Alec Salmond's doing for Scotland's sense of itself.

WH: This is one thing about Scotland, we're very schismatic and we're always breaking up and fighting among ourselves.

WP: So you haven't been to Ireland? (*laughter*)

WH: I can remember, again going back to this period in the seventies drinking in the Abbotsford and places like that, I remember Alec Salmond as a young politician. Everyone was talking a great game about what they were going to do. He did it. But now we've got something, it's up to us to take it forward and to build on it.

JH: Absolutely. I sometimes feel great despair when I look at the situation of Gaelic for instance, the situation of Scots and perhaps the main reason I espoused nationalism when I was very young was for cultural reasons – for political reasons as well but the cultural reasons came first. And now you see whole areas of Scotland in which Scots are in a minority. What's going to happen to Scots culture in these circumstances? I think independence or devolution has come too late. Independence will come too late but we've got somehow to battle on.

WH: That's one of the disappointing aspects. I think Salmond is above all a pragmatist, from speaking to Matthew Fitt about what's going on, you know there's a cross party sub-committee on Scots language. It's a talking shop I think. I don't think the SNP are really doing very much in that area and that's a big disappointment for me.

WP: Well, they still have a strong legacy from the Westminster MPs.

JH: Yes.

WH: They don't see the link, the importance of the cultural link.

JH: No, they always talk about the 'bread and butter' issues, as it were, which are of course important. But having established a position based on sound economic and political views, you then have to pursue what makes a country itself. What makes it a country worth living in – a country that's got its own ethos and its own way of doing things.

WP: Well, Yeats, with others, established the Abbey and drew in Synge and the others, Gogarty, Lady Gregory. The model has been different here. But this idea of moving from employment issues down, like Thatcher's theory of a trickle-down effect in economics, the kind of policies pursued by Blair and by Brown too, that if you just let the rich get richer... But the poor just get poorer. And it doesn't work culturally either. Ireland was not prospering when the great cultural advances were initiated. It almost has to work the other way round.

WH: You see, there's no way of quantifying the impact of the cultural aspects of Scottish writers, what influence they've had. In the 1980s James Robertson, he was running a magazine called *Radical Scotland*, and he asked me to review books and he published my poems at a time when no one else would. It was that anti-Thatcherite time, when Labour were getting in in Scotland and the Tories were getting in in England, you know. So *Radical Scotland* was set up, I think to be a propaganda vehicle of protest and alliance between nationalists and left wing labour. There was a lot going on at that time and after the first devolution referendum when everyone was very down and disappointedabout the outcome.

WP: What year was that ?

WH: The magazine was published in the early eighties.

JH: The first devolution referendum was '79.

WH: It was really because of that failure that I think things picked up.

WP: You think on balance it's better that we ended up where we are?

JH: It's very hard to say because what we were going to have got then was much less; but nonetheless through those Thatcher years there was such a collapse of the kind of confidence that had been growing, and a lot of people, writers, social activists of various kinds, withdrew, went into themselves, did their own thing, and I think it was at that point that there was a loss of a sense of a Scottish literary community.

WP: And that's never come back.

JH: No.

WP: John and I will be among the few who remember what it was like to have a society of fellows, though even I only experienced the tail end of it.

JH: Yes, many of whom you might have disagreed with, but nonetheless you felt there was that community.

WP: It was perhaps that one had a sense of a set of underlying shared values which could be taken for granted, the importance of the imagination, of its education.

WH: Have you both read the Alexander Scott biography?

JH: Yes, by David Robb, Dundee. It came out a couple of years ago.

WP: No, I haven't.

WH: It's worth reading. It was a very interesting book for me to read because I was kind of half-joking when I said that no-one else has shown up since I started writing poetry. But I feel I have been going it alone, really.

JH: Don't we all now?

WH: And I think it's a combination of things. For one, I'm pretty thrawn.

JH: Good.

WH: For two, I'm quite shy about things, which is its own form of conceit I guess, but so I'm not going to chap on doors or network.

JH: No, I can't do that sort of thing either.

WP: Not being able to do so is one of the hall marks of civilisation.

WH: So I'm really delighted to talk with you about poetry today.

WP: What would you like to talk about that we have not touched on?

WH: Well loads of stuff, how Celtic are getting on with their new manager. Now Hugh MacDiarmid wouldnae have approved of that.

JH: No, no. But that was one of the interesting things about him, his complete rejection of popular culture.

WH: There's that poem about 40,000 coming out of Ibrox after the debate between the two philosophers.

JH: Yes, there's a reference to that in the introduction to *Makars*.

WP: When you start to write a poem, or when the poem begins to emerge from wherever, is there a pattern to that, is it a musical phrase, a linguistic phrase, an idea or is it all of these or is there no pattern?

WH: Usually the poetry comes on me like a bout of the 'flu, you know, it's a compulsion.

WP: Flu's not a compulsion. That's a very weak analogy. (*laughter*)

JH: Well, you can't avoid it, it's compulsory in that sense.

WH: One of the really good things about being a kind of peripheral writer, I've spoken to Tom Hubbard about this, Tom's been prepared to make a lot of sacrifices to do what he wants to do, he's a very good pal of mine, and I've gone for teaching and a cushy job and a mortgage and everything like that and looked after the kids and...

WP: Well, if you're straight and married and have a family, what else do you do?

WH: That means that when I decide to write a poem, I can write about whatever the hell I like. I can choose; if I want to write a poem about Caedmon, there's nobody to say otherwise. If there's nobody out there who wants to read it, it doesn't matter and if there is someone, that's fantastic. I would hate to be tied down by being something like a writer in residence.

JH: I would never do that again.

WP: But you don't have to produce specific work if you're a writer in residence.

WH: Oh, I'm sure that you do.

WP: I never did. On the other hand, when I was a writer in residence I rarely wrote much.

JH: You don't have to produce writings. But you are in thrall to them in numbers of ways. It's a different thing if you've got a short-term job, but when you get involved in a permanent creative writing course, that's different. I know people who were creative writers who have now said: O well, now I just teach creative writing because I've got a family and so on. Once you do that, once you're involved in the full-time teaching of creative writing, you've had it as a creative writer.

WP: On the other hand, I learned an enormous amount from teaching creative writing classes.

JH: Yes, but it was never your central activity.

WH: What I am talking about is being thirled to it, tied down. Usually when I feel the urge to write, it's when I'm really busy, when I've got a big pile of marking.

JH: I think you need to be under a certain amount of pressure to write.

WH: Yes, I know guys and it is their job to write stuff to order and they come up with lots of things but I think I'm really lucky. I tend to fit stuff in during the holidays and when I can although in a way that's meant that I cannot give my full attention to it.

JH: Sam Maclean used to say that from the time that he came back from the war and became first of all head of department and then headmaster, he really almost stopped writing for about twenty years and he said, "You know, it might be that at the end of the

Summer holidays, a poem might just about be there." And then he had to get back. For him, obviously, he needed quite a long stretch of free time in order for poetry to happen. But there are some people who find it happens better under pressure.

WP: I don't know about that. Look at Rilke, ten years for the *Duino Elegies* to emerge. Sam took a long time because Sam took a long time. He would always have taken a long time. Do you not think so?

JH: Well, when he was at his peak he was writing huge amounts, very quickly.

WP: What about this, which I hadn't thought about before: when Chris began writing it was as a journalist, in South Wales. Sam never did that, he wrote when the poems came. Chris wrote because he felt he had to and always could keep on writing, it was a frame of mind in which he perhaps saw writing more as a profession and as always possible, a more instrumental view.

JH: Yes, but I think the lyrics came in a different way.

WP: Yes, I agree about that.

JH: I am still of the opinion that his greatest work is the early lyrics though I can admire the later poetry. I think his gift was essentially lyrical.

WP: Perhaps with all poets the real gift is a capacity for lyricism.

WH: In my experience, I've done a bit of teaching and I've been involved in folk music and I've been involved in poetry and I referred to this earlier: in Scotland, we are a wee country, there doesnae seem to be any tie ups between people that I meet when I play in the folk clubs and the literary world.

JH: Yes, I would say that that's something that has changed. When I first came on to the literary scene in the late sixties and the early seventies, they did. It was all part of this literary world. I helped to form a group called The Heretics, particularly to bring together poetry and folk music in a relaxed pub atmosphere but the thing was that there were people involved in that, like Stuart MacGregor, like Dolina Maclennan, my first wife, who moved in both these circles and people did at that time know each other, literary people and folk music people. They didn't all know each other but there was a considerable overlap and interlink.

WH: Not the case now.

WP: But something has changed over that forty years, something fundamental is missing.

WH: I try to address that. I think inevitably if you are a nationalist you are an idealist. It's been spoken about before; we need a subject in education, Scottish Studies, if we're going to break this reservation mentality, that of the former labour council schemes, you know, kids have got to learn about their background, the bad stuff as well as the good stuff, they've got to learn about their music, they've got to learn about their poetry, what's gone before. It's there in a kind of token way but as an English teacher I could get by without teaching any Scottish literature.

JH: Yes, I'm sure.

WH: I could prepare the kids for their Higher without really doing any.

JH: Is there now any mechanism in the curriculum for doing something specifically Scottish, in the Higher?

WH: There is if you want to. I've been doing Robin Jenkins, Scots War Poets, Fife Poets, anyone who is not Liz Lochhead, Morgan or

MacCaig. The reality of the situation, and I remember talking to people from the Henryson Society about this, and they were keen because Henryson is on the Advanced Highers list, for English, but he's there as an option. Now, no teacher in their right mind is going to touch him with a bargepole, because you can also do Edwin Morgan. Now if you're looking for route A and you are under pressure from your headmaster to get your kids A passes...

WP: Then you choose Morgan

WH: Yes, you won't take Henryson because you are not going to have to teach them all the medieval stuff.

JH: Exactly, there's always been, even when I was at school, a bias towards over-valuing the contemporary.

WH: It's a results factory now, the schools are compared and there are league tables and so you are under a lot of pressure and you will choose the things which will dumb it down a bit.

WP: We haven't talked at all about what you see for the future, about what's to come?

WH: Strawberry tarts I think. Everything's under review. I said to John, I haven't written anything for a wee while. As you know, my son died. That put a stop to things.

JH: It won't necessarily go on doing that. It is an experience which, perhaps quite indirectly, will maybe feed in to what you have to say at some time.

WP: What about this business of feeling that we are all still sending out poems into a void, poems that no-one reads?

WH: That's something our generation has to come to terms with, just because of the way culture has gone, or not gone, we've got to be prepared to accept, in almost medieval terms, a very small audience.

WP: It was never much different, with the exception of a historically very short period when poetry sold, perhaps the two hundred years from 1750–1950. But Erasmus could send his writings round Europe to those he thought would understand him in a matter of weeks.

WH: Having said that though, I often get labelled as a local poet, because I write about the pits. But when we do put things on, readings, concerts, they are well attended. I think there is a real audience there.

WP: I think there's a terrible hunger for identity.

WH: It's difficult sometimes if I write to a publisher in Edinburgh and they think, No we won't take you on because you're a local poet. Yet I'm sure my stuff outsells a lot of them

JH: Yes, I bet it does.

WP: A story which may be relevant is of Douglas Young, touring the Borders; a great classics scholar, he translated the Psalms into Scots.

JH: And Aristophanes, *The Puddocks.*

WP: And many other things. He gave a series of readings in the Borders, Selkirk and Melrose and some of the wee country villages. In some settlement somewhere, not a town, his audience was rural, mainly shepherds and he read them the Scots version of the twenty-third Psalm. And he said of these men, some old, all hardy, that there was not a dry eye in the house. Because they heard their identities given back to them in their own tongue and in the context of the sacred.

JH: Yes, he was a Fifer. He was from Tayport.

WP: I didn't know that. What about your general philosophical views, Willie.

WH: Well I went to catholic schools. I was an altar boy, choir boy and everything.

WP: Are you a religious man?

JH: Or spiritual?

WH: I don't know. I think that changes from day to day.

JH: I converted to catholicism when I was about forty and I wanted to become a monk at one time, but I'm now lapsed.

WP: Yes, but you never gave up being a presbyterian, did you?

JH: I gave up being a presbyterian a long time ago.

WP: You cannot just give up that degree of Scottish individualism. If you are really going to be a papist you need to be an Italian peasant.

JH: I'll never manage that.

WP: For me, it is hard to imagine a poet who, as they get older, does not find himself surrounded by ghosts and spirits.

WH: You would laugh at me for saying that (*to his wife, Mary, who has just come in*).

       I was an altar boy for Thomas Winning. He came back from the Scots College when I was in Bellshill and he drummed Catholicism out of me. (*laughter*)

6. ALASDAIR GRAY

Alasdair Gray (1934–2019): Writer of novels, plays, poems and translations. Painter and designer. Internationally knownfor his 1981 novel *Lanark*

The conversation took place at Alasdair's home in Glasgow on February 6th. 2015 with John Herdman and Walter Perrie.

JOHN HERDMAN: I was very interested in an earlier interview you did Alasdair, I can't remember for whom, when you were talking about the genesis of *Lanark* and you said that it was originally two novels, one being the more *Bildungsroman* type and the other being more modernist, almost Kafkaesque. That struck me as very interesting. I had wondered whether something like that might be the case. I think it was a very shrewd move in that it gave Scotland a Big Novel, which it had been looking for. I'm not saying this in any way to denigrate the novel but it did provide that. And possibly gave it a kind of impact which it might otherwise not have had if you had done, for instance, the *Bildungsroman* first.

ALASDAIR GRAY: You see, when I started, leaving aside that the first fictions I did were prose serial narratives told to my sister – we slept in adjacent bedrooms with the door open between – I had a fantasy life in which I imagined myself in all kinds of exciting situations from which I was aided by miraculous magical powers of intelligence and these stories were made up from bits of all the stories I had ever read or was learning or hearing. I was putting them together and adding them up and the only spine was a central character who was me at the time I was writing. The kinds of stories I eventually found I was most enjoying and most wanting to imitate, particularly about the age of eight or nine, I thought I am going to start writing them down. And I began writing stories which were versions of very silly children's tales of magic and I thought I want to write that so that it comes out in a way that I prefer to the way it does. I thought when I was writing one of these one day I'll get things out in a book. At that time I was probably about nine. The thing was at school I got good marks for 'compositions', for essays, you know. I found it easy if the subjects were given and of course, it was usually 'What you did during your Summer holidays'. I found on any given subject I could write quite fluently. And I became more and more ambitious, the more I read, the older I got. My earliest inclination was towards the magic, the strange, the weird, lost worlds. Oh, and I did encounter Edgar Allan Poe who horrified me but hypnotised me. I still reread him without the horror. I greatly admire his technique. But as I say, the marvellous and the strange and all the early H.G. Wells stories. I cottoned on to early science fiction stories as a modern, believable form of magic. But the stories I was interested in – and some of them I had heard on the Children's Hour dramatisations of *The Magic Bed Knob*; John Masefield's *The Midnight Folk* and *The Box of Delights* – are remarkably good novels. Well, they're written for children but I think any adult could appreciate the humour and invention in them. And of course the Alice books by Carroll. I realised I didn't want absolute fantasy and I was keen on the novels which started with somebody like someone I could identify with – a boy in an ordinary bourgeois, or petty-bourgeois in my case, or working class even – kind of home or surroundings, finding a magic door, an entrance. This was years before the Narnia one.

WALTER PERRIE: I was just thinking there of C. S. Lewis.

AG: I never caught up with him. I think these novels started appearing when I was in my early thirties, by when I had rather lost interest in them. But, the point was I came to realise that it was only in what you might call realities that I could have enjoyable sexual possibilities, though in fact I immersed myself a lot in the writings of Walter de la Mare. His short stories are remarkable, his novels even, the *Memoirs of a Midget*.

WP: He's quite fey isn't he?

AG: I wouldn't say fey. His stories never amount to giving anything
       approaching sexual satisfaction. There is always a pervading
       sense of loss in them. You never exactly enter magical kingdoms.
       There's a feeling that there might be one, that you are close to
       one but not that you'll find any precise satisfaction in them. And
       in his short stories his use of the supernatural isn't at all fey. In
       Seaton's Aunt, he's good at conveying terrible horrors. It is one of
       the best, in which Seaton is a school friend of the narrator, who
       takes him home; he lives with his aunt, an old, very powerful
       woman in her aspect and manners, and rich, she's got all the
       food and Edwardian conversation. But he has a horror of his aunt
       and you do finally come to the conclusion that she has been an
       emotional vampire. It ends with the narrator deciding to visit him
       because the last time he had seen him, Seaton was engaged to be
       married and he meets Seaton and his fiancé in the aunt's home.
       Sorry, I'm just remembering the bit in which he finds he has not
       been invited to the wedding and he's rather surprised, because
       he is the only friend, so far as he knows, which Seaton had. He
       revisits the house and meets the aunt who says; "Who are you?"
       and he says "Seaton's friend. I wondered has the marriage been
       postponed?" and she says "Between the two of us, it has." And she
       says something like "Excuse me, I'll have to leave." She goes away
       and he sits in this darkening room a long time. He gets up to ring
       for a servant or something and nobody comes. He opens the door
       and, she's blind now, and he hears her leaning over and saying
       to him; "Arthur, Arthur" – that's the name of his friend; "I don't
       think Arthur's here." And she shouts angrily; "Get out of here you
       terrible person. Go out! Leave me!" And he goes off through the
       village and stopping at a blacksmith's shop, he learns that Seaton
       is dead and he is left with the feeling that she has fed upon him in
       his life and is still feeding upon him in his death.

WP: Have you always had this fluency, Alasdair?

AG: I don't know. Sorry, I suppose this is an example of it. Yes! I've always known I talk too much. But the thing is that realising that the magic of the fantastical, the convincingly magical and fantastical that most appealed to me was not exactly that which hinted at something as other-worldly, even if it was diabolical, as De la Mare did.

WP: So it had to be something rooted in your day to day life?

AG: Well, or my political imagination.

WP: Why the political imagination?

AG: So many of the best – *Gulliver's Travels* for instance – are what Arnold called Criticism of Life. I am very fond of the third voyage involving the flying island of Laputa, which is not only a satire on the Royal Society, it's also a satire on England's domination of Ireland. And H. G. Wells, his science fictions, though it wasn't quite direct, are criticisms of British imperialism.

WP: Is this in the forties you're reading Wells?

AG: When I was still an adolescent, yes. They were broadcast; *The War of the Worlds*, and the BBC versions of Conan Doyle's *The Lost World,* which I heard when I was I suppose thirteen or fourteen. We discussed them and played games about them in the playground. We were all keen radio listeners.

JH: Radio was a great thing for children in those days. It was one of the prime sources of imagination.

WP: It's all aural so your imagination is not tied down to images.

AG: True, or rather, you are creating your own images. And of course you had the Third Programme which I cottoned on to early and listened as long as it lasted. You had *The Listener*, which reprinted some of the most interesting lectures or dialogues. And of course, at secondary school I did start reading Hardy and Dickens with great pleasure and appetite – well, not Hardy at first, but Dickens I found fascinating. He was dealing with what were accepted as realities, but a kind of heightened reality.

WP: Dickens is very strange at times.

AG: Oscar Wilde in one of his critical dialogues, maybe it's *The Decay of Lying* or *In Defence of Criticism* has two characters, posh young London men, discussing literature but one of them is opposing what he calls realism in fiction. And he regards Zola as an example of it, but the other says But you're very fond of the novels of Balzac. And he replies Balzac isn't a realist; everyone he describes is supercharged with willpower.

WP: Absolutely.

AG: I noticed in reading *Père Goriot*, that at this boarding house, you've got a collection of people sitting round the table and he describes it, quite convincingly, as a very ordinary boarding house in the 1830s or thereabouts, and these are very ordinary people. And gradually you realise that this poor old man is in fact the father of two daughters who are married to extraordinarily rich husbands. He himself has sacrificed everything in his life, and still does, to them. He is actually spied on by one of the other lodgers, who realises that, though apparently an old farmer or a peasant, he's a man of extraordinary physical strength, because he takes out some silver ornaments and utensils and with a rope, squeezes them down into one solid mass in order to raise money with them. And there's the bloke who's spying on him – they're all rather afraid of him – and he {Vautrin} turns out to be an absolute master criminal. Then you've got the young man {Rastignac} who's wanting to train himself in the law in order to support his decayed aristocratic mother and his sisters, and even two of the dimmest characters turn out to be police spies and informers. He can't stop making everybody as marvellously interesting as possible. In *Cousin Pons*, for instance, you've got this old bloke whose chief resource in life is actually to be a not very welcome parasite; he drops in on his relations at dinner time. But he has one talent, he can spot rather good things in antique shops and has built up a small collection. But at the very beginning, in order to ingratiate himself in this house where they tolerate him at meals, he gives the hostess "Here's a fan you might rather like. It's actually been painted by Watteau." But you find he's managed to build up a collection which contains priceless antiques; paintings by Leonardo, a small Michelangelo. You think, Oh, now...

WP: But there's a political side to Balzac that could be called realist. A characteristic feature of that period not just in French literature but in French life, is the invention of the violent police state, the ubiquitous police spies, not just under Napoleon but under the Restoration and subsequent regimes. This was very much in the public awareness at the time; it's in Victor Hugo, it's in Balzac, all part of the politics of the period.

AG: Yes, you're right and even the business in which this master criminal eventually becomes the head of the Paris police.

WP: Well, that was based on Fouché, Napoleon's head of the Paris police and there's that great remark of Chateaubriand's when he sees Fouché and Talleyrand, who was lame, at the Restoration, coming in to an audience arm in arm Vice supported on the arm of Crime. And this was Balzac's immediate background, a sort of heightened political reality, especially under Napoleon.

AG: I suppose what I was working towards saying was that I realised I increasingly wanted to read what referred to realities. My father, who left school at twelve, came from a family of readers, wanted me to be a reader. He kept buying second-hand books for me and subscribed to a thing called the Reader's Union, which was a book club, so that every month one got one of the books or a selection called *The Essential Hemingway*; there was another one called *The Essential James Joyce*, which had the whole of the *Portrait of the Artist as a Young Man*.

JH: Yes, I've got that.

AG: Reading that, you know, I was very much moved and excited by it.

WP: It was, even by present-day standards, very sophisticated stuff. But you also must have had an aptitude for it, even inasmuch as your memory for detail is obviously quite extraordinary. In the books you've mentioned, though I've read them, I wouldn't remember half the detail you describe.

JH: No, I wouldn't either.

AG: Well, I did it very early I suppose. And I'm slightly ashamed because I think I ought to remember more. In fact, I think one of the reasons I became more of a visual artist was to keep my memory of what I see rather than read.

JH: Did those two things go in parallel, the painting and the writing, from the very beginning?

AG: Yes. I suppose the earliest book my mother read to me that I would still reread, was Hans Andersen's fairy tales, and it was from a book that had lots of pictures in it. But of course I was very fond of comics, which in those days were mainly pictorial; the *Dandy* and the *Beano*. But among these Readers Union books that came to me, there was Kafka. By the time I went to art school I had sketched the start of the Thaw part of Lanark, the first chapter, and in the first year at art school – by that time I'd got on to Kafka – I'd read *The Trial* and *The Castle* and *America*, and a selection of his *Notebooks*, and therefore I imagined the start of *Lanark* with somebody coming to a city in which the sun hardly ever rose and only for a few bits at irregular moments. And it was a kind of caricature as Glasgow seemed to me while it was still a heavy industrial city. Because the sky was almost like a very solid lid over the city. As a tiny child I'd believed the sky was a ceiling and, as I describe near the start of *Lanark*, my father had a great deal of difficulty explaining to me that the world was a globe, not flat, and the sky wasn't a ceiling, because when I was drawing, I would first draw a brown line representing a floor or the earth, then a blue line representing the sky and then have houses and people and aeroplanes and clouds in between.

JH: It's a common misapprehension.

WP: I'm not sure it's a misapprehension.

JH: Well, it's not. That's our experience.

AG: But I remember after my father's attempt to explain, having a kind of fantasy, it may even have been a dream, I'm not sure, of travelling up and then coming to a ceiling, thinking what's on the other side? and getting through and going on and on. And he got through to me that there isn't a ceiling and space is infinite.

WP: Sounds like an intelligent father.

AG: Oh, yes. He judged himself to be inferior to me in knowledge and I think even suggested in intelligence. It's not true that he was my inferior in intelligence.

WP: Were you close?

AG: I would say he was more intelligent than me in his choice of a wife, in his conduct towards his two children and in how he managed his own life. But by the time I went to art school, I'd be in my first year, I had worked out what was going to be the story of the Thaw character; it was going to be Portrait of the

Artist as a Scottish Young Man, he would be a visual artist, to distinguish him from Joyce's Stephen Dedalus, and he wouldn't depart to hammer out the conscience of his race or anything like that, because he would find himself unable to complete the great artistic work that he'd conceived and he would commit suicide, possibly even murder. I'd worked that out and I can remember during my first art school holidays suggesting to my father that all my contemporaries were getting jobs for the school holidays and that, instead of becoming a tram conductor or anything, I would like to stay at home in order to write this novel. So he said, alright, and I started trying to write it and discovered I had no prose style. I thought that writing should be as fluent as you talked; Tristram Shandy had made a big impact – that sounds like somebody just talking. I thought – I'll do it like that – and I found I couldn't. One thing I wanted to write a story that was a definite narrative.

WP: With a beginning a middle and an end ?

AG: Not necessarily an end but certainly had a beginning and went forward in time. Anyway, by the end of that two and a half months or whatever it was, I'd managed to write the first chapter of the Thaw section.

WP: More or less as it is now?

AG: Yes.

WP: And at this point you're what, twenty?

AG: Nineteen, or eighteen. No I was seventeen when I went, I'd be eighteen then.

JH: Remarkable.

AG: And realising, this is going to take longer than I'd thought. Also at art school in my first year or three, I was keeping copious and detailed diaries because I thought this is going to be useful material, and then through my readings of Kafka I got this idea of somebody in an after-life state arriving in this city which was a kind of suburb of Hell, or Hell itself.

WP: Otherwise known as Glasgow...

AG: Well, Unthank, a kind of limbo in which, insofar as there appeared to be an industry, it was only constructing what seemed to be the shells of huge rocket bombs which nobody had any intention of ever employing. I'd written a chapter from the beginning of that one and I was thinking of both as two separate books. I wanted to write a book that contained all the elements that I'd enjoyed in other people's books, and then I read Tillyard's book *The English Epic and its Background*, and in that he was explaining how the epic form could contain every other literary form. It had to have a strong historical element, it had to embrace the whole gamut of literature.

WP: I wonder whether a whole generation may not have been seduced, in part by Tillyard's book, into a sort of false-epic writing, thinking of my own early efforts, of MacDiarmid, Tom Scott and others, seduced by this notion that somehow epic was the highest possible form.

AG: Yes, yes.

JH: And you had read Tillyard?

WP: Yes. It was A.W.S. Dubber who introduced me to Tillyard; he and Leavis were two of the primary critics of the day. We knew them very well.

AG: Well I did too, but I didn't go to university.

WP: No, this was at school.

AG: Well that was good then. My English teacher, Mr. Meikle, he never directed us towards reading criticism at all, but he did speak well and interestingly about literature.

WP: Is there a direct link, Alasdair, between all that you've been talking about, this mixture of finding a way forward into writing something which you had enjoyed in other people's books, which contained your own fantasies and so on, with the political dimension. Where does that begin to become evident to you, that you have a political line to follow as well?

AG: I think I've actually put this into the epilogue of *Lanark*; Tillyard indicated that most epics were written at a time when the author had a sense of a political initiative, introducing the possibility of a new world.

WP: Shelley, Byron ?

AG: Yes, but Milton. He stops short at Walter Scott. He regarded Gibbon's *Decline and Fall of the Roman Empire* as being Gibbon's epic, and a successful 18th century epic, even referring to its political dimension. Gibbon was, of course, quite shocked by the French Revolution because it seemed to be undoing everything that he had thought had been achieved. In one chapter he explains how European civilisation can no longer collapse or degenerate as the Roman Empire did, because it is no longer unified, you have so many different European states with so many different constitutions, and also taking the line that technology is so advanced that there is no danger of more barbarous nations outside our Pale taking us over, *{laughing}* not even America. His was a rather hopeful and complacent vision; he knew that some of these states, Switzerland and others, were republics and thought that the variety of different constitutions was a guarantee of stability. He also said that he thought that the Scottish novels of Sir Walter Scott almost amounted to a Scottish epic because if they were united, he was talking just about the Scottish novels, and certainly, their historical panorama is interesting and broad.

JH: They appealed to me at a very early age. I read about a dozen of them when I was between about eleven and thirteen. I hadn't come to Dickens at that stage.

AG: Scott was spoiled for me initially. I only started reading him with great interest when I was in my thirties and forties because they started us off with... ehm ..

WP: *Ivanhoe?*

AG: Yes, *Ivanhoe.*

WP: It put me off Scott too.

AG: Well, after I'd read a page and a half of him describing de Bois-Guilbert's armour, which, bye the bye was utterly unhistorical, because at that period he would have been wearing chain mail but he goes into the visors, the vambraces, and so on. But of course the education department had chosen that because it was showing how *{declaiming}* "The crude, defeated Anglo-Saxons eventually were inter-blended with the Norman conquerors, and so to form the English Language!" What a good thing for the Scots to learn about.! *{Laughter}* But when Scott was talking about the Portuguese classic, the *Luisiads*, in which he mentioned Camoens describing Vasco de Gama's journey to the Indies, which was of course the extension of classical Christianity over the world and how this was being blessed by visions of a Roman Catholic heaven and its saints, which he was doing it for, also had Neptune and the Nereids and the mermaids all on the side of it, it was at that point I thought that my *Lanark* novel was going to be more about politics, the politics of the modern world and particularly Scotland. At that time, you see, I believed the Labour Party was socialist. Well, after the War, I mean, it had implemented the Beveridge report.

WP: It was semi-socialist up until about 1950, until Gaitskell became leader.

AG: It was.

WP: On the other hand the Labour Party was founded out of various groupings, some of which were specifically anti-Marxist, like the Fabian Society.

AG: Well the Fabian Society appreciated Marx's definitions but, yes, the notion of revolution....

JH: Was the ILP anti-Marxist?

WP: Yes. Alasdair's exactly right, inasmuch as it was against the methodology of Marxism and it was anti-revolution. It was an assimilative, parliamentary approach.

AG: The Labour Party was made by the Fabians, who were definitely socialists, and by the trade unions. It was assumed by the founders and the Fabians that it had to be a union of trade unions.

WP: Surely, but British trade unions are not like those in Italy or France. Trade unions here have a very circumscribed political history.

AG: No, you're right. And there was also of course the fact that the Irish and Scottish nationalists were also part of this group and which were also rejected by the Labour Party very early on. Just as it absorbed the ILP and destroyed it, that too was destroyed. It's a complicated business. You had John MacLean, who Lenin appointed the first Bolshevik consul in Britain.

WP: In 1918?

AG: Yes, and Lenin told MacLean that he was looking forward to the British revolution starting in Scotland. Maclean told him There is no chance of a British revolution; you might have a Scottish revolution, but it won't take over England. And he actually said I refuse to let Moscow dictate to us.

WP: Just as Marx was very clear that the one place in Europe where a genuinely communist revolution could not happen was in Russia. There were no foundations for it, no proletariat. I'm interested Alasdair, in the nexus between your background in Scottish literature, where that comes from initially, and the political dimension, which seems to have been there from the beginning.

AG: Well my father was very strongly Labour, left-wing. His father had been was a Congregationalist in Bridgeton.

WP: A preacher?

AG: A lay preacher. He was a journeyman blacksmith. He did take Sunday School.

WP: Is this your father's father?

AG: Yes, I never met him. He died in the twenties, long before I was born. My father told me that when the congregation were getting together to build a new church, and were putting money toward it, his father couldn't afford to give any money but said he would give them nine years of service as a church officer, that is, cleaning it and so on. But he also said that his political heroes had been Gladstone and Keir Hardy. Of course, you had a lib-lab confederation, in the 1890s. The Congregationalists, of course, that was Oliver Cromwell's kirk. Apparently the minister invited Keir Hardy to preach a lay sermon in the Bridgeton

Congregationalist Church. I remember at art school when it was suggested for our monthly competition we paint an episode from Scottish history, I asked Dad about the period when Glasgow voted a majority of Labour MPs, in 1923 I think, and he told me about it and I got newspaper reports of the event; how a huge gathering of all the socialist groups, the socialist Sunday Schools which they had in those days; there was even John Wheatley's Young Men's Catholic Socialist Association, denounced by the Church, a vast collection of folk going to St Enoch's Station where the MPs would be departing for London and Jamie Maxton addressing all the supporters who were filling up St. Enoch's Square *{declaiming}* "When we return, the railways will be ours" – nationalisation!

JH: That never happened of course.

AG: Until the Second World War, when in fact a coalition, mainly Tory, government, in a state of panic nationalised everything that had been regarded as impossible.

JH: And how did Home Rule come into this?

WP: Well the Irish movements played a big part in this with the Fenian movements and Parnell. The Crofting movement was important in Scotland and that related too to the Land Acts in Ireland.

AG: Yes, that's true because there was a co-operation between them. And James Connolly was Scottish anyway. again, the notion of holding the harvest, you know the impact of scale of evictions in Ireland, though it wasn't as bad in Scotland.

WP: It was in some places. But Home Rule as a phrase and as a political goal comes into play from the Irish situation, and after Parnell, John Redmond and the Irish caucus more or less blackmailing Gladstone.

AG: Well, again, Gladstone, and a number of others, took the line that a nation with an empire as large as Britain's, why not let the Scots and the Irish look after themselves. It'll take some weight off us. It's funny thing to think that Churchill, when he was a liberal and had been assisting the Lloyd George measures that had brought in old age pensions, when the liberals were still considering Home Rule for Scotland, Winston Churchill in his impetuous way, said; "People think it will take a long while to bring it about. Nonsense! We could get that through in a few months." And if people had said, Yes, you go ahead and do it, he would have.

WP: When, Alasdair, did you come to read in the Scottish literary tradition?

AG: Later. What happened first was, as I said, I hadn't been enthusiastic about Scott, except, come to think of it, I had read with great pleasure *The Lady of the Lake*. But Stevenson of course I had read and I knew Burns pretty thoroughly.

WP: From home?

AG: Yes. And then in Riddrie Public Library I found Hogg's *Memoirs of a Justified Sinner*.

JH: You found that when you were in your teens?

AG: Yes. It was the edition that came out with an introduction by ... ehm

JH: Gide ?

AG: Yes. I was hugely impressed by that and then of course there was *The House with the Green Shutters* which, again, is a really great book. It has a few wee faults, the same faults as Dostoievski has when he starts.

JH: Was Dostoievski someone who interested you?

AG: Oh, very much. I think Turgenev first, because I was quite
        young when I read them. I was visiting Alexander's Bookshop
        in Broddick. We went on holiday to Pirnmill on Arran and I
        would cycle over to Broddick, because this general tobacconist-
        newsagents, the owner, Mr. Alexander, had quite a good collection
        of Penguin paperbacks of various kinds and I remember
        getting into conversation with him and him recommending me
        Turgenev's *On the Eve*, which is a great book.

JH: Yes.

AG: I was just thinking, one of the defects, perhaps the only defect
        really, in *The House with the Green Shutters* is that he has a wee
        side bit in which he's explaining how the Scots are and what
        Scottishness is, just as Dostoievski occasionally has wee bits in
        which he's explaining what Russianness is.

JH: When they were already showing it in what they were writing.

AG: Yes. I was writing the Thaw section and the *Lanark* section kind
        of simultaneously, And none ever quite drew ahead of the other.
        Well, it would for a while and I would go back.

JH: So in a sense they did have a common genesis or a common
        history that was running along the whole time; different poles of
        the same...

AG: Yes. What I was afraid of, and I was a very timid person sexually,
        and not very attractive either, and I thought; Oh dear, nobody
        could ever write properly about love, marriage, fatherhood, unless
        they've had some of that. And it doesn't look as if I'm going to get
        any. But then I did and with a vengeance. {laughter}

JH: So that was artistically liberating?

WP: Emotionally liberating?

JH: Well the two go together.

AG: Well they did in me certainly.

WP: You must in your day, Alasdair, have encountered most of the
       Scottish Renaissance people. Did you know Chris Grieve well?

AG: No. I met him first at Glasgow Art School. I had started a literary
       and debating society. Glasgow Art School, I suppose, as in most
       of these institutions, a few students get something going and
       whether other students keep it going afterwards depends on the
       students. I did start a literary and debating society because my
       school at Whitehill had one and it was one of my main ways of
       getting together with other folk. And at one of them we did invite
       Chris Grieve to give a reading.

WP: You would know his work by this time, about 1955?

AG: I was beginning to. I really did come to it later.

WP: At which point his career was very much in the doldrums, he had
       been half-forgotten.

JH: Yes, it's really about 1962 he had his seventieth birthday and there
       was a flurry of interest about then.

AG: A book of *Collected Poems* was brought out about then.

WP: There was a *Selected Poems* before that, edited by Oliver Brown, I
       think in 1955.

AG: Oliver Brown is one of those people who has been forgotten,
       utterly and unfairly. My wife, Morag, has a collection of

pamphlets of his and I've been meaning to fish them out to help me with this series of articles. *{for The National}*

JH: He was a man of great integrity.

AG: And also the capacity to investigate facts. For instance, there's a pamphlet about how many people are tied up with the arms industry, how many bishops and canons and members of the Church of England had shares in armaments. *{Arms and the men, 1942.}* He was good in all aspects. He was also witty. He had a very good essay in in Bill MacLellan's ... eh...

JH: *Scottish Life and Letters.*

AG: But there was also a book he brought out in which people were asked to write about some aspect of whatever it was and Oliver Brown was asked to write about political pamphlets. And he was very good on it, explaining how you had not to speak in large generalisations before you had mastered more material facts than your opponent had ever bothered to get. But, as soon as you had amassed the right number, you could therefore make statements and back them up to the full, and even become slightly playful about it. But to return to Chris Grieve, my first response was this is not a language I have ever talked or heard other people talk. And then, to my amazement, I found I couldn't forget it. And I read it thinking this is just language, resounding no doubt but surely the sense in it doesn't justify its alien-ness to my way of talking "There was nae reek i' the laverock's hoose...". Many have quoted it and come to the conclusion that it has a significance which is slightly different from mine. And then realising there were so many others. And more recently I've been looking into *The Kind of Poetry I Want.* So much of it is prosaic in almost a clichéd way.

JH: Yes, there's a strong didactic urge there.

AG: Oh yes, but I don't mind that and as he himself said, he was like a volcano, putting out a lot of rubbish and soot as well as heat and light.

WP: "My job, as I see it, has never been to lay a tit's egg, but to erupt like a volcano, emitting not only flame, but a lot of rubbish." *{Laughter.}* That was, I think, in a conversation with George Bruce many years ago.

AG: But reading *In Memoriam James Joyce*, and thinking this is somewhat prosaic and then you come across, what is it "Great vessels sink when pisspots stay afloat." *{More laughter.}*

JH: Is that his own line?

AG: I'm sure it is.

WP: There are passages in *In Memoriam* and in *Direadh* which are as fine as anything he ever wrote.

AG: And in *On a Raised Beach*, and the fact that there he's not pondering Jamieson's *Dictionary* but geology and again, the business of him, as T.S. Eliot had done, patching in extracts from other folk's books. Much later on, when I was being an artist-recorder for The People's Palace, in the mid-seventies, Michael Donnelly suggested we might draw him for The People's Palace and I said Yes, anytime. Grieve was unwell and was living with his son Michael and daughter-in-law in Hamilton Drive. We went along and I spoke to him a bit.

JH: There was a group that you were in with Philip Hobsbaum, you were involved with that from the start weren't you?

AG: I don't know about from the start. I first met Philip Hobsbaum in a pub in Byres Road, I think it was The Rubaiyat, and he was with Tom Leonard and Aonghas MacNeacail, Angus Nicolson as we called him then, and there was living with him Anne Stevenson, an American poet, who left him to his great grief a few years later. Anyway, we got on quite well together and then on a second occasion we all went, roughly the same party, to the lodgings of Angus Nicolson in order to hear a Pinter play. No, not a Pinter play, Pinter was producing it, it was a Beckett play, *A Single Voice*, a monologue, and Tom Leonard was very keen to hear it. And we were listening. I didn't find it a very fascinating monologue "Little body, erect in desert..." I forget how it went, but it was a single little body talking about itself and at a certain point Philip started huffing and puffing. I think in later years he allowed the wide estimation in which Beckett was held to ... well, it might have made him more patient. But he said "What are we listening to?" Nobody said we were listening. Then he said {*shouting*} "Why are we listening to this? This is hell, why are we listening to it?" At which Tom Leonard said "If you shut up and heard it, you might find out." Whereupon Hobsbaum suddenly became the most idiotic blimp of a highly conservative kind.

JH: Really?

AG: {*shouting*} "My taxes are paying for wah wah wah..." He was liable to explode, though he was not always exploding. He was frequently quite gentle. But the point was that it was dreadfully embarrassing. I may have been the only person who actually left the thing thinking I have met somebody that I genuinely hate, would prefer not to be alive. {*laughter*} And the next time I met him, it was in the Pewter Pot, and I will not explain what I said to him and what he said to me, all unforgivable, but we were standing adjacent and he said "I've been told you've written a rather good play. Would you mind lending it to me because I'd quite like to read it." "Oh yes, certainly." It was a play called *The Fall of Kelvin Walker* that had been produced on television, BBC, and it was almost well-produced except for the very ending, spoiled because they got a very bad actor for a very important, very small part. But anyway, I gave it to him and then I got a letter

207

saying "I believe that this is the best modern Scottish play that has been written since Barrie's *What Every Woman Wants*, and in some ways it's even better than that. I wonder if you'd mind attending a writing discussion group of writers who meet in my house about once a fortnight.". And he explained that each writer gave in something beforehand. At each meeting one of the writers would read out something of their own but it would have been distributed to the group in typescript form by Philip using the University facilities, so that when it was read out we would have already read it just as a printed text and thought about it, and therefore we could discuss it, explain what we liked in it and what we thought didn't work or could be improved. And he was the chairman. In fact, it was a very good system. He was a very good chairman; he wasn't a bully. He submitted one or two quite good poems of his own and he really handled it very well. Through it I met Jim Kelman. I hadn't known him before then, though I had known Tom Leonard.

WP: When was this, Alasdair?

AG: Certainly in the seventies. Liz Lochhead didn't attend this group but she'd met him at an earlier grouping.

WP: So seventy three-four?

AG: Yes.

JH: He obviously had qualities as a chairman which drew people together. I think he'd done something similar in Belfast, hadn't he?

AG: Yes, very successfully. Seamus Heaney has an essay on the subject in which he says that though there were writers in Belfast who knew about each other's existence, he felt it was only with the coming of Philip Hobsbaum that they became conscious of each other, you might say, as allies in an artistic enterprise.

JH: And this is very important because it's what is often lacking.
       There's a sort of amorphous situation in which people are all
       doing their different things and not realising what they have in
       common with other writers.

AG: Heaney said, and in my experience it was the case, that although
       there was much in Philip's manner that was resented, in the first
       place he was hugely interested in what people were writing in
       Belfast. He also took it for granted that they should be writing
       about their own culture and background and knowledge of
       things. He took seriously that statement of D. H. Lawrence saying
       "All good writing is local. All bad writing is provincial." And
       the provincial writer, I think he meant and I certainly believe, is
       the person who writes about his own experience but his main
       potential audience, it is somewhere more important.

JH: Yes.

AG: And Philip was prepared to take everybody's piece of writing at
       its own worth, that is, he would lead us into discussing a piece of
       work as a made object that was improvable. I've said this before;
       people who have started writing something that they hope will
       'live outside them' have generally broken through an inhibition,
       are often doing something that parents or friends will forgive
       them for, rather than admire them for, or, for that matter, take for
       granted. And therefore having achieved something, they are more
       touchy towards what they feel as a living thing to which they've
       given birth, rather than as an article of furniture which they have
       constructed. The point is therefore "I think you could change
       this sentence or that, or remove that phrase" – they think; "You're
       asking me to chop off my baby's fingers" when actually "We think
       if it's meant to be a coffee table, it should have shorter legs. And
       if they don't work, you can restore them to exactly the way they
       were."

WP: On the other hand, if you want a coffee table at all, you have to like coffee. So there has to be the emotional input as motive.

AG: Yes.

WP: But it's an understanding at the artifactual level that people are simply not taught.

AG: Not often, exactly.

WP: That's a pathetic failure of education.

AG: But he did convey that it was possible to criticise; you could criticise something cheerfully, even affectionately. Criticism can be creative not destructive.

WP: It's very difficult, writing poetry, to find anyone with whom one can have a genuine conversation about a text you're working on and to get useful comment.

AG: Philip was good at that kind of thing. Even in London before he went to Belfast, he was I think a leading part of a group.

JH: And is Philip still living?

AG: No, he died some years back.

JH: The other Hobsbawm, Eric, the historian, was his cousin, although they spelled their names differently. I didn't realise that Philip had died as well.

WP: What took you to your Dante translations, to so vast a project?

AG: I'm working on the fourteenth canto of *Paradiso*.

JH: They're wonderful.

AG: When I started it, I proposed to Canongate that I should write a book on independence for the coming referendum. Now, I don't really enjoy writing political criticism.

WP: But you feel it's your duty?

AG: Something like that, like going on protest demonstrations. It embarrassed me to go on them, but I felt dirty if I didn't. Anyway, I'd signed a contract to write this book on independence and I went to the Scottish National Library to get out some earlier writings or early materials and I was thinking I don't want to do this, I don't want to start it. But the notion of Dante had been in my head for a while, because, although I couldn't read it, I had tackled it in several translations. The one I most liked was John Ciardi's which came out in the fifties. {1954–70}. The more I've been working on it, the more I've respected every translation I've read, because mine is a paraphrase, it ain't a translation. I've read many; from Carey's, which was the earliest successful one, up to and including Dorothy Sayers, and she's good and her notes are very copious and enlightening, but, again, she uses the archaisms, the thees, thous, dost, all that kind of biblical prose.

JH: But she was an Edwardian.

AG: Yes, that would certainly fit the part. But the kind of prose that still survives of course in the King James translation of the Bible, which is so closely based on Tyndale's, which is almost a century earlier, is, as you can see from Shakespeare's plays, an obsolete prose. Shakespeare's characters don't go in for much in dosts and thous, etc. I think it was Gerard Manley Hopkins who was among the first to complain about some poets writing what he called Parnassian.

WP: That of course had already been heavily argued over in France where the *Parnassiens* followed on in reaction against the

Romantics; seeking to discipline poetic diction from a kind of sentimental, narrative wordiness; this is about 1860s and 70s.

AG: And so far as English poetry is concerned, I first came across it in one of Gerard Manley Hopkins' letters, in which he talks about Parnassian as people using a kind of diction that was obsolete and saying that a poem should be in a kind of speech in the diction that people use in everyday life.

WP: Just like his poems. *{laughter}*

AG: I know. He went on to say; the language can be heightened all you like, you should heighten it as much as you can, but you shouldn't depart from a vocabulary...

WP: Don't falsely archaise it.

AG: Yes, heighten it as much as Milton, if you like, but he wasn't archaising very much. Why am I raving about that? Yes, it had to do with finding that Ciardi was one of the later translators who had largely, though not completely, avoided archaisms, was using a normal vocabulary. The version I chiefly depend upon has been Sinclair's prose translation. *{1939–46}* Now he actually does use thous, thees, dosts to an extent I find rather irritating, but apart from that, since he's not wrestling to get a rhyme going, he's not wrestling, as I always do, to get ten syllables in each line. I've been reading quite a good translation of the *Inferno*, by Ciaran Carson; he's slightly slangy, slightly humorous, slightly Irish, as he should be – and is. But at the same time, you find him in the Wood of the Suicides and at one point, in order to maintain the rhyme, he calls this woodland a *bosky chase*. Now in terms of the dictionary this is straightforward language, *bosky* does mean woodland thickets, *chase* is a word for an area of woodland maintained for hunting. And in this Wood of the Suicides, you do have wild dogs pursuing human beings and chewing them up.

WP: Is the attraction of Dante for you that he is almost a kind of magic realist? Why Dante rather than any of the other great Europeans?

AG: I think it's just because of his influence. Another project I was hugely influenced by was a performance, I think a translation by Louis MacNeice, of Goethe's *Faust* on the Third Programme. It was spread over three evenings and went right through to the fifth or sixth books – I forget how many parts. I was fascinated by that. As a teenager I even planned writing a modern version of it. At secondary school they called me Professor, that was my nickname, it wasn't unfriendly, because they noticed that on some matters I did know more than the teachers. This wasn't held against me by anybody, not even the teachers. I found it quite easy. It starts with this dignified old professor, who has never enjoyed youth, never had sex, has never had aa these things that people tend to want. All he's got is fame for his erudition. Nietzsche's criticism of Goethe's Faust was that here was a German professor incapable of seducing a girl of the servant class without being supported by all the powers of Hell. *{laughter}* But anyway, I identified with this character. It may have been only eight or nine years ago I found myself writing that version. I got it printed. I even managed to get a production of it, although I haven't managed to get any production of it by a professional company. I got a full reading of it at the Edinburgh Festival by the clever expedient of inviting the writers I knew to take parts in it. It sold out. There's a friend of mine, he became my unofficial biographer, he's called Rodge Glass; I quite like him.

WP: Not an overly enthusiastic judgement.

AG: No, it's not. He wrote a book *Alasdair Gray; a secretary's biography* – he was my secretary for a while. I first met him in the nearly two academic years in which I was a third of a professor of creative writing.

WP: How had that come about?

AG: It was an arrangement we asked for. What had happened was
       they wanted a professor of creative writing. The creative writing
       course had been taught by members of the English Department,
       who were not known as poets or novelists or dramatists, so they
       thought Who can we get? What about Jim Kelman, he's had a
       Booker Prize and he actually teaches part time – creative writing
       at a university in Texas, so we'll ask him. Jim knew that if he took
       up that job, he'd have no time for creative writing. At the same
       time the money would be useful. His wife, Marie, said Why don't
       you ask Alasdair and Tom Leonard if they would share the job
       with you and then they've got three professors and each would get
       a third of a professor's salary. We should never have accepted it
       but we did. I was seduced by the fact that my parents as socialists
       and aa that believed that {declaiming} "The highest forms of
       social life were doctors who combated disease and illness, labour
       politicians who combated poverty and social inequality, teachers
       who combated ignorance." and, of course, the highest form of
       teaching life would be a university professor.

JH: Of course you would be living up to your school nickname too.

AG::   Yes. I was saying Rodge Glass. I gave him a small part in the play.
       {giggling}

WP: Gretschen!

AG: No, a toady! {laughter} My point is that my first act of the play is
       all of it derived from the start of Goethe's play. It starts off with a
       prologue; the interview in which God comes to Earth in order to
       find out what's going on. And of course he talks to Satan who, as
       in the Book of Job, is really God's chief of secret police. And you've
       got Mephistopheles – not Satan – saying Well, it's a real mess,
       isn't it. I feel almost sorry for human beings. What a pity you gave
       them power of reason. You'd think they would use it to avoid dirt

but in fact they use it to stick their noses in it. And God says Well, what do you think of my servant Faust? He says Oh, he's one of the most miserable sods there are. God says you can't deny that he's a good man. Aye, right, but give me the chance of playing a bit with him, he'll soon give you up. And God says Well, go ahead. Do your best. I have that bit in and it's rhymed, I think quite successfully, and then I move into the first act. In my version God is simply a centre of light at the back and Mephistopheles bends down and gives expression of exaggerated adoration which no one could possibly believe in. Then God starts speaking to him and Mephistopheles jumps up and gives a Nazi salute, which I was told wouldn't be allowed on the stage nowadays. The one thing that I don't have in my first act, is him signing a pact in his blood. The way I'm taking it is that Nick is out to seduce Faust by offering him all that Faust can desire, which includes – I think I call her Elsa - one of his students. And Faust accepts. Mephistopheles begins by restoring his youth, making him handsome. Sorry, I shouldn't be trying to recapitulate a thing that is in print. The point is that he will corrupt Faust. What I have against Goethe's version is that though his Faust is utterly corrupt; he seduces a girl, he abandons her, she commits infanticide "Oh, sorry about that!" She's condemned to death for it. He charges back hoping to spring her out of jail with Mephistopheles' help, and she refuses to go with him, along with "That man" because she has never liked Mephistopheles. So he has to leave her to die.

WP: Do you not think there's an element of the real Goethe in all that?

AG: Oh yes, and his Faust matches. It's almost a parody of Goethe's career. With Mephistopheles' help Faust saves the credit of the emperor of all Europe, the Holy Roman Empire, by inventing paper money. He extends his power using magical weapons to quell civil wars. He goes back in time to seduce Helen of Troy and then he becomes a major landowner, he acquires the seashores in order to build dykes in order to create a purer, better home for the whole of mankind, though he's doing it by evictions, driving old people out of their house and setting fire to it. And what's more it's based largely on piracy. But this is all being done by his assistant, Mephistopheles. Faust doesn't seem to notice the horror and disaster. He's a real nineteenth-century imperialist capitalist. Goethe knows what he's doing. Yet at the very end the bargain has been that he shall only finally become Satan's if he suddenly wishes to hold the passing moment, to say *Stay for me now, thou art so fair*. He has said at the very beginning You can seize me if for one moment I stop striving for extra, for more. And at the moment he hears these excavations going on, which are actually lemurs digging a tomb in front of him. He believes that actually this is part of the excavations to create a new land below sea level which will be a home for future humanity, who will bless his existence, and at that moment he says I almost feel I could say *Stay for a while thou art so fair*. He's blind. And at that moment Satan says Ha, got you! And the devil's Hell breaks loose to carry him off. His soul is like a butterfly to be grabbed. At that moment Heaven opens and the angels appear singing in order to redeem Faust and they pour down showers of sweet-smelling roses and you've got Satan/Mephistopheles getting to be seduced himself, he says Ah, wait a minute – forgetting about the urgent business of grabbing Faust's soul and taking it off to the hell he so richly deserves. He finds the sight of the angels so seductive, he actually ends by saying Oh, turn round, let me see your bums and you'll be irresistible. At that moment they do, they turn their backs on him but they have seized the soul of Faust and so disappear and it ends with Mephistopheles saying what amounts to Fooled again, as usual! Then you have the final act which Goethe grabbed off Dante in which the soul of Faust is shown ascending through circles of blessedness as Dante was escorted up by Beatrice in the *Paradiso* and he passes the circles of the wise contemplatives, the circles of the saints, etc. There's nae hint of God in the prologue at the very beginning of this. There is no hint of God at the end because at the very height he reaches the empyrean and it seems to be purely female. There's even an indication that Faust had been drawn up to this female deity or cluster of deities or whatever at the top – and She probably includes the soul of Gretschen. But the final line is The eternal feminine eternally draws us upward and he who unfailing still strives on, we have the power to free. In other words, a Hitler or Stalin could have said I've never had a moment's peace in my life. Do you think I'm enjoying being myself? You know, I found that ending sickening.

7. MARGARET BENNETT

Margaret Bennett, 1946: Folklorist, historian, singer and storyteller

This conversation took place at Margaret's home at Locherlour, near Ochtertyre, on September 15, 2013. Present were William Hershaw and Walter Perrie.

WILLIAM HERSHAW: Let's begin with when you were growing up. I gather you had a lot of music around you in the family,

MARGARET BENNETT: Yes. My mother's from Skye for some generations, and her people are Stewarts. My father, whose name was George Bennett, came from a Glasgow Irish background, County Armagh; he grew up in Glasgow and in his teenage years spent a lot of time with an aunt in Menstrie. He was a very good musician and was also very, very keen on poetry and words. He was a great reader and was a member of a book club. We had a tilly lamp then – no electricity– and the books came by post, and these names would appear on the book-shelf one by one: Neville Shute, Alastair Maclean, and so on. He was also a really keen Burns man and he'd be invited to Burns suppers and to give the Immortal Memory. In those days Burns Suppers were men only.

WALTER PERRIE: Had your father come from Armagh?

MB: No, he was born in Glasgow in 1917 and his father was born in Armagh and there were seven brothers came over. I never did ask exactly what the prompt was but then there were various economic conditions.

WP: Protestant or catholic?

MB: Northern Ireland, Protestant, Orange and Masons from County Armagh – Portadown, Portrush, Tangradee were names we heard in childhood. He had spent boyhood holidays there, setting out from Glasgow every summer with his Dad, my grandfather, to visit family. But living in Skye was a world away, and in the fifties folk didn't have money or cars to go travelling. My father also felt wary of taking us into what seemed to him to be a very unsettled community; in childhood he had felt the tensions, heard the whisperings ('keep the boy away if these people come....'). He abhorred sectarianism. Growing up in Skye our lives were very much rooted in my mother's old family homestead, a croft in Glenconon, Uig, the north end.

Her's was the day of the ceilidh house. I don't think there was ever a day without some kind of music or singing. But my mother's people were very literate as well. It was that kind of paradox an outsider sees when he walks in the door; what might seem like material impoverishment and yet poverty is often something that other people label, not the people whose lives are there. They thought they were rich beyond measure. She's ninety-four, and to this day she says, "I had an idyllic childhood". No electricity, of course. She was born in 1919 and they didn't get electricity until my childhood. My mother was a singer and her parents sang. Her grandfather, Peter Stewart, was recorded by Marjory Kennedy-Fraser, who went to Skye about 1909 and there are eleven songs that he recorded for her.

WH: On wax cylinder?

MB: Yes. In fact my son Martyn used a digitized version on Glenlyon. It opens the track and anybody of faint heart might think they had a faulty album for it crackles, crackles, crackles, but it's the whole point of the continuing tradition. I have three sisters and we were quite honestly surrounded by music. The four of us used to sing together, we were always singing.

WP: What language was that in?

MB: Gaelic songs from my mother, but a lot in English because my
      father insisted we should speak only English. I was born after the
      War and my oldest sister was born in 1944. My father was in the
      army, in France, and when he came home he was just devastated
      that she wouldn't speak to him. But he hadn't taken on board that
      perhaps any child who hadn't seen their father for months or
      years might not know him – and she only spoke Gaelic. She had
      no English at all and my mother afterwards, she said, "Well he
      was angry actually, and he said, 'Why didn't you speak English
      at least?'" And she said, "Well, I just didn't think you could speak
      English to a baby, they wouldn't understand it." (laughter)

WP: Was your father an Irish speaker?

MB: No, he wasn't; his folk, being from County Armagh, in their day
      Irish Gaelic meant Catholic and low education and backward. In
      fairness to him, he did attempt to learn Scottish Gaelic and he did
      write some of his wartime letters home in Gaelic but his attempts
      to speak it were another matter. I think even to this day the Gael
      is intolerant of somebody speaking his language with a less than
      Gaelic sound, which is a pity.

WP: There is sometimes a kind of Gaelic fascism about the language
      which I find, among younger people in particular.

MB: Indeed, and now the tables are turning because things have
      changed in Gaelic in points of spelling and case agreement and
      all the rest of it. And my mother, who's very literate and had
      been dux of the school, says: "Well, here I am, over ninety, and
      people from America are correcting my Gaelic. And people in a
      parliamentary position having learnt it and have a degree in it
      and they're correcting how I spell it." However, as children we
      heard Gaelic and pretty well all our songs were Gaelic. People
      would come into the house and my awareness of poetry as well as

song being a part of that world was from a neighbour, who went by the name of *An Sgiobair* [the Skipper] – we didn't appreciate it then, but he was actually a very fine bard, Iain Nicolson, and he used to talk in verse sometimes. My grandparent's house was a real 'taigh céilidh' and there would be a discussion; it could be anything, something you heard on the radio, the weather or some political situation or some emotional concern, and the *Sgiobair* would begin his sentence with something like, "O uil, mar a thuirt Mairi Mhòr nan Òran" [oh well, as Mary MacPherson of the songs said] and then you would get twenty lines of what she said on that occasion – or Duncan Bàn. Duncan Bàn was a great favourite. The *Sgiobair* just had a head full of it, thousands of lines all off by heart, it really was the oral tradition. My grandfather was a great reader and he would read not only Gaelic and English, he would also read Greek. He was conversant with classical Greek, and he would check his Greek New Testament to see if the minister had the interpretation quite right. And to think that he grew up in a thatched house with an earthen floor.

WP: But the influence of the Bible on the Gaidhealtacht was enormous.

MB: Yes, and that was an incentive for education, that you should read the Word.

WP: Sam Maclean said to me that when finally they did get round to translating the Bible, and in particular the New Testament, that that was what saved Gaelic from extinction. {Referring to the fact that it both maintained a wide range of vocabulary and that it also carried such authority}

MB: I hadn't thought of it in those terms. We certainly had family worship in the house, every night; this was in my grandparents' house. I spent as much time as possible with my grandparents, I was more at ease there than I was in my parents' house. My parents might not like to hear that. My father died two years ago but I think that even now both of them would understand that, knowing me, who I am now.

WP: So he was well into his nineties?

MB: Yes, my father was ninety-two when he died. My mother is still with us, she's ninety-four. Grandparents sometimes have more time for children than the parents, who are always busy, busy. My father was a civil engineer but he was never too busy for music and was a very good piper.

WP: That was a thing I was going to ask you. You said he was a musician.

MB: Yes, he was a piper, but when he was growing up in Glasgow in the thirties, it was the time of the dance bands. He was a superb ballroom dancer. People used to go to ballroom dancing lessons and he had a cousin who was a professional dancer so he was her partner. And of course moving to Skye with his kind of background in dancing, he thought country dancing was a bit heedrum, hodrum, hoochter, teuchter. The schools in those days also taught quicksteps and foxtrots and I remember a visiting band came to play at a wedding but when they announced a tango, nobody got up except my dad and my oldest sister. People just sat and watched. Everybody watches Strictly Come Dancing but he would have been able to go on that programme, he was so good. He could play clarinet as well as pipes and he played piano by ear and, to my shame, we used to say – badly. But he was a good piper for he won a couple of medals at Cowal.

Everybody thinks their own upbringing was ordinary. We moved to Lewis when I was in primary seven, then my entire secondary school except my last year was in Lewis. I have friends there I still see and they used to say to us "We thought that you had a most

223

unusual house-hold, classical music, o my word!" And I think my father bought the first stereo on Lewis. He was a real gadget guy.

WP: Where was this?

MB: Just on the isthmus on the way out to the Eye Peninsula (Point); we stayed at the bottom of the croft of the bard Murdo MacFarlane, that part near Melbost. That isthmus is the reason we went there, because it was calculated that by the end of the twentieth century Point would be an island if it weren't conserved, so my father was the engineer who built the sea walls. I should have mentioned that when we were on Skye, he worked on the hydro-electric power station, he built the big power house at Storr Lochs.

WP: That was when the big station at Cruachan was getting built. Was he involved in that?

MB: No, but he had uncles who came over from Ireland and were involved in earlier projects.

WP: So this is the fifties we're talking about Storr Lochs.

MB: Yes, and in the previous generation, he had uncles, his father's people, who had worked on the Forth Rail Bridge and others who worked on viaducts. That's possibly why the Bennetts came over, years back.

WH: So it was in the family.

MB: Yes, it definitely was. He thought that I was going to be an engineer, but ...

WP: So were you a disappointment?

MB: Well, in some senses, yes, in others, no. I mean, I did all the right things at school (apart from misbehaving). I chose physics and chemistry, he used to pride himself on bringing me into his engineering office when the draughtsmen were there. And he would say, "Now Margaret, I want you to calculate the volume that we're going to excavate from this site. And this is the profile of it."I quite liked it actually and sometimes I would go out surveying with him. I'm not sure I was overly keen on the mud or swampy ground, but he'd say, "Never mind your bloody feet getting wet! Keep that theodolite still." But it was all part of the adventure.

WH: When you were young, did you have any inkling about where your path would lead you or did it just kind of happen?

MB: I had absolutely no idea of what I was going to do. I didn't even know the word folklorist, and as for being a writer, that would have been out of the question because at school I was neither good at it, nor did I like it. I was so attuned to listening and, looking back on it, I think I had dyslexic tendencies, not that would permanently impair my writing or reading but ones that they would refer to as maturational. I used to see words backwards – I had this left-right thing, like 'saw' and 'was'; for years they looked the same to me. I never got the hang of it till I was in my early teens.

WP: Are you right-handed?

MB: Yes, interestingly, my son had the same thing so that when it was his turn at school and all the other kids were reading extremely well and I was reading to him, the teacher was saying, "And you a teacher?" And I said: "Look, I'm not worried". He had an incredibly retentive memory for stories, pictures, tunes, he'd remember every detail. I'm not saying that I could do that and I wasn't as aware as I am now that I did have a very retentive memory. So reading was no big deal, if I listened very carefully I would catch it anyway.

WH: I was really interested that, I think in the eighties, you were in the Scottish Education Department and you were trying to bring folklore into education in a way that would help less able children, children with learning difficulties.

MB: Yes, that happened maybe more by default than design. When I reached the end of school, I didn't actually get the Highers I wanted because right in the middle of the exams we were moving from Lewis to Shetland, I wanted to go to Aberdeen University to study geography, cultural geography. I had set my sights on this as I found that how people lived was fascinating – why they settled where they did. I knew I didn't want to study statistics, I was more interested in what their story about it was.

WP: People rather than ideas?

MB: No, I liked their ideas too, because without people you can't have ideas. My two grandfathers, for example, one was a crofter-fisherman and the other grandfather was a blacksmith, time-served 'boiler-maker'. Both full of ideas, and both men of few words. (I didn't obviously inherit that trait!) Anyway, the night before I had a couple of my Highers to sit, my parents had this massive farewell party at the house. There was songs and music and laughter in our house till three or four in the morning and not a few glass things to clear away in the morning. Anyway, that night before the Highers, I remember lying in bed crying because I couldn't sleep and my father came in – and he was not one to show emotion – and he sat down on my bed and I was upset, "Daddy, I have to get up in the morning to catch the bus." And he said, "O, don't worry. Just lie in the bed and I'll take you in in the morning in time for your exam." So guess who was up and about but let the bus go, and guess who didn't get up to take me in for the exam? So I was on the road thumbing a lift. It wasn't the best frame of mind to sit the exam and I knew I wouldn't pass (I got 'compensatory O levels'). We moved to Shetland and I became quite rebellious – I was really quite disgusted and I flatly refused to school in Lerwick until the rector came knocking at the door.

WP: Was it a drinking family?

MB: No, my Dad liked a dram but I hardly ever saw him the worse for wear. But that night, we were leaving at the end of the week, and his pals were all there, each with a half bottle in their pocket. Even at New Year I never saw him drunk and he was not what I'd call a dicey drunk.

WP: Not aggressive or disagreeable?

MB: Not at all, but he could be disagreeable for plenty of other reasons. He was quite short-tempered. Sometimes I think I was a little bit scared of him.

WP: Lots of people who have led very creative lives often seem to have had a teacher or mentor, someone who set them on that particular path. Was that the case with you?

MB: Not till I got to university, except in Lewis I did have an English teacher who made literature live for me, a man called John Scott. He was a terrific Burns man and we didn't think anything of learning the whole of Tam O'Shanter – and this is in Stornoway. We learned poems by heart but that was part of our culture anyway. For me, Burns came alive in the classroom but at home too. There was a lot in Scottish literature that drew me, although I wasn't about to read it all for myself. I didn't think that I would have any career in literature or that I had anything to contribute, but it was a source of enjoyment. At the end of school I thought, what will I do? My elder sister had gone to Jordanhill to be a teacher and I thought I might as well do the same. I quite like children and I am a patient person and I'm creative, although I wouldn't have put it in all those words. But I had a wonderful

salutary lesson when I was at Jordanhill, in my first year. We had
a class on modern literature and I wasn't quite mature enough to
appreciate modern literature and especially not Virginia Woolf.
I thought, well, if this exam has any fairness at all, it'll cater for
people like me, there'll be a choice. Hemingway was in there
and various others and, lo and behold, this exam painted me
into a corner. Whatever avenue I went down, whatever section
I went to, I had to do a Virginia Woolf question. So I failed
spectacularly. What I took from that was that it was the best thing
that could have happened. I had never experienced that kind of
belly-flop failure with something that had never given me any
trouble. Imagine failing English, for goodness sake, that's what it
amounted to. I began to look at things in a different light. I don't
remember studying furiously but I remember being just a little bit
more methodical. I never missed a lecture. I loved the discussions
afterwards and I loved the freedom it gave me to explore things
for various projects. So when I finished Jordanhill, to my great
surprise, it was with distinctions and merits and so on.

WP: How long was that course?

MB: Three tri-semester years. I remember feeling a slightly less worthy
citizen than all my graduate friends who has M.A. after their
names. But I didn't mind. I actually enjoyed it. Then my father
emigrated to Canada. He'd reached the top of the ladder in civil
engineering and he didn't want to be a big fish in a little sea. He
decided he didn't want to hang up his hard hat and would apply
somewhere they needed good engineers and would appreciate
him.

WP: When are we talking about?

MB: 1966. I was in my second year at Jordanhill and my father had
gone to Newfoundland. I had no notion of visiting him because
he and I used to spark and fall out. I was going to go to Israel, to a
kibbutz for the Summer until that Seven-Day War broke out and

all plans were cancelled. I had been scrimping and saving the fare and I thought, well, I have to do something; I'll just go and visit father. And when I went to Newfoundland, gosh – that was the beginning of a new education. My father worked in a place that was 110 miles of dirt road off the main highway, so that's where we lived. And several communities were very short of teachers, so I was asked if I'd stay and teach but I wasn't yet qualified – neither were most of the teachers and some had barely finished high school. This was the end of my second year at Jordanhill, a year before I qualified as a teacher.

Geographically the area was a challenge and I met people who had never known electricity, or seen electric lights, like maybe going back to the twenties on Skye. While I was there I heard that they had just opened a department of Folklore Studies at the university, the only English-speaking folklore department in Canada at that time. I was fascinated by this. My Dad took me to St. John's (he had a meeting anyhow) and we went in to the university so I found out a bit about it. I thought that maybe I could come back and study there. I told you about missing the Highers – I think my father always felt a little bit guilty, or maybe he felt a bit of responsibility in that I didn't actually follow the path I had hoped to. He also knew I didn't feel stretched at Jordanhill. I liked it enormously but I didn't feel stretched. So, I said to him, "I'd like to come back," and he said, "Then just come back." Well, I couldn't do a postgraduate degree without a first one. They would give me two years credit towards a four-year degree but I'd have to do two more years just to get a B.A.(Ed.). After that I might do a postgraduate degree in folklore, but I was starting at square one and thinking to myself this is longer than medicine. But it didn't take quite that long, because when I started in the third year I found it too easy. I had all these courses and one by one, within the first two weeks, I asked if I could be reassessed – and they agreed, acknowledging that their original assessment might not have been apt.

WP: I can't see that happening nowadays.

MB: No, it wouldn't. There was a mediating body for foreign students,
      set up to look at your work from the previous college and then
      assess where to put you. Basically, what they said was, "We may
      have put you in the wrong place, so we'll do an oral exam and a
      panel will decide." One of the exams was in French. Well, that's
      easy enough. All you do is sit there and speak French. I never
      studied French at Jordanhill, so this was from a French teacher
      in Lewis who never spoke a word of English in class after third
      year. And my English Studies was certainly up to it and so also the
      educational psychology courses I did at Jordanhill. I was a bit of a
      sponge, so that I retained things. So I did a year as an 'Education
      major', intending to teach, and got to do one course in folklore,
      which was really what I want to do, and came out with a degree.
      I don't think I hoped for a cushy number studying Folklore
      but I wanted something I could really love. The Introduction
      to Folklore was one of the most challenging courses I ever did
      and the professor, who was very demanding, was the strictest,
      grumpiest man you ever met!

WP: Who was he?

MB: His name was Herbert Halpert and he had been, in the forties
      along with Alan Lomax, named as one of the two greatest
      folklorists of their time. He had been taught by the anthropologist
      Ruth Benedict. His other teacher was G.L. Kitteridge, who was the
      son-in-law of Professor Child. Franz Boas was his other influence,
      the great anthropologist who became 'the father of American
      Folklore'. So Halpert was at the cutting edge and extremely
      well-read and, interestingly, a friend of Hamish Henderson's.
      He was an army man (American Airforce, actually) who, during
      the war, like Henderson, had collected. It wasn't so much songs,
      it was stories and he had a big collection of them. He had an
      encyclopaedic mind. I forgot to say I had met Hamish by that

time. I met him when I was a student at Jordanhill. I joined a folk club the minute I could, there were lots then. Glasgow University had one and Jordanhill had a separate one. Sometimes we'd team up and we all went through to Edinburgh. I was eighteen I think. The first time I went who should meet us but Hamish and he took us to the School of Scottish Studies. This would have been about 1964–5.

I was, believe it or not, quite shy in those days. Hamish was such a brilliant man, though he came under criticism, even in his own department, for his unusual hours and his unusual office – up in Forrest Road (Sandy Bell's). But having known him in those days, I can assure you I learned more in that unusual office and in those unusual hours... The (official) office was quite amazing. Before I ever met Hamish I was longing to see this place and we got down to the basement with all his tapes. I had whispered to a friend of mine on the stairs that my mother had been recorded by somebody here.

WP: Was that Calum Maclean?

MB: No, it was John MacInnes in 1953, and when we got to the basement this friend of mine, who was a mature student from Aberdeen and who knew Jeannie Robertson extremely well, and was quite vocal – because he had something to say – in the middle of it all said: "Noo, there's a lassie here whase mither wis fae Skye and she says her mither wis recordet bi somebody here. Is there ony wey ye could fin they recordins? It wis mair than ten years ago. Whit wis yer mither's name?" So I told him and in seconds he (HH) had the tape off the shelf and was reeling it onto the machine, and there was my mother singing.

WP: Extraordinary!

MB: Well it was and, thinking back, I gained a little centimetre of status among my peers. They thought, "Oh, maybe she is from something worthwhile after all." When you grow up on the islands, I think island children have little or no confidence.

WP: I would have said the opposite, but that it's a different kind of confidence, which you must have had or you wouldn't have been able to do all the things you did. At some level, you must have had a degree of self-trust.

MB: Yes, and part of it was innocence. The other thing was my father, he encouraged us to ask questions, which helps. But there was a big differnece between Lewis and Skye. Skye is rather different now because it is full of incomers, but in my day, coming from Skye, I noticed the levels of confidence in Lewis.

WP: And what was the difference?

MB: A forthrightness and a willingness to speak out – and to be right, by the way. The school had a really teriffic debating society, which I joined – it used to be packed out – and that boosted confidence far beyond the classroom.

WP: And was any of that down to the evangelical movements, an *daoine*?

MB: No, I don't think it was that. There's a joke on Skye that there are some things that don't exist, and one of them is a Lewisman lacking self-confidence. But to go back to the recording; I got so much out of that day and then we had a huge night in Sandy Bell's. Actually it was the year Hamish composed [sings] "They have sentenced the men of Rivonia" – 'Free Mandela'. I think the ink was still wet. He had us all singing it. He was very charismatic. He seemed hundreds of years older but, when I think about it, he was only in his forties.

WP: But had seen a lot of the world.

MB: And he had such humility, Walter. I have always thought this, and more as I grow older, that one of the distinguishing marks of a great human being is someone who doesn't have to tell you of anything he did that made him great in the eyes of the world: "It's not by gold or costly claes I take my estimate o man. But when you see a friend in need, ye reach forth a helping hand."

WP: So what do you think of the idea that the tradition is impersonal, modest, so that, if your concern is with the tradition, you cannot put yourself in front of it. It's about the objectivity of the tradition; a song, a story, scholarship, but it's not about personality, not about you.

MB: How well expressed. It's something I have often said, the same sentiment, same belief that if you put yourself before your subject, whether it's the tradition or poetry or anything, you will be unable to make a mark anyhow, because you're so busy trying to impress. It's about forgetting self. But then I think too that when you are blessed with a passion for the subject, I really do love

it, then there's no question of putting self first. You are in this whole cosmology, you almost don't exist – and Hamish I think epitomised that. He knew the tradition intimately but he never name-dropped or referred to anything to impress you, or that he knew this or that. For him it had all just been grist to the mill and for you, the listener, you're benefiting from the product of all that.

WP: Hamish also had a kind of class confidence, that comes from a semi-aristocratic attitude.

MB: Yes, he did, and that, I suppose was a combination of the school he went to and the fact of his enforced exile from Perthshire, hence his clinging to everything Scottish. The fact that granny sent *The Sunday Post* or articles and clipped things out, and he would save it all up. That too is the experience of the exile, everything of the homeland becomes important. I think of when I moved to Canada, I used to save all *The Scotsman* calendars – they had pictures of home – and little bits and pieces. But to go back; what makes a good researcher is that no path is too narrow or twisted not to follow.

WH: Was this at the time when you were in the Codroy Valley in Newfoundland?

MB: When I was there I was aware, as was my mother, she said she saw things that had gone from Scotland even before her time – traditions her mother used to talk about as being in the past. It was quite incredible.

WH: How was it you got to the valley ?

MB: Well, I did my one year teaching – then I wanted do a post graduate degree in Folklore, so I asked the head of the department, Professor Halpert, (Herbert Halpert, H.H. two H.H.s in my life) –although I said that Halpert was grumpy, he was the most inspiring man, he was incredible.

WP: So he was the mentor?

MB: Yes, without a shadow of a doubt, he was the mentor. He was a great field-worker – his own fieldwork recordings were exemplary, as were his notes and supporting research. And his standards were, oh, there was no compromise, no half-measure. He was extremely strict, but not in the least unreasonable. He was demanding, very clear about objectives and the training was going to be rigorous. When I went to ask if he would consider taking me as a graduate student, he said, "Come back in a year and if you can convince me that you have a project for a master's degree that I think is really worthwhile, then we'll talk." So, I had a year to find something (still teaching) and lots of choice.

But in a wonderful way my father's job led me along the right
path. My father by this time had moved from the place down the
peninsula and he was working on laying out a new oil refinery
at a place called Come-by-Chance. There was nowhere in the
whole area where they could sink an artesian well. In he comes
with this hazel rod he's cut from a tree and he's going along and
folk saying "The Lord, Jeez, would you look at that Scotsman with
the hazel stick! What the hell does he think he's going to stick
down there for water?" And next my father is making these marks
on the ground and said, "Aye, that's it, sink the well there." And
they had this most amazing well. It's the traditional way, though
nobody really knows why water divining works. I remember
Halpert being very excited: "You've got an engineer who believes
in it, that's great!" I would go and visit my father just about once
a month, because I was in St. John's. This particular time he was
staying at a "motel", but you should have seen it; it was a wee
row of shacks. And he had a Christmas party for all the men –
and it was all men. But he'd already decided that I was going to
sing. And he played pipes and that was a great celebration. And
there was a man there and my father said, "Now, I don't want to
introduce you to this man, though I normally would." My father
was one for courtesy in manners and formality, which maybe gave
us a bit of confidence. He said, "His name is Hector MacIsaac and
he's from St. Andrews and he's full of Gaelic." And of course, the
first thing I said was, "Gaelic? St. Andrews? Never!" Ach, he said,
it's not St. Andrews Scotland, it's St Andrews Newfoundland. Just
go over and speak to him in Gaelic. My father, for the first time,
wishing I were fluent. So I went over as I was bidden, reached out
my hand, and I had enough Gaelic. And this man, who probably
would be in his middle sixties, was almost in tears and he shook
my hand until I thought it was going to come off: "I never thought
I'd meet anybody of your age who has the Gaelic." (He called
it Gaylic) And I asked him where he was from and he said the
west coast. It was another four hundred miles on the west side of
the province and the year my Dad went the road had just been
completed. And he said; Oh, the place is full of Gaelic, full of it.

They were from Scotland, from the real old country, from Moidart and Canna. And they were all catholic, every last one. So this was quite a change from what I had grown up with. And they were full of music. So I decided I would have to go and track them down. There was a short TV programme called "Cameras on the Codroy Valley". I saw this man playing pipes, singing Gaelic songs and waulking songs. I'd never seen men singing waulking songs and I thought; I must go and see them.

I went to the University; I think have a project, it's to collect the Gaelic songs of Newfoundland. And Halpert said: "And where are you going to find these?" I told him, and he said: "Margaret, have you read the newest book, I suggest you do and look about the third chapter that's about the Codroy Valley and that will tell you how much Gaelic is there." It was written by a journalist, a fifth generation Newfoundlander, who said: "Gaelic was once known here but it died out in the 1930s, about the same time as Micmac." I was like the cat that caught the canary and back to Halpert I went and said, "No, he does say it's gone, but I can assure you it's not." And he said, "Well if you can convince me and if you bring some evidence we will talk." So I got a scholarship, that's how I could afford it, and my Dad helped with my accommodation. I stayed in a boarding house and shared a room, a bed, in fact, with the landlady's daughter and, do you know, I soon discovered that my landlady could neither read nor write.

WP: Were they there because there was a catholic affinity, because Newfoundland was mainly settled by catholic Irish?

MB: No, that's not why they went. What happened was that during the waves of clearances in Scotland they were shipped off – from 1773 onwards – to Nova Scotia, because they weren't welcome on the American side. The Irish went earlier but what happened was they were all promised cleared land, and they went out in dire poverty. A group of them, who went later in the 1830s, when they got there, were bitterly disappointed to discover there was no land. They were lined up to be servants on the land of one of the big MacDonald landowners, so they were not going to be tenant farmers.

WP: Serfs, essentially.

MB: Exactly. What happened was – they felt free enough to express their disappointment. In Nova Scotia there were a lot of Gaelic-speaking priests. They had a number of Irish priests who had learned Scottish Gaelic and had gone there. This particular priest gathered this group together and told them there's land in Newfoundland and it's fertile. It's better than the land on Prince Edward island and there are grants of land and if you go there you will get them, and, in great faith, they went. As it happened, the area they went to was the only part of Newfoundland that wasn't settled for the fishing. The Irish went for the fishing, but the Scots, it was specifically for the land and to this day they call it the Garden of Newfoundland. It's very fertile, a little alluvial plain and I don't think I ever met any of them who didn't say it was the best thing they could ever have done. They were beside French, Micmac, English and Irish settlers, so it was quite a mix, with a fascinating effect. They had a way of living among, and together with, all those languages, and Gaelic was the best preserved, apart from English, for that's obviously going to come through the wireless eventually. But Gaelic lasted longer than French, and Irish vanished in the area, Micmac vanished. But there are just two or three speakers left now. So here they are all those years later.

WP: And did these people represent a different strand in the tradition?

MB: Well, I took the first recordings back to Scotland with me. I thought; I'll have to ask my grandfather this, because as a fisherman-crofter he had fished in and out of Canna and that area – there was a herring station there. I was very close to my grandfather and I thought I'd just play a wee trick: I'll play this tape and say, :Seanair, (grandfather) any idea where this man is from?" Then when he gets it wrong I'll go ha ha ha. He listened and he listened and he says, "Well, I was herring fishing and we used to land a catch at Canna and they sound very like the men from Canna. In fact, there's a wee island beside Canna, Sanday island," – I'd never heard of it – "that man sounds as if he's from there."

WP: That's an extraordinary capacity to identify a voice to that degree of proximity.

MB: Isn't it! Absolutely extraordinary, and my jaw dropped. When you think of it though, voices are so distinctive, a bit like hands, they're all the same but they're all very different. I think if you were to play a dozen recordings of your friends, or even of everybody you've ever known in your life, for a second, you'd be amazed, you could probably name every single one of them. The human mind is amazing. So yes, they had retained the tradition quite incredibly – stories, and songs that MacInnes helped me to identify.

WH: And you say that was at a time when the road was coming in and opening up the place. Did that spell the end?

MB: Probably it did. The Trans-Canada Highway went through in 1965. I made my first recordings in sixty-seven. But they got electricity in 1962. Unlike in Scotland when we got electricity, it took another twenty years for us to get a fridge and goodness knows how long to have a telly. I left home, I wasn't quite eighteen, and television was not a feature of life. But in the Codroy Valley they literally got television the next week as it was all over Canada. As this old man said to me, "When the television came in the front door, the story-telling went out the back." It's killed so much. I don't think the wireless did so much. My memory of wireless is that it was very important.

WP: Well, especially during the War.

MB: We didn't have electricity and you had to buy a battery, this massive accumulator and this voltage thing. It must have weighed a ton and the wireless was kept in my grandfather's house for three things: for the news, and the shipping forecast, and Scottish dance music and Gaelic songs.

WP: Exactly as in my own grandparents' house.

MB: And did you clear back the chairs and dance on a Saturday night?

WP: No.

MB: We did, and the cousins would arrive and there was a dance in the house. I asked some of the people in Newfoundland and the first time they listened to a radio broadcast was just before the War. But they would go to each other's houses like they did with the television. That too in its own funny way was a social occasion. It didn't dilute the social activity but it changed what they heard.

WP: But hearing what were, in some way, metropolitan voices must have changed the way they heard themselves?

MB: Yes, but that took a lot longer. One of my projects I never thought anybody would do, never mind me because you'd have to live awfully long to do this, I recorded the same family over four generations and traced how they made music and the repertoire of songs. It was all Gaelic-speaking in the first generation and then a mixture and even a macaronic mixture of songs. But with a big repertoire of songs they heard on the radio, including country music, which is very popular, and it's popular in the Western Isles too and in Ireland.

WP: But country music derives in large part from the Scots-Irish tradition, much of it from Ulster.

MB: Yes, it must, there's such an affinity. Even the ornament of the voice. If you think of Dolly Parton, she has a very ornamented style of singing Go to the Outer Hebrides, especially Lewis, and this ornamented style of singing is all part of it. So they're very much at home now singing country songs in Gaelic, Ceòl Country they call it. I think the same thing was happening in Scotland, even somebody like Jeannie Robertson could sing American songs and Jane Turriff, who died recently was a big fan of Jimmy Rogers. She had brothers, I think, who'd bought the gramophone records. This just goes to show that the earlier you hear a sound, the more certainly you can reproduce it. She was expert at yodelling the same songs as Jimmy Rogers. She was a bit like Mary Martin and Lonely Goatherd and she would flip from her singing Boston Burglar or an old Scots ballad to her American influence.

WP: These events in your life that you have been talking about came at a very interesting time because up until the early sixties everything that came across on television, even if it came from Glasgow or Edinburgh, was metropolitan, and people were desperate to hear something Scottish and it didn't happen that often. Then people like Andy Stewart came along. I remember when Scottish Soldier came out (in 1960) it was an instantaneous hit because it was about a specifically Scottish identity and was still within touching distance of the War. I was in Hamilton at the time, when Mrs Ewing's campaign was going on. She was elected in 1967. Suddenly, within a decade, the whole notion of it being respectable to assert a Scottish identity took off, culturally, politically.

MB: I think that's probably right because Scotland has suffered from the Scottish Cringe, and a Tartan Cringe, even worse I would say.

WP: Blame Walter Scott.

MB: No, I can't and I'll tell you why. I used to think that but then I realised I only thought that because everybody else said it. Reading the introduction to *The Minstrelsy of the Scottish Borders* and Paul Scott's work on Walter Scott, I realised that I hadn't really been looking at it other than superficially. When Walter Scott was given the job of stage-managing the visit of King George IV, the first monarch to visit Scotland since the Act of Proscription was repealed, he took the opportunity to have him dressed in the very garb that had been banned by Parliament, albeit during his great-grandfather's reign. We seldom stop to think what banning Highland garb meant in those days; we need only consider the intensity of feelings about banning any form of dress, whether it be hijab or burkha when, technically, other dress options are available. For the Highlander, no other option existed – it was not only the garments that were banned but the very fabric. All their woven cloth was some form of tartan or check, and in the immediate aftermath some were trying to make alien garments out of sacking. So if we look again at Walter Scott's plans to dress the new king in this fabric, it was an absolute tour de force! And if, in the years that followed the whole thing took off, it seems ridiculous to blame an individual for the 'whole tartan mess' as some call it. But I can't agree it's a mess, not even when I see it on enormous figures parading round an American games field. I feel that their insistence on wearing it is a reflection of something much deeper.

WP: Another means of asserting an identity which had become questionable. But in the Lowlands, it was Ramsay, Fergusson and Burns who resurrected Scots as a respectable literary medium and Scott is interesting in that regard because although he has many Scots-speaking characters, the narrative is always in English.

MB: And I make of that that Scott wanted the world to read the books. The Scots as a nation are so good at doing themselves down. They have a national costume the whole world envies and say, "O, I wadna be seen deid in that."

WP: I don't think that's the case now though.

MB: No, not now. Less than ten years ago I went to a huge gathering on Scottish Identity at the new conference centre in Edinburgh. The main speakers, James Hunter, Tom Devine, a whole platform of them, and each had twenty minutes. I'm sorry to say, Tom Devine spent his twenty minutes tartan bashing and I thought, how dare you? I admire many aspects of Tom Devine's work, it was St. Andrew's Day, and to my great disappointment James Hunter, when questioned, seemed obliged to agree. I wanted to stand up in that massive hall, with over a thousand people and say, "Look, I wear tartan. I'm wearing it now and I'm proud to wear tartan." But then I thought, Margaret, sit where you are, because that would be misinterpreted. It's not about me. That's only a few years ago. My Dad wore the kilt on the hill. But of course, he was a pipe bandsman and he liked the kilt.

WH: Something I wanted to ask you, Margaret: Walter was talking about Andy Stewart and the sixties. What do you think about Scottish Studies as a discrete subject, because it has been proposed.

MB: By the Scottish Executive? Well, it's not before time that Scottish children, young people learn about their own. When you think about the absolute greats we have in every century, every decade; take any decade, the 1980s. If you were to go to the Queen's Hall: Sorley Maclean; Norman MacCaig; William Montgomerie; Hamish Henderson. It was like the Enlightenment and we have had so many times when there have been great opportunities to have young people meet them and say "This is the great literature of Scotland." And it hasn't happened. Everybody knows about Wilfred Owen. Does anybody know about Hamish Henderson? No.

WP: Or Chris Grieve?

MB: Exactly. I left school and I had never heard of the man. The only
        reason I knew about Hamish Henderson was that my mother
        knew of him. My mother was tuned in to tradition and because
        she'd been recorded by the School of Scottish Studies. Everybody
        had heard of it by that time, probably thanks to Calum Maclean.

WP: I had meant to ask you if you ever knew Calum Maclean.

MB: I didn't ever meet him but I've been thinking about this quite a
        lot – there was no training for folklorists in Scotland, not even in
        Hamish's day and certainly not in John's day, when he began at the
        School. But when Calum began, 1951, he had already been trained
        by the Irish Folklore Commission to the highest of standards –
        Sean O'Sullivan's *Handbook of Irish Folklore* would train anybody
        in the world to be meticulous. Interestingly, that was the same
        handbook used to train us in Newfoundland as folklorists, back to
        Halpert again, he literally wouldn't let us go out recording again
        unless we had completely catalogued whatever we did. There was
        none of this stuff about being out having a great time and stick
        the tape on the shelf and forget about it. No, it all had to be done
        there and then.

WH: I asked because, as you know, there is a problem now. There's been
        this vacuum; they have no teachers who can be confident in Scots
        language, Scottish history, Scottish music. So where do you begin?

MB: I know. I wring my hands over this. I wish I had the answer.
        Right now I teach folklore at the Conservatoire. But although I
        am waiting for bright new graduates coming from the School of
        Scottish Studies to take over from me, there's something that's
        not happening. Let me go back a bit; that department's basically
        for the whole tradition but everything's been carved up, it's in
        boxes and there haven't been enough paths between each little

box, houses for Scots, Gaelic and English languages – that doesn't represent who we are, or what we aspire to be – people who can share tradition, people who can be enriched by our differences as well as our commonalities.

WH: Things don't join up a lot. That's something we've spoken about, Walter. I know that among younger members in my own English department, there's a terrific lack of confidence. It's not a lack of will.

MB: That's interesting because I haven't recently spent enough time in secondary schools. I did teach (1976–1983) but I taught special education and maybe I would bring in the folklore. Do you remember in the early eighties there was the Warnock Report? Things were changing in the curriculum and there was to be more conversation between disciplines. They were looking for modules that they might add to the English class and the history class and they might even speak to one another. I was aware then how difficult it was for teachers because I had been hired at Kingussie High School as a special education teacher. That happened really by accident; I had come back from Canada. I knew I didn't want to spend the rest of my life there although I had fantastic training and I did finish my master's and taught and had been offered a college job. But I felt I wanted to come back and bring up my son with a Scottish education. What I didn't know was that Scottish education had changed a lot since I had turned my back for the ten years before coming home. A lot of things were homogenized. For a start, gone were the ABC classes because they didn't want to label kids, but they were trying to level out everything.

WP: So this is when comprehensive education began.

MB: That's the word I'm looking for, yes. I think there was always a need for those who were lagging behind to have special attention, not just to let them drag behind and just stick them in a corner with a colouring book or whatever they did.

WP: But no longer catering for the gifted and they did away with the kind of rigour you get from the classics.

MB: Exactly. And they abolished standards in many things, they dumbed down an awful lot, right across the board. They began to use mindless questionnaire sheets, tick boxes, work books, etc. And took away from what I call creative teaching. When they changed to comprehensive education there were always a few kids who were going to turn into the biggest troublemakers, because they still didn't cope with complete dyslexics and complete attention seekers and so on.

WP: But did much of that nonsense not come from the education colleges?

MB: It must have. Nobody wanted to touch those jobs in special ed. When I came back, I couldn't get a job, there was a glut of teachers. They said; would you teach in a special school? We'll try you out in Glasgow, near Ibrox football stadium and then they had one for mild mental handicap. And I said I would have a go.

WP: It was very low status, wasn't it?

MB: Very. And I discovered when I went into an ordinary school afterwards, some of the kids were thinking, "I'm no havin her. She teaches special ed. She cannae be much use."

WP: Yes, I remember those attitudes.

MB: So I started off in the one for mild mental handicaps and then I realised that half the world has a mild mental handicap and the big need there was for material that would allow children to live and to function usefully. The only way I could do that was to consider how our forebears did this or that. So I devised a programme more relevant to life – in a tenement flat, or on a croft, and, in a way, it was using folklore where it was a reality for the

245

children. We weren't, for example, calculating how much water was in their bath – just fill the bath and get in. These arithmetic problems they used to create are not really relevant to life. I was looking for something that was real. So I began to try to find things from tradition that would fit. Stories, but also, if it was to do with maths, for example, they actually would go to the post office. Or if it was to do with reading, there's got to be something they're going to read. So I started off with things like menus. I'd teach them living skills, like how to answer the 'phone. That's basic but beyond that, when I went to teach people who didn't have mental handicaps but were really struggling, I had children of gamekeepers, hoteliers, farmers, you name it. So I thought, this has to be relevant to their tradition, so maths would be mixing sheep dip, how would you mix a gallon. And then you would talk about the various breeds of sheep and what do you do with the wool and the exports, so it was real to them. So, tradition and stories – did you hear the one about…. and the next thing was the place would be full of laughter. And there's a song about this and we'd do that too. So my classes in Kingussie are remembered by the people who were there. We did everything from how to mend a shinty ball – with two needles and waxed linen thread, my grandfather showed me – and they didn't know, so they thought that was great – and they were all keen shinty players. Then I'd tell them the story of how Cuchulainn could whack that shinty ball from Scotland to Ireland. How far is that? It was the sort of education that kids, quite literally, had centuries ago. I know it worked because when the school was closed on snowy days and blizzards, they would come anyway. Do you remember the strikes of the eighties? I was persona non grata because I felt I couldn't go on strike. The children said I couldn't and we went in but we didn't do any formal school work.

WP: C.J. Jung remarks that most serious pathologies are only really curable if you can find the right story to share with the person – their story.

MB: Yes, I like that, their story. That's profound. People have to be able
      to relate.

WP: It comes back to who we think we are, who we can say we are.
      And the tradition is an accumulation of all those responses across
      the centuries.

MB: In many cases young teachers lack a confidence in their own
      culture and that deeply saddens me. It's much easier for many
      people to collapse into a chair and watch game shows.

WH: There was a story on the radio this week that, apparently someone
      is detecting that in Glasgow some people are beginning to speak
      with a sort of Cockneyfied accent, they think through watching
      East Enders and so on. I suppose on the other hand that language
      is always changing and you cannot preserve things for ever.

MB: And yet, if you allow too many changes, we are going to lose Scots.
      I'm going to sound like a terrible bigot but the last few times I've
      listened to the news on Radio Scotland, when maybe I've been in
      the car, I've all-but turned it off. No, I've said, leave it on. Go and
      listen again and transcribe it and send it to the BBC.

WP: Because?

MB: Because the pronunciation was American – on BBC Scotland!
      Every word with double T had a double D, as a madder of fact.
      What are they trying to do? If one were to write and object, you
      would be accused of having some kind of fascist idea. I don't, I just
      feel that I value what we have in Scotland so much, I don't want
      to see it homogenised. The lowest common denominator is not
      necessarily the point at which all of us function best.

WP: Are you optimistic about the future of the tradition?

MB: Yes. What gives me the optimism is, well, several things: my own students – I only have maybe thirty in all at the Conservatoire. First of all, they're all musicians, so they come into the class not sure what to expect and perhaps with a slight disappointment they might have to pick up a pencil and put their instrument down – Is that woman going to talk for an hour? But then I see their body language and their faces, they're tuning in and I always invite them to draw something from their own past – and in seconds you have some saying: 'Oh yes, my grandfather told me such and such'. They start to actually value that they do have a great line of tradition. I've seen some great pieces of work produced just from that germination of ideas, including a fantastic set of recordings of an Irish fiddler that grew out of a class in which I had said that some people said they had heard tunes from the fairies. This girl put her hand up and said, "My grandfather said he learned a tune from the fairies." I thought everybody was going to snort and snigger but they didn't, they kind of went – really? I don't have an airy-fairy attitude to life. People ask me about ghosts and I say: when I see one I'll certainly believe in it. Until then, I'm not going to tell someone else who says they saw one that they didn't see it. That's a universal concept (ghosts) but Scottish tradition has its own distinguishing characteristics, so many voices, so many colours, so many textures, so imagine making all that monochromatic.

WP: Sam [Sorley] Maclean used to say of the Gaelic literary tradition that, in contrast to its debasement into sentimentality at the hands of people like Fiona Macleod or even the early Yeats, the tradition itself was hard, crystalline in its clarity, because it was looking at its real world from very close up.

MB: That's right. And the more I learn about it, the more I realise how little I know.

WP: Do you see a link between your subject and Scotland's political future, most obviously, the impending referendum?

MB: I've got great hopes for Scotland and, now and again, a twinge
      of doubt. It's not doubt that we can't go it alone, it's fear I think,
      that we mess up and that people should do things for the right
      reasons. I remember Hamish saying a long time ago that pride in
      nationhood should never be based on dislike of another nation,
      otherwise you have nothing to be proud of. But I don't want to
      leave Willie's question about Scottish Studies behind, because,
      unless we bring in to this new Scotland the hopes we have for
      Scotland, for our identity as expressed in education, but not an
      education that looks only at ourselves. It's an education of the
      sort that we had in, say, George Buchanan's day, when they knew
      about the world... as Europeans. And in their tapestry of language
      and culture could still identify which colours were theirs. I wish
      I knew some solution to how to change the confidence aspect of
      teachers.

WH: Grace Notes, the music and the publications, is partly addressing
      that. [Grace Notes Scotland runs projects and workshops; Grace
      Note Publications publishes Gaelic and Scots books.]

MB: Yes. A few years ago I started this little charity, Grace Notes
      Scotland, dedicated to handing on tradition; tradition is like a
      song or a story; you can give it away and give it away and still
      always have it. So it doesn't ever diminish what you have. It may
      enrich your enjoyment when you realise that someone else is
      enjoying it. Grace Notes, I called it that because it's a musical
      analogy, the gracenote is the ornament; the tune can exist without
      it. You can live without traditional customs like our New Year
      celebrations or our shortbread or whatever, but you cannot
      live without air and water. But it's the colour of life. They're not
      essential for you to stay alive, but they are essential if your mind
      wants to stay clear, and it's what gives us our identity as a people.
      So the gracenotes are the ones that come for free and you can
      have as many of them as you want. And I liked the word grace
      as well, in its biblical aspect grace is something that's free – and
      its antithesis, disgrace. It's all from the same source, to give it

freely. It's something I hope can happen now. I try to concentrate on planning holiday and week-end workshops which we call Bridging Tradition. For most of my life we have suffered from this Scots/Gaelic divide and if you steer a safe English path in the middle you'll be understood by both. But I don't actually think it's always been like that. In Burns's day when he travelled in the Highlands, his Gaelic tunes came through. In Walter Scott's day, he used Gaelic words too; he didn't have a clue how to spell them but at least he used the words and phrases.

WP: But there's another strand in that history, which is that the whole development of the centralised institutions of Lowland Scotland, Crown, Church, legal system and all the apparatus that went with that, was predicated upon the destruction of the Lordship of the Isles, and particularly on the destruction of the culture that subtended the Lordship. So, for example, the SSPCK, their behaviour would disgrace the Nazis.

MB: As far as their attitude to Gaelic goes, I agree. In fact, I think they should accept responsibility for the demise of the language much more than folk south of the border.

WP: So there's a fundamental problem inasmuch as the Lowland culture, which, essentially, won the battle, eventually lost out to an even more metropolitan culture. And that whole history has produced a long series of economic and cultural crises in Scotland with the result that the people actually capable of receiving your grace notes are quite a small elite. And that's part of this problem of confidence.

MB: I probably haven't addressed that, Walter. I have looked at it from my end of the spectrum. I don't come from what I regard as an elite, either economically or socially. In fact, I come from the Highland peasant culture that must be, as John MacInnes used to say, we're the black people of Scotland.

WP: But it wasn't a peasant culture, it was aristocratic.

MB: Yes, but we didn't appreciate that. By the time we arrived, we'd already been through this crisis of confidence, through the Clearances and heavens knows what. In fact, in my mother's generation, I know when she went into Glasgow in the 1930s, she used to get quite distressed at the number of times she heard the phrase 'heather growing out of your ears'. Now that may seem funny and in Glaswegian it probably is. But to a girl of eighteen, sensitive to coming to a new town, it's not. So they hesitated to speak in their own language and often they were told it's completely rude to speak your own language when the rest of us can't understand you.

WP: You know Ruari MacThomais – Derrick Thomson?

MB: Yes, I met him a few times.

WP: A prominent Gaelic scholar, editor of *Gairm*, but I don't believe his children knew Gaelic.

MB: There's an example of what I'm on about, although he wasn't the only well- known Gael who didn't teach his children Gaelic. I said to my mother, "Surely you could have spoken Gaelic to your children?" Oh, no, no, it would have caused too much of a row. They used to hear, "You'll get on better if you have just good English." One thing at Jordanhill I remember, in one of my psychology of education classes, our lecturer told the whole assembly, mostly they were women, and he said, "A high standard of English is essential and it's absolutely certain that if a child has two languages, they'll be inadequate in both as far as vocabulary is concerned." And we believed it because he said so! Then I thought, "Hold on, think of Maclean, think of MacInnes, articulate and eloquent." It's just the opposite.

WP: Do you think of yourself as a religious person?

MB: Religious, no, spiritual, yes. Growing up in a house with an atheist father – he abhorred the bigotry of Northern Ireland. Number one on in their list of "Thou Shallt Nots" was "Thou Shall not get involved with a Catholic". He felt that the whole Church/ State thing had been so damaging that he became, he was, a real Marxist, typical of his generation, typical Red Clydeside. My mother would say, "Your father used to be a raving communist!" But yet, my father, I know, came to the point where he admitted that , during the war, which for him was a pretty horrendous, he kept his Bible – it's like a folktale – in his left hand breast pocket.

WP: To deflect the stray bullet...

MB: Exactly. But I also discovered he read it – between that and the Rubaiyat of Omar Khayyam.

WP: Sounds like he was an immensely well-read man

MB: Oh yes, and he could quote at a moment. But I never rated it until I was much older. I think I took it for granted. It was my friends would notice. But I did have enough intelligent conversation with him, he was the intelligent one. And he said, "I realised when I was in extreme danger I prayed to Christ I would get out of here alive." Well, you don't pray unless you have somebody, a greater power, to pray to. But spirituality: I mentioned that at my grandparents' there was family worship in the house every night and I never saw my grandfather get up in the morning but he was on his knees and praying, and my grandmother too. Out of bed, on to your knees. I suppose I tried to emulate that from a young age, because I would kneel down beside him. All my life I felt that a spiritual dimension was essential to me. I have had plenty of times when I have abandoned it, not on purpose but probably because I thought there was something more exciting out there. Then I think, everything is fleeting and that I need something. When I quietly left the Free Church, I remember thinking, it's not for me. I felt in my grandfather's day they had austerity but it wasn't narrowness, it was that these sort of guidelines kept them alive and there was a morality about it that wasn't just denial.

It would have challenged the earlier ministers living in manses and in the 1850s famine, living off labour. I eventually drifted; the Church of Scotland, I tried that out for a wee while and that wasn't for me either, especially when they began to project words on to a screen. I thought, excuse me, I look at a screen all day, I do not want to look at one now. They accuse the catholic religion of being ritualistic, this is just as ritualistic with its three hymns and a prayer. It became formulaic. It was Martyn actually who eventually said, go down to Old St. Paul's, the acoustics are fantastic and the music, and I went, to the old Scottish episcopal church, and to my huge surprise, discovered a kind of peace that I really was looking for.

WP: So you became an Episcopalian.

MB: Yes, though I never joined.

WP: You don't take communion?

MB: I do, because you are invited. When life dishes you up some pretty hard knocks it's hard to tackle every single day's whatever it is. I think I have to be grounded in a spiritual dimension for it to make any sense to me. I remember Richard Holloway asking me one time (on a radio interview_ if there was anything I felt that gave me strength and I said, yes, there is and it's not on my knees asking for mercy or favour or healing.

WP: A new bicycle?

MB: Exactly. [laughter] It's more a training of my thoughts to look at what I have to be thankful for; so if I begin my day with thankfulness – literally for waking up and being thankful for the new day, even if it's pouring down rain, I think, this is another opportunity to be thankful. And if you are thankful, I feel there must be a recipient of the thanks.

WP: Well, though it's not exceptional to Gaelic spirituality, you'll find it among Canadian native peoples, it is marked by a sense of continuity between who your people are, and those who were, and those to come – a sense of who it's for and to whom you are responsible. Do you feel that?

MB: Yes, you mention Celtic spirituality and perhaps I hadn't even noticed that on that path I was exploring there is a big aspect of Celtic spirituality, inasmuch as I was looking for something that made sense to me, to my innermost being. I'm a very slow reader, so I take a long time to get through something I've chosen to read. It could take months; and one of those was Alexander Carmichael's *Carmina Gadelica*, in both Gaelic and translation. And I began to realise there was nothing they did, from wakening in the morning to sleeping at night, but that they had this wonderful, simple recognition of another dimension, beyond self:if it was lighting the fire, of ourselves we cannot create fire – you can take that match and strike it, but it is not you who creates that fire, it's something else. So also, planting seeds, whatever it is, making the cloth, weaving.

They acknowledged that there was a greater power in everything. So when they launched a boat, only that greater power would keep it in the water. I felt comfortable with that.

WP: Well, look at 'Birlinn Chlann Raghnaill'

MB: Yes, and that made me feel that; I don't believe we'd have had a Reformation or the need for one if we hadn't had a Synod of Whitby.

WP: Possibly, but highly speculative...

MB: Of course, but I feel the Celt, the Gael, if we had kept our Celtic
      spirituality, whether it was in Northumberland or Perthshire, I
      think we would have saved ourselves an awful lot of strife and
      heartache, including Moslem/Christian conflict, which seems to
      have roots in the Crusades.

WP: And in Western exploitation of the Middle East.

MB: Yes, that too.

WP: Are you ever aware of the presence of the dead?

MB: Well, if I feel the presence of the dead, that's paradoxical to
      me. I feel the presence, very much so, of those who have gone
      before. To lose a child, it has to be the hardest blow, the most
      unimaginable pain and anguish, and people will say, "Oh, I
      understand," and the simple fact is, No, they do not and they
      never will. But then I acknowledge that the one you lost can still
      make you laugh and smile and share things. And you realise that
      the moment that you are in is only there in that moment, but you
      relive it many times, you know that many times. Something that
      happened last night or when you were two or twelve or whenever,
      that moment stays with you, and yet you will never recapture that
      actual moment. But you will recapture pretty well all of what it
      was and sometimes it even becomes brighter in the passing – that
      to me is a very spiritual thing. It's more like those who have gone
      before are not the dead, the dead are with me, it's the alive, the
      living.

WP: I believe the whole pseudo-scientific notion of time, which
      derives from Aristotle, is false to our human experience.
      Aristotle's, and the scientific view, assumes that time is infinitely
      divisible (therefore, measurable) – and it's not. Our real lives are

experienced as cascades of – a wave motion if you like, of peaks and troughs of emotional intensities, of desolations, joys. And that seems inherent in many Gaelic songs. I'm thinking specifically of song such as 'An Ataireachd Ard' or 'Don Chuthaig'. And, again, it's about an awareness of the generations returning, or not, about continuity. I don't feel that people who grow up in the relentlessly urban, contemporary world have any sense of that continuity, and they are atomised and diminished by its loss.

MB: I think that's right but when you asked about having hope, I sometimes see in the young students that I work with, they're usually 18-25, sometimes a little older, that they live in this awful world of consumerism and the must-haves. So that within our lifetimes a celebration like Christmas: in our day your dad worked on Christmas Day. It wasn't even a holiday, and then, suddenly, we're almost where it is in America. I teach a section of my folklore class on customs and celebration of customs – and there's a musical aspect in all of it of course. So when we talk about Christmas I always have them perform one of these Galoshan plays. I might do the Armagh Rhymer one. And they all get their parts and, of course, the next thing is we're all helpless laughing, because it is hilarious. And I tell them "That was it, that was Christmas! And by the way, you might get a present, it could be a pair of knitted socks maybe with a red trim, or just nothing. Would you like that for this coming Christmas or this mass of stuff, with ipads or whatever?" And to a person among my students, not one opted for the modern Christmas. Because after the moment of 'look what I've got', it's gone, whereas the deeper dimension of celebration and of the intangible is much more important.

WP: And was it like that on the Islands?

MB: Yes, even after the Reformation. The first of May was Beltane (latha Bealtainn). It was a very important time on the land, the changing of the seasons, the meeting of light and dark.

WP: Yeats is good on that.

MB: Yes, I often think that Sorley modelled his recitation on Yeats. Angus Calder has an interesting statement, I'll find the quote: "Gaelic revival was not exceptional in a Europe where Basques and Sardinians were asserting their linguistic peculiarity... but the stature of Sorley Maclean, the Gaelic poet... became quite extraordinary, as Lowlanders, taking note of his international fame, honoured the major living exponent of a dying tongue which they had often been brought up to despise." (Angus Calder, *Revolving Culture*, p.10)

WP: And just before that Gordon Wright had brought out *Four Pointsof a Saltire*. It was Sorley and Willie Neill and Stuart MacGregor. Who was the other Gaelic poet?

MB: Was it George Campbell Hay?

WH Yes, it Campbell Hay, and who was the other one?

MB: It wasn't Derrick Thomson, was it?

WP: No, Sorley had no time for Derrick.

MB: He possibly did some harm to the younger generation's perception of traditional poetry. When I think of poets who get bypassed now, 20th century poets: Donald John MacDonald, an amazing poet, or the Paisley bard, Donald MacIntyre, they don't get international reputations – and Norman Maclean of the comedian mind – genius mind – told me that when he was at university, the students at Glasgow used to take their Gaelic issues not to the academics but to Donald MacIntyre, because he was such an incredibly knowledgeable man, totally conversant in centuries of his own culture.

WP: Derick was a very shrewd man but who was part of that metropolitan elite, if you can have such a thing in Glasgow. He was a great political operator.

MB: You can. But it says something if someone doesn't teach their own children their language. He had a great focus because *Gairm* out came every quarter, and it even had Gaelic lessons in it, presumably for adult learners. I wasn't allowed to learn Gaelic at school because I wasn't a Gaelic-speaker. You could do French and Latin. And you could do French or Gaelic. I wanted to learn French but I also wanted to learn Gaelic. Do you speak it at home? No. Well, if you don't speak it, you can't learn it. So that prevailed and I wasn't allowed to learn any Gaelic. But in my last year of school in Stornoway, I happened to disagree with the Gaelic teacher who was addressing the senior pupils about our excellent education. Following my father's advice, never be afraid to ask questions, I put my hand up, and said "Sir, I disagree; I am going to leave school without the one subject I wanted to learn." For my cheek (he said) I would stay behind till 5 o'clock every day and, as a punishment, would do homework every night for a week. The punishment was to work through the lessons in Gairm – thanks Derrick! But due credit to the Gaelic teacher, who stayed after school for several weeks as he saw how keen I was. Perhaps he recognised I had been denied a birthright; if we lose our languages, Gaelic or Scots, we lose our identity.

8. JOHN HERDMAN

John Herdman, 1941: Novelist, short story writer and critic.Co-founder of *Fras* Magazine and Publications

The conversation took place at John's home in Edinburgh on March third, 2020 with Richie McCaffery and Walter Perrie.

WALTER PERRIE: To get us under way John, will you begin by telling us a little about your ancestry? Not necessarily your immediate predecessors but how you see yourself in terms of your ancestry?

JOHN HERDMAN: Well, I see myself as a Scot of the Scots really, although some people think my name's not Scottish but it is – a mixture of Lowland and Highland, probably East Lothian being the major location in recent generations. My father was a grain importer in Leith and my mother's family were tea merchants in Leith. So, very much a nineteenth century bourgeois background. The only distinguished person in my more remote ancestry was a famous medical writer of my own name, John Herdman from Saltoun, who became a society doctor in London and later lived in Northumberland and was author of a number of medical works which are still sought after, I understand. Then on my mother's side I've a great aunt who was a rather famous suffragist and peace-woman in the First World War. Her name was Chrystal Macmillan and there's a building called after her in George Square, Edinburgh. They are my most notable forebears. But I think, going back a generation or two, they're mostly typical rural Scottish farmers, bleachers, millers in a small way, that sort of thing.

RICHIE McCAFFERY: You've already mentioned your father, William Herdman, grain importer, who you describe in *Another Country* as a man of two parts, two sides, a classic Edinburgh type. As such I'm going to inevitably ask about your debt to doubleness and duality: I notice in the background that you have a copy of the *One O'clock Gun*. I remember an issue of it which was about duality in Edinburgh, describing it as 'Edina's plague', the sort of thing that was easily used by the tourism board to market Edinburgh. I know there's a long tradition of this – Robert Louis Stevenson describing the city as being of two parts, one part alive and one part encased in stone, David Daiches' *Paradox of Scottish Culture* and G. Gregory Smith's concept of the 'Caledonian anti-syzygy'. Do you think this is a peculiarly Scottish and maybe even Edinburgh phenomenon because of its history or does it have a wider application? Is this something you'd apply to Scottish literature or could it be applied equally to European literature?

JH: I think it definitely can, yes. I quite take the point of the article in *The Gun* that it's been overstated in recent years or it's become a cliché, nonetheless there's often truth in clichés. I think actually of my father as a bit of an example of the Deacon Brodie type because on the surface he was a very much a conventional man of his own class. But he also was a drinker in Rose Street pubs who would talk to anybody and indeed my first contacts with literature were strangely enough through him, though the last thing he wanted was for me to become a writer. But he'd met Tom Scott in, I think, Paddy's Bar and Tom Scott gave me an introduction to MacDiarmid in 1963. But yes, I think in general there is truth in the doppelgänger thing. I've written a book about it so I don't want to elaborate on it too much because it's all there. It's certainly Scottish, certainly European.

WP: Yes, the golem.

JH: The golem, yes and E.T.A Hoffmann was one of the masters and Dostoevsky too.

WP: Years ago I did some work into the philosophical origins of *The Drunk Man* and corresponded with Chris Grieve about it and the fundamental texts were Dostoevsky's *The Double* and *The Underground Man* and Nietzsche's *Zarathustra*. *Zarathustra* in particular, with Chris and Edwin Muir, was a key text from 1910 through to maybe 1930 in Scottish poetry. But that's obviously part of your background as well.

JH: It's part of my background certainly and that shows in my first book *Descent*. I think it was reading *Zarathustra* that finally sparked off the tone in which I decided to write it. It was influenced by other works like Rilke's *Notebooks of Malte Laurids Brigge* and Rimbaud's *Une Saison en Enfer* and also Jung's *Psychology and Religion* but the actual sparking point was the style of Nietzsche.

WP: What do you make of it now?

JH: I haven't read it for quite some time. I think Nietzsche was a great destructive force. It's easy to sneer nowadays at the Superman and all of that but I think he was a great analyst of society as it was and is today and a great destructive analyst and that seems to me now to be a strength.

WP: He was the kind of figure who gave to other writers the notion of a heroic destiny and that was his attraction I think for Chris Grieve. One reason I was asking about your ancestry was I have the impression in reading you that there is a kind of lurking eminence in the background, which is the *Gaidhealtachd*, and when I'm reading you I'm reminded surprisingly often of Neil Gunn, who also has this intrusion in his writing of the completely unprepared for, the supernatural or whatever it is, while presenting it in the language of the truth-teller, the simple narrator who is just telling the story but underhand there are being slipped in all kinds of bizarre things. This seems to me very much of the *Gaeltacht* and very much a kind of background presence in your own writing.

JH: Well I'd agree because when one of my books came out somebody said to me, they've all got the same kind of movement which is from the city (Edinburgh usually) to the Gaidhealtachd / Highlands and then back again. It's certainly a pattern in three or four of my books. It happens in *A Truth Lover*, it happens in *Pagan's Pilgrimage*. It doesn't happen in *Imelda* but it does happen in *Ghostwriting* and it happens in *The Sinister Cabaret* and I'm not quite sure whether to give the first place to cultural factors there or psychological factors. In some ways it's maybe about some kind of a failed escape from the pull of Edinburgh, which has always been very strong for me, the pull of the city and the pull of Edinburgh and then there's a pull away from it which seems to fail.

WP: A golden age elsewhere?

JH: A golden age? An ideal society perhaps elsewhere, yes. A freedom from the city and from urban life which I felt very immersed in from my childhood I suppose.

WP: What do you make of Neil Gunn?

JH: For some reason he's someone I've never got into in a deep way. I've read some of his books...

WP: *Butcher's Broom* I think is probably his great book, that and perhaps *The Well at the World's End*. The writing is more subtle than you might think.

JH: I'm sure it is. I must say I've read three or four. I've read *Silver Darlings*, I've read *Highland River*, *The Serpent*, I haven't read any of the later ones.

WP: Those are the most popular ones. He was certainly highly regarded by both Chris Grieve and Edwin Muir. So who do you admire of that period?

JH: I don't say I don't admire Gunn but I'm not personally particularly drawn to his work.

WP: What about Gibbon?

JH: Yes, I admire Gibbon.

WP: I would rather read Gunn than Gibbon by quite a long way actually. I think the writing is more...

JH: It's more subtle. Gibbon was a linguistic virtuoso. I mean I admire Fionn MacColla actually.

WP: Well, I would have more hesitation about that. Politically, yes, he's a firebrand.

JH: Yes, I think that I said somewhere, I describe him as a writer of genius who never became a great novelist. He was an extraordinary stylist, an extraordinarily powerful and exact stylist. He had a very subtle mind, he could portray psychologically a character in a few strokes with tremendous accuracy, he'd note gestures and the way people moved and spoke but he had difficulty with structure. I think his obsession with trying to put forward his ideas compromised his position as a novelist.

RM: You were an early and vocal champion of his work and shortly after he died in *Brunton's Miscellany* you wrote about his unpublished work. We only have a limited insight into him because he was only able to publish a few books, but there remain these other novels. *The Ministers* was latterly published and also *Move Up, John*.

JH: I edited that and introduced it.

RM: What about *Facing the Muzhik*?

JH: *Facing the Muzhik* was really unpublishable. It was a curious
      attempt to mix ideas with a John Buchan type thriller which didn't
      work at all and I think he knew it. There's always a temptation
      when a writer leaves a lot of unpublished work to assume that it
      ought to have been published. But I think he actually knew that
      some of this stuff wasn't good enough. He did sort of finish the
      Reformation novel *Move Up, John*; he didn't finish *The Ministers*
      though it was possible to knock it into a shape and make it appear
      finished, but it wasn't finished.

RM: But this applies to you too, because you have a body of
      unpublished work yourself. One thing I noticed you mention in a
      few interviews is your spiritual autobiography of the 1980s which
      you say 'mercifully' remains unpublished. Why do you say that?

JH: Because I think I would now find it embarrassing. It was written
      from a very particular perspective of the religious position I had
      adopted at that time and it retrospectively tries to interpret my
      history in terms of leading up to that which I now think is actually
      very dubious.

RM: As we were saying over lunch about Tom Scott's engagement
      with Catholicism leading to 'The Paschal Candill' – although
      it was something he recanted and latterly disowned, it's still a
      fascinating poem and it does contribute to his body of work
      because it gives us a more vulnerable view of this rather
      hectoring, loud, very-sure-of-himself figure. As Alasdair Gray
      might have said: 'Let posterity judge'.

JH: Let posterity judge, but there are certain things that you perhaps
      just don't want posterity to judge.

WP: Or know about!

JH: Or know about even, yes. I feel about that book that it's striving
      too much after a position that I can't now objectively justify,

I mean the position I took there, the religious position I took there; I'm just no longer in that position. I think what was invalid about that book was the attempt to introject that stance into my past. There's also an unpublished novel that might best remain unpublished. I was looking at my papers recently in the National Library, and apart from the fact that I plundered it for later, better works, it's not good enough.

RM: You say 'plunder'. I get a sense throughout your work as it evolves that you cannibalise things, you take things, so we get recurring characters like 'Wee Davie' or you add, such as in *Ghostwriting*, the coda that is 'Tom na Croiche'.

JH: Yes, that's right, I do cannibalise, I do go back. I've used quite a lot of stuff from unpublished work in later books. *Pagan's Pilgrimage* contains quite a lot of that abandoned novel.

WP: But that's how the process goes on. All these efforts one makes of identifying with a position or an idea or whatever over the course of a life, they're all simply staging posts along the way because where you end up is *with the work*, what you want to be judged on is the best of that, the rest is irrelevant.

JH: Yes, I'd agree with that.

RM: 'Tom na Croiche'; that short story seems to raise some very interesting questions about reality and about fictional characters and how even a character that is created in the mind of the writer, a world created by the writer, isn't purely limited to those pages, that it might have an agency or ability to go on living outside of that? You seem to ask these questions in 'Tom na Croiche', when the protagonist spends this nightmarish night in a Highland shieling, having all these devilish visions of what went before in fact, fiction and legend.

JH: Yes, I sometimes wonder, whether the world that we experience in dreams isn't actually in some way real, an alternative universe that's actually real. That's partly what that was about. What I compare in 'Tom na Croiche', are the two cases, the story of ritual infanticide in *Ghostwriting* and another absolutely true story I came across much later in a doctor's waiting room, in an article about a case that's extraordinarily like the one I described in *Ghostwriting*, the parallels are extraordinary. I don't know whether I had actually read about the case myself long before and it was a subliminal memory.

RM: There's a communal consciousness being dredged up.

JH: Yes, the communal consciousness... you see, *The Sinister Cabaret* was a book that was written almost completely out of dreams because I began to ask myself how dream consciousness relates to waking consciousness, you've got an overt waking consciousness and you've got a dream consciousness, but after all they come from the same psyche.

WP: They come from different levels of consciousness, different layers.

JH: Oh yes, but I was wondering whether you could make some kind of a logical story, a journey, by trying to find the connections between different dreams, that's what I tried to do in *The Sinister Cabaret*. I thought I could, I thought that if I arranged them in a particular way, they'd make sense as a coherent story, which incidentally involved again that movement from the city to the Highlands and back again.

WP: You're very much a city boy.

JH: A city boy and specifically an Edinburgh person.

RM: We're sitting here in your flat surrounded by antique items that might have been inherited?

JH: The furniture? Yes, all of it.

RM: There's a passage in *A Truth Lover* where you, via the protagonist Duncan Straiton, write so powerfully and evocatively about the effect his family history has on him, how he stands at the graves of his ancestors and 'my flesh has crept to the grand words to which their souls thrilled'. It's a passage of great force and tenderness. I know family was almost a religion to Sorley MacLean.

WP: That is core to the Gaidhealtachd, the notion of ancestry. Now when Sam (MacLean) was headmaster at Plockton it was said that he could tell you the ancestry of each of his pupils for at least two hundred years. And I'm sure that was right, it was such a small, local community.

RM: Ancestry, family heritage and history means a great deal to me but it doesn't necessarily mean much to other writers, some of whom try to disown it. I'm more drawn to the writers who actively embrace it.

JH: Yes, I very much agree with that.

RM: You've written a great deal of your admiration for Bob Dylan, an early study of his work *Voice Without Restraint* and you consider him a very great genius. Do you think that in some of your writing you lay bread crumbs for readers in the sense that you quote him without acknowledging it? In *The Sinister Cabaret* you have in the dialogue one character saying 'It's not dark yet' and the other replying 'But it's getting there' (from the song 'Not Dark Yet' from *Time out of Mind*). Have you planted these little things to appeal to an ideal reader or a reader who has been where you've been? You also mentioned *Slow Train Coming* and that of course is also the album that's about a religious crisis. Do you identify with that religious crisis? It being the 1980s?

JH: I do, yes, I do. I had a religious crisis myself in the late 1970s, just about the time of 'Slow Train Coming' and the result of that was I became a Catholic, not a born again Christian. But I became a Catholic and remained so for about twenty years. But I do refer to Dylan on a number of occasions. I think he is the paradigmatic genius of our time as Shakespeare was for his time.

WP: That is a large claim!

JH: It is.

RM: I do think this plays to what Hamish Henderson called 'a false antithesis'. The folksong flytings in *The Scotsman* in the 1960s seemed to be based on this idea that there was a high culture and a low culture and never the twain shall meet, when both of them were symbiotically related and needed each other for their own existence.

JH: Exactly, and I think Dylan combines both of these things and I think I cottoned onto him, if I may say so, very early on. My sister brought back an EP in 1964 and I said to myself immediately: this guy is different. I was quite well versed in popular music at the time but this guy was quite different and it took me about fifteen years to write a book about him. The difference was the sharpness of his insight and the way in which it was expressed and the way in which the music and message were perfectly married. He was also clearly someone who was influenced by literature although he used to play that down. In that little record I remember seeing influences from the young Brecht for instance. But that's not the point of it, the point of it is really the startling quality of his insight, the economy with which he expressed it and the marriage of words and music in a unique way. But I think he's often underestimated as a great melodist as well. On Radio 3 the other day I heard someone querying whether we have any good tunes left. Well of course classical music in the modern sense I don't think does have any good tunes left, the tunes have gone to people like Dylan who's an incredible melodist.

WP: So you associate him with the 1930s, which is the last great period of political activism in the arts where it actually mattered? You mentioned Brecht.

JH: Yes, Brecht's early work, in the late twenties, even the early twenties.

RM: But I'd say there's something in your admiration for Dylan in the way that you elegantly and memorably turn a sentence. You obviously admire Dylan's lyrics and you're clearly a prose stylist; in fact, in an interview with Macdonald Daly in 1999 you said 'I think I was born with a feel for prose style but not for structure'.

JH: Yes, that's right.

RM: You're downplaying yourself by saying 'I was born without talent for structure' because your novels are most elaborately crafted. As soon as the reader thinks that they've got some sort of stable footing, you pull the rug on them.

JH: I think structure did come to me, but it came later. Because most of my earlier work was quite episodic.

WP: That's still clear, your propensity for shortness.

JH: Yes, that's kind of inbred, but from *Imelda* onwards I'd say that my books came to me much more as a whole, not in an episodic way, though they may still have episodes in them but the structure came to me in a much more organic way I think from that point onwards.

WP: And the attraction of Maupassant is ?

JH: That he's easy to translate.

WP: That's cheating!

JH: That's the main one I'd say. I wouldn't say that I have any deep affinity with Maupassant. I keep choosing him partly for merely practical reasons, that's he's translatable, that I've got a couple of copies of his books in the house.

RM: Just to return to plot and structure for a moment; Ian Rankin has a novella called *The Traveller's Companion* which is about a PhD student obsessed with Robert Louis Stevenson, going to Paris and finding somebody who claims to have the original draft of *The Strange Case of Dr Jekyll and Mr Hyde* and the novella unfolds in a rather predictable and linear fashion, you can see it all coming a mile off, even its twists, whereas your novels seem to be far more cleverly and wittily crafted. I remember reading Edwin Morgan in interview talking about writing his long poem sequence *The New Divan* and he said that he turned to Hafiz and Sufi mysticism because in the West we like to work a reader too hard, to guide them forcefully and rigidly to a conclusion. I don't know if you can relate to that feeling?

JH: Yes, that's more in the English tradition specifically, more than the Western tradition. I don't think it's true of European literature. I've been quite influenced by people like Hoffmann, Kafka, Beckett.

WP: Dickens?

JH: No, I didn't read Dickens until about twenty years ago.

WP: I mention Dickens because he's full of really bizarre moments which are wholly unpredictable and not part of the story but they just suddenly intrude themselves. That might be part of the episodic nature of his writing, originally for magazines, in instalments.

JH: Dickens is by no means typical of English fiction. Not at all. I actually should have known Dickens since my youth because he was my special subject in my last year at university and I went into the exam having read only one Dickens novel.

WP: Excellent, well done! Now I think we're agreed that fundamentally, you're dysfunctional?

JH: Yes.

WP: But you attribute your dysfunctionality subjectively. It's therefore always accompanied by guilt, secretiveness, sometimes self-loathing. Two points; Catholics see the world as object, they see evil as objective. Protestants by and large internalise it, as a personal problem in one way or another. I'm interested in how you relate that subjectivity… You see, one cannot help but think of another writer, especially one I've known as long as I have you, except in terms of one's own writing. I think mine is in a sense more simplistic; that my poetry presents the problem of evil as objective, as out there, as in the world, as political. I'm interested in how you connect that internalisation, which is the substance of your writing, that subjectivism, with your politics, which, by and large, we share, but from very different perspectives. Do you agree with that analysis?

JH: I do yes. Well, I suppose politics, the only politics that I was ever interested in, was the politics of Scottish independence really.

WP: But you come to this from a bourgeois background with a Cambridge education. I remember you telling me, maybe in Trevor Royle's company, that both of you had had these relatively privileged educations but both left school and university with an almost complete ignorance of the Scottish tradition.

JH: Certainly at school, total ignoring of the Scottish tradition. It was actually, ironically, at Cambridge that I discovered my own

Scottishness, became aware of myself as a Scot. And I suppose it was in part a desire for some kind of internal stability... identity, as you say, internally I was at odds with myself and didn't really know who I was or what I wanted to be. Well, I did know what I wanted to be, I wanted to be a writer. I found it difficult in lots of ways, engaging with reality, I had a tendency to want to escape from certain aspects of reality. I suppose my embracing of Scottish nationalism was partly an identity thing, partly a desire to do something more active, something that wasn't internalised.

RM: Maybe it's outsiderness. I know you once criticised Alexander Scott in *Akros* for calling you a 'convert' to Scots and you paraphrased Leavis: 'what does that mean? You don't even know what that means'. I grew up within thirty miles of the border with Scotland and I'd never heard a word of Scots and then at university I was presented with *A Drunk Man Looks at the Thistle* and *Under the Eildon Tree* and I hadn't a clue how to understand them and it was the challenge of that defamiliarisation that fired me up. But it was also so close to home, it felt criminal that I didn't understand it. So you took yourself out of the thick of it, it was only in Cambridge in the midst of all these very privileged, braying voices that you came round to it?

JH: Exactly, and I realised very quickly that Scots spoke to me, that although my parents would use only occasional Scots words, I had a tacit knowledge of Scots because it was in a sense in the 1950s more around you in Edinburgh, it was all around you and I had a tacit understanding of Scots from the beginning.

WP: In any case, the rhythms and syntax of Scots are not those of English. I had this discussion many years ago with Duncan Glen. I can't remember if it was Alexander Scott who accused me, of my Scots, having been dictionary learned, which of course unlike Alexander Scott's, it wasn't, I'd grown up with it. If I write a poem in what Duncan would have called English, it's never an Englishman's English, I've never written a poem in an Englishman's English. Sometimes maybe a pastiche of an Irishman's English, sub-Yeats.

RM: It's the Sydney Goodsir Smith line: 'Wha' the deil speaks like King Lear?' English is just as synthetic as Scots when it's in the hands of authors and poets.

JH: All literary language is synthetic, yes, and of course MacDiarmid's is synthetic.

RM: One thing I picked up on there was that from very early on you had a sense that you wanted to be a writer; I was reading your introduction to Walter's book *Decagon* and in it you write that these poems have an 'unchallengeable right to be recognised'. I get a sense from both of you that you have a very clear sense of yourselves, your vocations as poets and writers, besides the vagaries of literary fashion. Did that arrive early on, or was it something you had to work to achieve, this conviction that nothing's going to put you off.

JH: Well I think the urge was there without the conviction when I was about seven or eight, I started writing then and went on until I went to my public school, as they call it, when I was thirteen and then I became sort of brainwashed into thinking I was going to become an advocate, that I wanted to become an advocate. But as soon as I was released from that place this desire to be an artist kept jumping back. For a bit I wanted to be a composer when I was eleven or twelve. I have a good ear for music but I could never play an instrument. I don't want to say anything too negative about my schooling because apart from ignorance of my own culture I was well educated. It was like that at boarding school, it was a feeling of being released and I realised quite quickly that I the only thing I wanted to be was a writer, I think the thing that really sparked it off was reading *Ulysses*, which I did in my first term at Cambridge when I should have been doing History. I read *Ulysses* instead and changed my subject to English the next term.

273

RM: So you said that you were being groomed to be an advocate, to enter the legal profession. I was wondering why so many of your stories involve members of the upper middle classes, the legal classes of Edinburgh getting themselves into sticky situations.

JH: Well, it's sort of an alternative life really, I suppose. Donald Humbie, the protagonist of *The Sinister Cabaret* is really the reverse of me. He's someone who has actually become an advocate but who really would have liked to have become a writer and I'm a person who became a writer and wonder whether I wouldn't have been better off becoming an advocate.

RM: Well, it's like what you say in *A Truth Lover*, if you train to become a judge then you choose to be a judge and you circumscribe yourself to a limited narrative in the sense that the defendant is limited too, they're guilty by nature of who they are, or are seen to be.

JH: Yes, one reason why I chose not to become an advocate, apart from that I wanted to become a writer and nothing else, was that I couldn't envisage presenting a case in court which I didn't actually believe in.

RM: In *The Sinister Cabaret*, Donald Humbie suffers at the hands of academics, his early interest in writing is snuffed out by Dr Swinger Swann 'of the School of Literary Fashion at the Pictish University of Lesmahagow', who leads him on by saying 'I can introduce you to a publisher' and then he quickly backtracks when he realises the young Donald can't write something fashionable. That's one of the things that I find very entertaining because I share your mistrust of academia and I like seeing that in some of your stories, obviously one of the funniest examples is 'The Devil and Dr Tuberose'.

WP: I think you've picked up on something fundamental; maybe about both of us, but certainly about John, which is that he's a bit like a terrier with a bone that he won't leave alone and he just keeps worrying away at the same bone for decade after decade.

JH: It's the only bone there is! But I'm not sure what the bone is.

WP: There's something fundamental about the way in which you interact with the world, you internalise it. Perhaps that's what makes you a novelist rather than a poet, because the narrative is foregrounded but language is not. Let me put something to you: people lose their sense of the strangeness of the world because it is buffered by language. Language immunises them against seeing just how strange the whole place is; your kind of narrative does the opposite thing in a sense, unwinds the familiarity of what we call day to day reality.

JH: I'm not sure what you're asking.

WP: I'm asking about style, your relationship with language, you quote the French symbolist Rimbaud in particular. They foreground language; the novelist, in the way you tell novels, doesn't. You present your narrators as truth tellers.

JH: Not just truth tellers but unreliable truth tellers. I think that one element in a lot of my work is parody, it's literary parody. I realise that possibly one of the contributory reasons why my writing hasn't caught on with the general public is that a lot of my writing is literary parody. Not merely that of course, but it's an element of the whole.

RM: I'm thinking of Brecht, for instance; in a book on Brecht by Walter Benjamin, Brecht is put on mock trial and when he's interrogated he admits that he and his work are never totally in earnest. There's a sense that the most serious modernist writers of the twentieth century have always had this element of laughter, of play. It's like Margaret Tait's wonderful film portrait of Hugh MacDiarmid. There's this footage of his throwing this stone in a burn, after he's recited his one of his 'Hymns to Lenin' – and then turns to the camera and starts laughing. It's this idea of play all the time.

JH: Yes, that's been very important for me. There are writers about whom, when you invoke their name, there's a hush of dead seriousness; Dostoevsky, Kafka, Beckett. Now for myself, a lot of what attracted me to those three writers is that they're great comic writers. A lot of people don't see that, they don't recognise it. "Beckett is a deeply pessimistic writer", well maybe he is, but he's also an extremely funny writer. And Kafka can be an extremely funny writer, and Dostoevsky is often an extremely funny writer.

WP: The role of humour is? In these cases, what's humour doing, what's being funny doing?

JH: It's sending up the absurdity, it's invoking the absurdity of everyday life.

RM: But there's something that's uniquely Scottish about your approach, this deflationary approach. Here's a moment of high-seriousness, so let's puncture it. There's one moment that's particularly telling in your short story 'Emperor Bolingbroke III'. The first paragraph is setting the scene of this decadent, lotus eating emperor, engorged on food and then, all of a sudden, he says to his servant: 'See's a big Newcastle an' a packet o' salted peanuts, hen'. This is the 1970s when you wrote this, had you entirely envisaged the career of Frank Kuppner, for instance? It seemed to have been lifted from his work, but he only began to publish in the 1980s, it's like a scene straight out of Kuppner's poetry.

JH: Yes, I was probably there before he was. I came across him probably about that time. I saw that piece as a parody of orientalism, cutting it down to size.

WP: Humour is always subversive, yes?

JH: Yes.

WP: But what's it subversive of, apart from banality, which is why I was asking about the way in which language buffers people against the sense of the strangeness of the world.

JH: To give you an example: what is it that I find hilariously funny about the scene in Dostoevsky's 'The Devils' in which Stavrogin does this: he's in a club, a gentlemen's club, and an old gentleman says, talking to some other fellows: 'They will not lead me by the nose sir, they will not lead me by the nose'. Immediately Stavrogin crosses the room and gets hold of the man by the nose and succeeds in leading him across the room by the nose. I think Beckett and Kafka do this sort of thing as well. It's taking a thing to its logical conclusion, taking the absurdities and banalities to their logical conclusion and playing them out. What would it be like if I behaved as I would like to behave in this social situation? And a lot of Dostoevsky's scandal scenes are based on that idea and I suppose I've imitated that or tried to reproduce it in my own modest way. What is the logical conclusion of the things that people do and what people say.

WP: It's subversive of convention. I was hoping for something more, I was looking for not just the subversion of Establishment mores.

JH: I think it is more than that. It's what lies behind establishment mores, which is the way people are or might be, or think they are.

WP: Perhaps this is where the novelist has access to the exploration of different subjectivities in a way that a serious poet doesn't quite. Take the examples of either Chris Grieve or Yeats, or Rilke if you like. They never pretend to be anyone but who they are.

JH: What about Yeats's masks?

WP: But I think the masks for Yeats were real. They were the throwing off of day to day trivia, of burdensome personal life, but that's not the art. He wants the art to somehow transcend that. In my view the three great poets of the twentieth century are Rilke, Yeats and Paul Valéry. Few even run them close and they all have this similar approach to the outsideness of creating the aesthetic object, it's entirely objective, whereas in your work, in the novelist's work, to which I'm in some ways foreign, it's the exploration of subjectivity which actually creates the objectivity, exploring different possibilities of feeling for example.

JH: Yes, well Rilke himself does this in *Malte Laurids Brigge*.

WP: Which is his prose work.

JH: Yes exactly, it's a different genre altogether. I've often asked myself why I'm not a poet because I've actually got a facility for verse, I've got a facility for instance for nonsense verse.

RM: As in *The Sinister Cabaret* for instance.

JH: But I've never felt that I had, or would have, the capacity to be a poet and I've never been drawn to writing poetry and I've never been able to quite work out why but it's to do with the area we're talking about.

WP: And I think it's fundamental. It's one or the other and not really both. The only prose I've written for example is non-fiction. I cannot imagine myself writing a novel or a short story.

JH: If you look at it the other way round, Joyce started out as a poet. His poetry is pleasant but most of it's of no permanent significance at all and he must have realised that very quickly.

WP: He was also a singer of course, with a great lyric gift.

JH: He also had the capacity to write poetically, when he started out. In his epiphanies he wrote what I suppose are prose poems. I once thought of writing a PhD thesis on Joyce's epiphanies and their relations to his aesthetics and the tradition of the prose poem in French. I didn't but that's an interesting case in point, I think, that Joyce was a flimsy poet actually.

WP: That's a well-chosen expression, John.

JH: Because he was a massive novelist.

RM: Your short story 'Fates' strikes me as a prose poem. What would you say there's about 150 words to that?

JH: Yes, that's a prose poem. I can write little prose poems like that, I've been drawn to the prose poem at various times. Baudelaire, Rimbaud, also Kafka and Borges, Kafka's little parables.

RM: We're ganging up against you and accusing you of failing to be a poet but I don't blame you in any way because one of the stories which most affected me in *Imelda* is 'Acquainted with Grief' – a well-known biblical phrase which Edwin Muir played on when he described followers of MacDiarmid as 'men of sorrows and acquainted with Grieve'. I don't know when you wrote it, but it was published in 1993 and it's a pitch-perfect observation of how poets still go about it in social situations. I've been to many a literary event and they're still exactly the same, only maybe slightly more aggressively self-publicising. Is there a sense that you are consciously trying to put yourself apart from that world.

JH: I suppose I was. I was writing about an actual person in that story who, although he's dead, must remain nameless. It was written in 1988 because I know it was the first thing I wrote after not writing any fiction at all for virtually ten years which is when I was in my religious period and was thinking of becoming a monk.

WP: It came quite close, didn't it? You thought about it very seriously.

JH: I thought about it very seriously and I actually tried. About six years after my first marriage broke up I did try and go and become a monk for about five weeks. My friend David Black – D. M. Black the poet – said after I'd failed in my vocation, "To be released from a fantasy is always tonic".

WP: Well, you know Wittgenstein's great remark about the best thing a philosopher can do is to make a really fundamental mistake and for it to be recognised as a mistake because that closes off entire avenues of misguided exploration.

JH: Yes, and it can close off entire areas of feeling that become 'might have beens'.

WP: Don't you agree that feeling is a fundamental mode of thought? And that it's fundamental to literature?

JH: Yes. Intuition is fundamental to literature, feeling and intuition.

WP: I'll rephrase that: 'feelings', our capacity for feelings, which is also at the root of imagination.

JH: Yes, In 'The Devil and Dr Tuberose' it wasn't an accident that I had Dr Tuberose talking about Coleridge's distinction between fancy and imagination, which of course is an extremely well-worn topic but nonetheless an important one.

WP: I was re-reading the introduction by Macdonald Daly to your *Four Tales* where he mentions that you spent a year travelling in 1959–1960. Where did you go and was it important?

JH: It was, yes. I had two trips, the first to Paris and Switzerland.

RM: Like in *A Truth Lover* ?

JH: Yes, it comes out of that. The second was a trip right around
       Europe, to Eastern Europe as far as Istanbul. It was a kind of a
       grand tour done in a non-grand tour way, by car and camping.

WP: You were twenty-one or something?

JH: I was nineteen. Then I also did my James Joyce thing, I taught in
       Zurich for the summer as well, that was in 1964 a year after I left
       university.

RM: I get the impression with a lot of your writing, it might sound
       facile or even fatuous to say it, but a lot of your real life
       experiences have informed what you've written. There are certain
       aspects in all your novels, novellas, short-stories where there's a
       roman-à-clef element. 'Clapperton' for instance, the angry letters
       come directly out of your stramash with Ronald Macdonald
       Douglas over the editorship and direction of *Catalyst*.

JH: They do yes, oh very directly yes. Especially in that early work
       I very directly used my own experiences though it would be a
       mistake to think it all of it came from my own experiences, there
       are things that I fabricated as well. It was a sort of projection of
       my own experiences.

WP: Have you any projects in hand?

JH: No, I'm afraid I don't. I haven't given up wilfully. I just haven't
       written any fiction now for close on fifteen years.

WP: But you've done some translation. Do you find that helpful?

JH: Yes, exercise keeps the brain moving.

RM: In the case of Ernest Dowson it was what kept him in drink,
       Leonard Smithers paying him to translate from the French when
       he could no longer write, was too drunk to write. I think you've

anticipated what I was going to say because we've overlooked *Another Country*, which I think is a startling book, an amazing book, nobody has really made any attempt to properly map that time in terms of both politics and literature. For somebody who I feel has been side-lined or overlooked as a writer, I don't know if you'd agree with that?

JH: Absolutely.

RM: Does it give you any sense of pleasure or satisfaction to know that there are some people taking up the mantle. For instance, the Heretics have been revived. Craig Gibson and Peter Burnett, on the basis of reading *Another Country* decided that you were such a valuable figure they were going to revive the Heretics and promote your work as well.

JH: I'm delighted. Peter is about to re-issue *Imelda* as an eBook and an audio-book and as a print-on-demand paperback as well. So that's very pleasing to me. Yes, I think these things do come around eventually.

WP: You just have to live long enough.

JH: Yes, it's whether I want to though!

RM: So, you're saying you haven't written for fifteen years. Anthony Burgess once described T S Eliot's output as 'costive' and that word stuck in my head as being so judgmental. I remember there was an article written about you in 1993 and somebody criticised Trevor Royle for missing you out of the first edition of his big Macmillan book on Scottish literature. He defended himself by saying that 'John's been niggardly with his talent'. I'm the sort of person who thinks if you write one good poem, story or novella that makes your existence worthwhile.

WP: You judge writers only by their best.

JH: I agree with that too. I think my best work was written after that. *Imelda*, *My Wife's Lovers*, *Ghostwriting*, *The Sinister Cabaret* all came after that. Before that I had ten years of relative silence so it's understandable that someone should say that and I probably would have felt that about myself at that time. Don't think I'd use that word but yes, I was disappointed with myself.

WP: That's really what I recognise looking back. You were disappointed not so much as angry and frustrated perhaps.

JH: Yes, I found it very hard to find my real voice. I think I did find it with those novels from the early 1990s onwards.

RM: But the idea of being garlanded, lavished with awards. It seems to me your writing is above that or your stance as a writer is above that. You say that this prize culture is 'a terrible disease'.

JH: Well, it's very interesting thinking about blurbs of writers' lives, they used to say things like 'He was successively a brick-layer, a dish-washer, a lumberjack, etc, etc'. Now it's a list of what prizes they've won. You think, oh yes, all these people have won all these prizes and they've all been 'acclaimed'. And publishers say 'Oh well, we'll wait until you're acclaimed and then do something about it'.

RM: Time and time again, all of the writers I've come across and the ones that really excite me are the side-lined, overlooked, neglected. It seems to be on the periphery that the only interesting stuff takes place.

WP: The social world has changed. With the loss of patronage, what happened in place of the loss of large-scale patronage, aristocrats and the Church, was a kind of small-scale patronage. So, had Yeats not had the connections he had, had Eliot not had the connections he had, it would have taken them longer and with greater difficulty to achieve what they did. One needs people to help one along the way, even now, and without that you're stuck.

JH: I feel I've never had that.

WP: I have to the extent I wouldn't have had a degree had it not been for Professor W. H. Walsh. In my first year I'd been first in my classes and then completely fucked up... for illness and other reasons. But Walsh made sure I got a degree – he arranged a sort of personal cramming – because he (the department) knew you were bright, were worth the effort. I don't believe that would happen now in the academic world. It would be seen as favouritism or stigmatised as elitist. I suppose too I've had the patronage of both James Merrill and Robin Magowan, his friend and nephew. Without that, I would have missed out on quite a lot. But none of this affects a public perception. What I'm talking about is what affects the work in private; without that encouragement and sometimes just the sheer fact of having enough money. Without that, nothing much can happen. So, thirty-odd years ago, the Ingram-Merrill Foundation gave me $10,000; it saw me through another year or two.

RM: To go back to the prize culture issue. How do you square that with your role as a judge for the Saltire Prize, the non-fiction strand? Do you see the Saltire prize as doing something different?

JH: For non-fiction, it's probably more innocuous than it is for fiction, less invidious but for the creative arts I think it's completely invidious, because there's no possible standard of comparison. Every work is trying to do something different and how you can compare one with another qualitatively, I don't know.

WP: Did you know George Davie? He was an extraordinary man and his wife, Elspeth, was a short story writer.

JH: Slightly, yes. *The Democratic Intellect*, I re-read it last year actually, very interesting, yes. I was at Hawthornden with Elspeth Davie.

RM: And who else were you with at that time?

JH: There were only three of us, who was the third ? There was a guy called Richard Rayner who went to America.

RM: Which room were you in?

JH: Well, I've been there twice, the first, I think mine was the one up the tower. Have you been there?

RM: Yes, I've been there, I was in Boswell, in the attic.

JH: Was it Johnson? I wouldn't like to think of Johnson trying to get up there. The second time I was there I was lower down but I can't remember the names of either of the rooms I was in. And I'm thinking of trying to go again.

RM: It's still open even though Drue Heinz is now dead, her Trust is carrying on with it.

WP: You've displayed over your lifetime and career a remarkable consistency, as I've said before. Jung suggests, David Black was at one time a Jungian, that you spend the first half of your life accommodating yourself to the world, whether it's in terms of family or a career in the way most people do. Force of circumstances. But in order to grow you need to spend the second half of your life undoing all that and becoming precisely what that first half has excluded, has prevented you from being.

JH: Yes, I think that's probably true, you begin to relive your life, instead of looking forwards you look backwards, what might I have done, what should I have done?

WP: But also perhaps if you spent your life establishing yourself as, let's say, a banker or an advocate or writer or whatever it may be. In terms of worldly success you will pay a price for that course and the price of growing up is to undo that because in the process of achieving just that, you have neglected other things that might be important.

JH: The price of growing older, that's true.

RM: Sorry to digress, but I'd like to talk a little more about your most recent novel *The Sinister Cabaret*. Walter and I are in agreement that it's one of your strongest works. I'm interested in the role of absurdism in the book. I think again this shows your debt to European writing. I read a lot of Dutch and Flemish writers and that sort of absurdist humour is something that we don't seem to do very well in the UK with a few notable exceptions.

JH: That's right. I was very strongly drawn to absurdism in the 1960s, very strongly. Beckett was the greatest one I think but surrealist absurdism has always been a very strong factor in my writing and certainly it's come into its own in *The Sinister Cabaret*.

RM: I'm thinking of the orgy of vigilante violence at the end of the book. It's so absurd it's hilarious. It's when 'The Sinister Cabaret' troupe meet with their grizzly and far-fetched ends, none of the inhabitants of this sleepy town seem to bat an eyelid. Their reaction seems to be 'Oh well fair enough, this person's been trampled to death, this one's been gutted with a sword and this one's been drowned in a slurry pit'!

WP: Surrealism lies behind all of the great French poetry of the 1920s and early 1930s; Éluard, Aragon and others. Surrealism lost its way because of political events in the 1930s, so, from 1936 onwards Éluard and others reject surrealism in order to say something more directly about other people's worlds rather than their own subjectivism – which takes me back to this recurrent theme of the relationship between the subjective realities of writing, particularly a novelist's form of writing, and the political activism of writing, or painting, as you'll find in Picasso, Éluard and so on.

JH: Well as to what they used to call 'engagement' in writing, I was politically active as a Scottish nationalist for a long time but I felt even then that the only contribution I could make, the only way that I could forward that with my imaginative writing was to contribute to a Scottish tradition and a Scottish literature.

WP: The writing itself is an assertion of identity which supersedes the trivialities of political activism. It's the opposite of the position taken by, for example, Sartre, but I'm on your side with this. The integrity of the work, at the end of the day, is what counts, whether other people see it or not.

JH: Quite. I was quite an admirer of Brecht when I was younger. I still am. I now think that he was a greater poet when he was younger. He was a greater poet altogether than he was a playwright. And I don't think he was better when he was politically engaged.

WP: I don't think they're separable, with Brecht, as with Yeats, except perhaps for the very early Yeats.

JH: I think there's quite a strong element that Brecht willed himself to be a populist writer, a Marxist writer.

WP: Yes, because the dichotomies arose in that moment. People felt that they *had* to make choices, not just with Stalinism and the war in particular of course, but in the immediate post-War period in the struggle for hegemony over Western Europe. So Sartre and others made specific choices to, as it were, bastardise their intelligence in order to support the Communist Party at any price, seeing that as the greater issue. Hindsight says he was wrong.

JH: Which Chris Grieve didn't do actually.

WP: Oh, he had a different position. He used to say 'Do you know, when the rest of the world was leaving the Communist Party, I joined'; in 1956 on the Soviet invasion of Hungary. But by then, his great period had passed, not that that mattered so much because he was carrying with him that authority. He must have had a huge impact on both of us. For me he was relatively local. But his nationalism and politics were a profound influence. And he was a huge presence, a charming, courteous elderly gentleman, until you touched the wrong nerve. And then you suddenly had the voice of historic Scotland thundered at you.

RM: You were saying, John, that maybe people underestimate you as a comic writer, I'm still laughing thinking about the bar-room scene in *The Sinister Cabaret* where the drinkers try to refer to themselves by their nicknames and then the barman says 'No, no, no, this ...

JH: is the Night of the Patronymics', yes. [Begins to recite from *The Sinister Cabaret*] 'See, most of the year I'm Kenny Squeezebox, but no today. Today I'm Coinneach Eachainn Uilleim an Clarsair Odhar. Same for everybody. Only exception is Big Hieronymus there. He's a Dutchman, and the Dutch don't have patronymics. He mostly gets called Geronimo, but there's a few cry him Jerome. He disnae like Jerry.'

RM: So, you're saying you haven't written anything in fifteen years, that's obviously not quite true.

JH: Nothing imaginative, or at least very little.

RM: In the interview with Hugh MacPherson for the *Scottish Book Collector* in 1992 you were also a little bit unsure of your future as a writer and you said 'I'd like to further integrate my religious and literary concerns'. Do you feel now that you've not got as much to say or do you feel like you've achieved this, you've integrated these concerns?

JH: Well, I would say to the extent that I have, I would now call them spiritual rather than religious. Perhaps a bit. I think since 1992 I've probably produced my best work.

RM: And what would you cite as your best piece of work?

JH: Well, the one that came to me most whole and was to me most satisfying to write and to have produced was *Imelda* but that was probably because I had less difficulty with it than with anything else. I see those last three novels as a trilogy which I think quite highly of and I also think quite highly of the last book of short stories, *My Wife's Lovers* which I think is all good work. Before that I think there were only two or three stories that I would now want to be collected: 'Clapperton', 'The Devil and Dr. Tuberose' and 'The Man Below'. Perhaps a very few more.

RM: Yes, I rate *Imelda* highly and I think that's your most successful study in the Scottish gothic. I felt like I was in the presence of an updated James Hogg on reading that.

JH: Well, I couldn't wish for anything better.

RM: Also I had this same feeling at times in *Pagan's Pilgrimage*, when the bookish bogeyman Raith appears beyond the dyke, hissing and he's sent packing by Pagan's sudden self-assertiveness. I think that was a very Hoggian moment.

JH: Then again, it's also parodic of the double motif. I still like *Pagan's Pilgrimage*, I feel it's more episodic than the later work. I don't mean that necessarily pejoratively but it's different.

WP: If it's the case that in order to write well, you both have to be kicked about enough and cherished enough – to have both. Good writing somehow needs to come out of a feeling that you have a position in the world, a role in the world, as well as enough discontent to prod you into writing.

JH: I've certainly got plenty of that! I don't feel I've had enough nurturing as a writer. I don't feel I've had enough critical support, publishing support, particularly publishing support. I'm very grateful – with one exception – to all the publishers that have published me but most of them have not had the capacity to distribute the books as they should have been distributed.

WP: What you're basically saying is that you don't feel you're famous enough.

JH: Yes. Or rather not me but the writing.

WP: Quite, because as a writer one wants to have an influence but it won't necessarily be in one's own generation. So one looks forward to a crystallisation of the best of what one can do, which is where I hope you're going. And I have some confidence in that. You were full of self-doubt when I first met you in 1970.

JH: Well, I've never really doubted my capacity as a writer. I think probably about the late 1970s I had a blip when I thought 'it's not where I'm going to go anymore' and it was to do with religion but I got back on track.

WP: We have both have had quite long periods of relative silence. Perhaps a necessary reformulation of strategies as well tactics – as well as just who one is. I think we're similar in that I never had any serious doubts about who or what I am in that respect. I made a decision when I was seventeen, I was going to spend the rest of my life doing this, for long or short.

JH: I did too, when I was about nineteen.

RM: I have to say as the younger aspirant looking at you that's what one of the qualities that I admire in both of you.

WP: It's not of itself admirable, you know; McGonagall probably felt similarly.

JH: He certainly did!

RM: As I say, you don't need to be showered with prizes and you don't need legions of fans, you just need a handful of intelligent readers or sympathetic readers.

JH: Yes, exactly.

WP: We both have our own audiences I think.

JH: It's important to feel that one can actually get to these, perhaps necessarily small number of people, that you're being heard by somebody.

WP: Poetry's even more difficult.

JH: I'm sure it is. Donald Campbell once said something to me which I found was quite supportive...

WP: And Donald's genre was not in being supportive!

JH: No it wasn't always. He said, and I found it quite comforting: 'John', he said 'You're just not the kind of writer that wins prizes' which I took as a compliment and it was intended as such.

WP: Something else I said to you was that we've probably, between us, known most of the interesting people, certainly in the Scottish literary world over the last half century, we haven't missed many out.

JH: Indeed. Though I didn't know Neil Gunn.

RM: The only one of that 'seven poets' generation I got to meet was Edwin Morgan and by the time I met him it was hard to talk because he was very deaf. He was ninety, it was the year before he died. I went to see him at Clarence Court in Glasgow. I sort of feel a little hard done by.

JH: It's strange to think you never knew any of these people.

RM: I do think I was born far too late.

WP: No, you have come at the right time.

JH: It's another curious thing, this business of the moment at which you're born. The degree to which you're a prisoner of the moment at which you were born and you can't do certain things because of that simple circumstance.

WP: But that's also the gift, to make something of that. There's a great line in Tolkien where Gandalf advises one of the hobbits that all we can do is make the best of the time that is given us.

JH: That's one of the things that fascinates me about Dylan. I think he found a new mode or exploited to its utmost a new mode of art and he was the right person at the right time, who could do that as Shakespeare was in his time.

WP: Luck, you need luck.

RM: It's interesting that you've singled out *Slow Train Coming* and then 'Not Dark Yet' from the *Time Out of Mind* album. They were both produced after a relatively short, by your standards, period of silence, or reconsidering things. He was thought of as a spent force and then he came out with *Time Out of Mind* which was a beautifully elegiac, haunting album.

JH: He's continually been thought of as a spent force. Like what
       you were saying, Walter, about being remembered for your best
       work. After a period of silence then he suddenly comes out with
       Tempest, I mean the title song is absolutely excoriating. It's about
       the Titanic but it's not, it's about our civilisation.

RM: It's polysemous veritism, as Tom Scott might have said!

WP: I've become aware, especially after my last trip to the States, that
       Americans cannot hear certain voices in my work, that America
       has lost the capacity for certain voices. It could no longer produce
       a Longfellow. It could no longer produce...

RM: The rhapsodies of Whitman?

WP: Not just Whitman. It has lost a direct connection with its ancestry.
       Much of what still subsists in the English language tradition is
       now alien to them.

JH: Yes, I agree with that. American literature doesn't much speak to
       me after Poe.

WP: It was brought to mind by what you were saying about Bob Dylan.

JH: He stepped in to say things that can't be said in the old language.

WP: Exactly so. I tell you one way to think of it; that America has lost,
       or given up, a capacity for high voice.

JH: Yes, and he says the high voice things in a low voice. I believe that
       it's absolutely true what has been said, that almost any emotional
       state you can be in, Dylan's given it voice.

WP: In relation to older voices, you and I on a rare occasion might still
       be party to, let's say, a ceilidh, a real one.

JH: Do such things still exist?

WP: Yes, thanks to Margaret Bennett, I was at one not very long ago, where song and story can still touch you as they have done people for centuries, that's still perhaps available to us because we're on the European fringe and because of all kinds of historical accident. That's no longer available in metropolitan culture, even in France I think it's disappeared or is disappearing. It disappeared perhaps with the Félibriges reviving Occitan, with the loss of regional languages.

RM: The film script of 'Imelda', what became of that?

JH: Oh, it's still lying in a drawer, still waiting for someone to take it on.

RM: I could well imagine it as a film.

JH: The dual narratives would be the difficult part of the filming process. There's also someone who's interested in *The Sinister Cabaret*. It's now ten years since he wrote a film script of it. It's a very long shot, but you never know.

WP: Tell me a wee bit, if you will, John, about the evolution of your politics. I'm thinking back to *Catalyst* when I first knew you and we knew a lot of lunatics in common, including Ronald MacDonald Douglas, Major Boothby and a number of others. Major Boothby was the only man in the universe, who on trial in the high court for treason or gun-running who would have cited Chris Grieve as his character reference.

JH: Probably the only man also to have helped Chris Grieve out by lending him a set of false teeth.

WP: I told Trevor Royle that anecdote the other day and I don't think he believed it, but I know it to be true. Tell me a bit about that evolution. I have no doubt that Britain is not a democracy. The United Kingdom, there's no way in its present dispensation that it's a genuine democracy. But nationalism when we were younger was regarded as an oddity.

JH: It was first of all an expression of my surprised consciousness when I went to Cambridge and discovered that I wasn't like other people there, that I was a Scot and had a different experience and a different background and the next thing was my attraction to Irish literature, Joyce, Yeats, Beckett. And although neither Joyce nor Beckett were Irish nationalists...

WP: But they were in the sense of being Irish cultural nationalists.

JH: They were, yes, and I suppose I would start by saying that I started as a cultural nationalist but I also took fully on board the MacDiarmid political dimension, which included to that extent being pretty left-wing to begin with. Now I would say I'm neither left nor right wing.

WP: How would you distinguish them now? Going back to the 1950s and 1960s, even the 1970s, had we then had a majority of nationalist MPs in Scotland that was the mandate for independence. That position has been surrendered.

JH: That has been surrendered. I've been saying that for the last two decades. That ought to have given us independence now according to the SNP's original and repeatedly stated position.

WP: How would you distinguish between right and left now, looking at nationalist politics nowadays? Given that the policies pursued by the present (Scottish) government are what one might call European social democratic.

JH: I have to say that the present excessive preoccupations of the Scottish government with social justice issues I just find boring.

WP: Would you agree that they have lost the plot to this extent, that they have confused government with the national cause?

JH: Yes, which is an inevitable development I think. I always envisaged what I wanted for the development of a movement towards independence was along the Irish lines after 1916, which they could do now. You know, we've got these institutions, the Irish had to create them after 1918. We now have them. The Irish created for instance a complete local government structure from 1920 or so.

WP: I'm wondering how that plays across in your work. This is what I was driving at earlier.

JH: I don't know that my work has particularly concerned itself with politics.

WP: No, it hasn't. But in some of your letters and articles and reviews it quite rightly has, especially going back a few years. But of course I know, maybe others don't, but I know perfectly well that that (political stance) hasn't changed.

RM: I'm thinking how controversial your piece in Duncan Glen's *Whither Scotland* was at the time.

JH: That piece was written in 1970. Yes, I think I was considered to be outré.

RM: But I read it now, not having been through what you've been through, and it strikes me as the voice of utter reason and sanity. This is obvious, it's still going on the worship of money and economics above everything else, leading to, you said, 'cultural erosion' but it's a far greater erosion than that.

JH: I think in some of my *Catalyst* articles I also spoke about the environment as early as 1968/1969 and there's a lot about that in

Pagan's Pilgrimage written in the mid-1970s. Although I would dissent from some of the language in which I expressed it. I think that I can modestly say that I've been prophetic in some of the things I wrote as a young man, and nothing of their essence would I dissent from now. One's hope as a writer of any kind, of course, is that the work will be able to speak to and be recognised by readers beyond the era in which it was written.

SELECT BIBLIOGRAPHIES

INTRODUCTION: WALTER PERRIE

Books & Poetry Pamphlets

1. *The Ages of Water*. Grace Note Publications, 2020.

2. *Sorceries*. Fras, 2018.

3. *Vigils - Poems*. Fras, 2015.

4. *Double First* (poems with William Hershaw). Fras, 2011.

5. *Lyrics & Tales in Twa Tongues*. Fras, 2010,

6. *Twelve Fables of Jean de La Fontaine: made owre intil Scots*. Fras, 2007.

7. *Decagon: Selected Poems 1995-2005*, with an introduction by John Herdman. Fras, 2005.

8. *From Milady's Wood and Other Poems*. Scottish Cultural Press, 1997.

9. *Roads that Move: a Journey through eastern Europe*. Mainstream, 1991.

10. *Concerning the Dragon* (Poems). Black Pennel Press, 1984.

11. *Out of Conflict: Essays on Literature and Ideas*. Borderline Press, 1982.

12. *By Moon and Sun*. Canongate, 1980.

13. *A Lamentation for the Children*. (SAC book award 1978). Canongate, 1978.

14. *Surge Aquilo* (Poems in Scots). Akros, 1977.

15. *Poem on a Winter Night*. MacDonald, 1976.

16. *Metaphysics & Poetry* (with Hugh MacDiarmid). Lothlorien, 1975.

Criticism

1. *Nietzsche, Dostoievsky & MacDiarmid's Drunk Man*. Bessarion, 2021.

2. *A Minding for Merrill*. Bessarion, 2017.

3. *The Fog of War; Edward Thomas' Adlestrop*. Fras 28, 2017.

4. *The Imperceptible Miss Dickinson*. Fras 26, 2016.

5. *Auden's Political Vision,* in Bold, A. (ed) *W.H. Auden: The Far Interior*. NewYork: Barnes & Noble, 1985.

6. 'Mrs Spark's Verse', in Bold, A. (ed) *Muriel Spark: An Odd Capacity for Vision*. New York: Barnes & Noble, 1984.

7. 'The Byronic Philosophy', in Bold, A. (ed) *Byron Wrath & Rhyme*. New York: Barnes & Noble, 1983.

8. *The Essential Grigson*. Lines Review 87, 1983.

9. *Edwin Morgan*. Chapman 37, 1983.

I. DONALD CAMPBELL

Poetry:

1. *Heard in the Cougait*. Ochtertyre: Grace Note Publications, 2017.

2. *Fugitives*. Ochtertyre: Grace Note Publications, 2015.

3. *Homage to Rob Donn*. Fras Publications, 2007.

4. *Selected Poems: 1970–1990*. Galliard, 1990.

5. *Blether: a collection of poems*. Akros, 1979.

6. *Murals*. Lothlorien, 1975.

7. *Rhymes 'n Reasons*. Reprographia, 1972.

8. *Poems*. Akros, 1971.

Plays:

1. *Till all the seas run dry*. Capercaillie Books, 2007.

2. *Blackfriars Wynd*. Netherbow Arts Centre, 1980.

3. *The widows of Clyth,* Paul Harris, 1979.

4. *Somerville the soldier*. Paul Harris, 1978.

5. *The Jesuit*. Paul Harris, 1976.

Other:

1. *Edinburgh: A Cultural and Literary History*. Signal Books, 2003.

2. *Playing for Scotland: A History of the Scottish Stage 1715–1965*. Mercat Press, 1996.

3. *A Brighter Sunshine : One Hundred Years of the Edinburgh Royal Lyceum*. Polygon, 1983.

2. DUNCAN GLEN

Books & Poetry Pamphlets

1. *Collected Poems 1965–2005.* Akros, 2006.

2. *Echoes. Frae Classical and Italian Poetry.* Edinburgh: Akros, 1992.

3. *A Journey Into Scotland: Poems.* Edinburgh: Akros, 1991

4. *Selected Poems 1965–1990.* Edinburgh: Akros, 1991.

5. *The Autobiography of a Poet.* Edinburgh: Ramsay Head Press, 1986.

6. *The Turn of the Earth.* Nottingham: Akros, 1985.

7. *The Stones of Time.* Nottingham: Duncan Glen, 1984.

8. *The State of Scotland.* Nottingham: Duncan Glen, 1983.

9. *Realities Poems.* Nottingham: Akros, 1980.

10. *A Bibliography of Scottish Poets from Stevenson to 1974.* Preston, Lancashire: Akros, 1974.

11. *A Cled Score.* Preston, Lancashire: Akros, 1974.

12. *Hugh MacDiarmid: A Critical Survey.* Scottish Academic Press, 1972.

13. *Clydesdale: A Sequence o Poems.* Preston, Lancashire: Akros, 1971.

14. *In Appearances.* Preston, Lancashire: Akros, 1971.

15. *Hugh MacDiarmid and the Scottish Renaissance.* Edinburgh: Chambers, 1964.

3. TESSA RANSFORD

Books & Poetry Pamphlets

1. *A Good Cause.* Edinburgh: Luath, 2015.

2. *Scotia Nova: poems for the early days of a better nation.* Ed., by Alistair Findlay and Tessa Ransford. Edinburgh: Luath, 2014.

3. *Made in Edinburgh: poems and evocations of Holyrood Park.* Edinburgh: Luath, 2014.

4. *Rug of a Thousand Colours* (with Iyad Hayatleh. Edinburgh: Luath Press, 2012.

5. *Don't mention this to anyone: poems and fragments of life in the Punjab.* Edinburgh: Luath, 2012.

6. *'Tis Sixty Years Since: The 1951 Edinburgh people's Festival Ceilidh and the Scottish Folk Revival,* ed., by Eberhard Bort. Ochtertyre: Grace Note Publications, 2011.

7. *Poems & Angels.* Wisdomfield, 2011.

8. *Borne on the Carrying Stream: The Legacy of Hamish Henderson,* ed., by Eberhard Bort. Ochtertyre: Grace Note Publications, 2010.

9. *Not Just Moonshine: new and selected poems.* Edinburgh: Luath, 2008.

10. *Sonnet selection with eight Rilke lyrics translated.* Kirkcaldy: Akros Publications, 2007.

11. *Shades of Green.* Kirkcaldy: Akros Publications, 2005.

12. *The Nightingale Question: five poets from Saxony.* Ed., Tessa Ransford. Exeter: Shearsman Books, 2004.

13. *Noteworthy Selection.* Kirkcaldy: Akros Publications, 2002.

14. *Natural Selection.* Kirkcaldy: Akros Publications, 2001.

15. *Indian Selection.* Kirkcaldy: Akros Publications, 2000.

16. *Scottish Selection.* Kirkcaldy: Akros Publications, 1998.

17. *When it works it feels like play.* Edinburgh: Ramsay Head Press, 1998.

18. *Medusa Dozen and other poems.* Edinburgh: Ramsay Head Press, 1994.

19. *Seven Valleys.* Edinburgh: Ramsay Head Press, 1991.

20. *A Dancing Innocence.* Edinburgh: Macdonald Publishers, 1988.

21. *Shadows from the Greater Hill.* Edinburgh: Ramsay Head Press, 1987.

22. *Fools and Angels.* Edinburgh: Ramsay Head Press, 1984.

23. *Light of the Mind.* Edinburgh: Ramsay Head Press, 1980.

24. *While it is Yet Day.* London: Quarto Press, 1977.

25. *Poetry of Persons.* Feltham: Quarto Press, 1976.

4. TREVOR ROYLE

Books

1. *Facing the Bear: Scotland and the Cold War*. Edinburgh: Birlinn, 2019.

2. *Culloden: Scotland's Last Battle and the Creation of the British Empire.* Little Brown, London, 2016; Palgrave, New York, 2017.

3. *The Kitchener Enigma.* London: Michael Joseph, 1985; The History Press, 2016.

4. *Bayonets. Bearskins and Body Armour: Welsh Guards 1915–2015.* London: Front Line, 2015.

5. *Britain's Lost Regiments: The Band of Brothers Time has Forgotten.* London: Aurum Press, 2014.

6. *Isn't All this Bloody: Scottish Prose of the First World War*, editor. Edinburgh: Birlinn, 2014.

7. *A Time of Tyrants: Scotland and the Second World War*. Edinburgh: Birlinn, 2011.

8. *Montgomery: Lessons in Leadership from the Soldier's General.* New York: Palgrave Macmillan, 2010.

9. *The Road to Bosworth Field: A New History of the Wars of the Roses.* London: Little Brown, 2009; Abacus, 2010.

10. *The Argyll and Sutherland Highlanders.* Edinburgh: Mainstream, 2009.

11. *The Cameronians: A Concise History.* Edinburgh: Mainstream, 2009.

12. *Lancaster Against York: The Wars of the Roses and the Foundation of Modern Britain.* New York: Palgrave, 2008.

13. *The Gordon Highlanders: A Concise History.* Edinburgh: Mainstream, 2008.

14. *The King's Own Scottish Borderers: A Concise History.* Edinburgh: Mainstream, 2008.

15. *The Royal Highland Fusiliers: A Concise History.* Edinburgh: Mainstream, 2007.

16. *Queen's Own Highlanders: A Concise History.* Edinburgh: Mainstream, 2007).

17. *The Flowers of the Forest: Scotland and the First World War*. Edinburgh: Birlinn, 2006; rev ed, 2019.

18. *The Royal Scots: A Concise History*. Edinburgh: Mainstream, 2006.

19. *The Black Watch: A Concise History*. Edinburgh: Mainstream, 2006.

20. *Patton: Old Blood and Guts. London:* Weidenfeld & Nicolson, 2005.

21. *Civil War: The Wars of the Three Kingdoms 1638–1660*. London: Little Brown, 2004; New York: Palgrave Macmillan, 2005; London: Abacus, 2004.

22. *We'll Support You Ever More: The Impertinent Saga of Scottish Fitba'.* Ed., with Ian Archer. London: Souvenir Press, 1976; Edinburgh: Mainstream, 2000.

23. *Scottish War Stories*, ed. Edinburgh: Polygon, 1999.

24. *Crimea: The Great Crimean War 1854–1856.* London: Little Brown, 1999; New York: St Martin's, 2000; London: Abacus, 2000.

25. *Winds of Change: The End of Empire in Africa*. London: John Murray, 1996.

26. *Orde Wingate: Irregular Soldier*. London: Weidenfeld and Nicolson, 1995; Phoenix 1998; Front Line Books, 2010.

27. *Glubb Pasha: The Life and Times of Sir John Bagot Glubb, Commander of the Arab Legion*. London: Little Brown, 1992; Abacus, 1993.

28. *Mainstream Companion to Scottish Literature*. Edinburgh: Mainstream, 1993.

29. *A Dictionary of Military Quotations*. London: Routledge, 1990; New York: Simon & Schuster, 1991; Glasgow: Harvill Collins, 1992.

30. *Anatomy of a Regiment: Ceremony and Soldiering in the Welsh Guards*. London: Michael Joseph, 1990.

31. *In Flanders Fields: Scottish Poetry and Prose of the First World War*, ed. Edinburgh: Mainstream, 1990.

32. *The Last Days of the Raj*. London: Michael Joseph, 1988; Coronet, Sevenoaks, 1989; John Murray, 1997.

33. *War Report: The War Correspondent's View of Battle from the Crimea to the Falklands*. Edinburgh: Mainstream, 1987; London: Grafton, 1988.

34. *The Best Years of Their Lives: The National Service Experience, 1945–1963*. London: Michael Joseph, 1986; Coronet, Sevenoaks, 1987; John Murray, 1997; Andre Deutsch.

35. *Death before Dishonour: The True Story of Fighting Mac*. Edinburgh: Mainstream, 1982; New York: St Martin's, 1983.

36. *The Macmillan Companion to Scottish Literature*.London: Macmillan, 1983; Detroit: Gale Research, 1983.

37. *James and Jim: The Biography of James Kennaway*. Edinburgh: Mainstream, 1983.

38. *Edinburgh*. Edinburgh: Spur Books, 1982.

39. *A Diary of Edinburgh*, with Richard Demarco. Edinburgh: Polygon, 1981.

40. *Precipitous City: The Story of Literary Edinburgh*. Edinburgh: Mainstream, 1980; New York: Taplinger 1980.

41. *Jock Tamson's Bairns: Essays on a Scots Childhood*, ed. London: Hamish Hamilton, 1977.

Radio and Stage:

1. Radio Drama

`Magnificat', Radio 3 (1984); `Old Alliances', Radio 4 (1986); `Foreigners', Radio 4 (1987); `Huntingtower' by John Buchan, Radio 4 (1988); `A Man Flourishing' by Sam Hanna Bell, Radio 4 (1989); `Pavilion on the Links' by R.L. Stevenson, Radio 4 (1990); `The Suicide Club' by R.L. Stevenson, Radio 4 (1992); 'Tunes of Glory' by James Kennaway, Radio 4 (1995).

2. Stage Play

`Buchan of Tweedsmuir', Borders Festival (1991).

5. WILLIAM HERSHAW

Poetry Collections:

1. *Earth Bound Companions*, Illustrated by Les McConnell. Ochtertyre: Grace Note Publications, 2021.

2. *Saul Vaigers, A Calendar of Scottish Saints 2021*, illustrated by Les McConnell. Ochtertyre: Grace Note Publications, 2021.

3. *The Sair Road*. Ochtertyre: Grace Note Publications, 2018.

4. *Buirds*, with illustrations by Hugh Bryden and Fiona Morton. Roncadora Press, 2017.

5. *Stars Are The Aizles, Selected Poems In Scots.* Neepheid Publications, 2017.

6. *Postcairds Fae Woodwick Mill, Orkney Poems in Scots.* Ochtertyre: Grace Note Publications, 2015.

7. *Double First* with Walter Perrie. Fras Publications, 2012.

8. *Happyland*. Fras Publications, 2011.

9. *Johnny Aathin*. Windfall Publications, 2010.

10. *Makars*. Kirkcaldy: Akros Publications, 2006.

11. *Fifty Fife Sonnets*. Kirkcaldy: Akros Publications, 2005.

12. *The Cowdenbeath Man*. Scottish Cultural Press, 1997.

13. *Four Fife Poets/Fower Brigs Ti A Kinrick* with John Brewster, Harvey Holton, Tom Hubbard. Aberdeen University Press, 1988.

Selected Poetry Anthologies:

1. *A Kist of Thistles*. Culture Matters, 2020.

2. *Scotia Nova*. Luath Press, 2014.

3. *The Smeddum Test, 21st Century Poems in Scots.* Kennedy and Boyd, 2012.

4. *Skein of Geese – Poems from the 2008 Stanza Festival.* Stanza Publications.

5. *Scotlands – Poets and the Nation.* Carcanet, 2004.

6. *Dream State – The New Scottish Poets.* Polygon, 1994.

Drama:

1. *The Tempest in Scots*. Ochtertyre: Grace Note Publications, 2016.

2. *Michael Scot of Balwearie, A Ballad Play in Scots.* Ochtertyre: Grace Note Publications, 2016.

Novel:

1. *Tammy Norrie, The House Daemon Of Seahouses*. Ochtertyre: Grace Note Publications, 2014.

Music:

1. *Michael, A Ballad Play In Scots, The Bowhill Players*. Scotsoun, 2021.

2. *Introducing... The Blues Makkars*. Neepheid Records, 2020.

3. *Peewits, The Bowhill Players*. Scotsoun, 2020.

4. *Cage Load Of Men – The Joe Corrie Project, The Bowhill Players*. Fife Council/Birnam CD, 2013.

5. *A Song Cycle For Craigencalt Ecology Centre, The Hershaws*. Dances With Whippets Records/Birnam CD, 2009.

6. *A Fish Laid At The Door, The Hershaws*. Dances With Whippets Records/Birnam CD, 2002.

6. ALASDAIR GRAY

Novels:

1. *Old Men in Love: John Tunnock's Posthumous Papers*. Bloomsbury, 2007.

2. *Mavis Belfrage: A Love Story and Four Shorter Tales*. Bloomsbury. 1996.

3. *A History Maker*. Canongate Books, 1994.

4. *To Tales True and Tall*. Bloomsbury, 1993.

5. *Why Scots Should Rule Scotland*. Canongate Press, 1992.

6. *Poor Things*. Bloomsbury, 1992.

7. *McGrotty and Ludmilla*. Dog & Bone, 1990.

8. *Something Leather*. Edinburgh: Canongate Books, 1990

9. *The Fall of Kelvin Walker*. Edinburgh: Canongate Books, 1985

10. *1982 Janine*. London: Jonathan Cape, 1984.

11. *Lanark: A Life in 4 Books*. Edinburgh: Canongate Press, 1981.

Short stories:

1. *Every Short Story by Alasdair Gray 1951–2012*. Canongate, 2012.

2. *The Ends of Our Tethers: 13 Sorry Stories*. Canongate Books, 2004.

3. *Ten Tales Tall & True.* Bloomsbury, 1993.

4. *Lean Tales (1985)* with James Kelman and Agnes Owens. London: Jonathan Cape Ltd., 1995.

5. *Unlikely Stories, Mostly.* Canongate Books, 1983.

Theatre:

1. *Fleck.* Two Ravens Press, 2011.

2. *A Gray Play Book.* Luath, 2009.

Poems:

1. *Hell: Dante's Divine Trilogy Part One.* Dante Alighieri, Alasdair Gray (translator). Canongate Books, 2018.

2. *Guts Minced with Oatmeal : Ten Late Poems.* Fras, 2018.

7. MARGARET BENNETT

Books:

1. *Scottish Customs from the Cradle to the Grav.,* Edinburgh: Polygon, 1992. (many reprints); Second edition. Birlinn, 2004. Third edition, 2019.

2. *We are the Engineers! A History of Scottish Working People,* Ochtertyre: Grace Note Publications, 2015.

3. *Eilean Uaine Thiriodh Beatha:* Òrain *agus Ceòl Ethel NicChaluim – The Green Isle of Tiree The Life: Songs and Music of Ethel MacCallum* (with CD for teachers and students and musical transcriptions by Eric Rice). Ochtertyre: Grace Note Publications, 2014.

4. *Nell Hannah: Aye Singin an Spinnin Yarns.* Ochtertyre: Grace Note Publications, 2013.

5. *Jerome: Just One More Song! Local, Social and Political History in the Repertoire of a Newfoundland-Irish Singer,* (with CD, co-recorded with Kenneth S. Goldstein). Ochtertyre: Grace Note Publications, 2012.

6. *'In Our day...' Reminiscences and Songs from Rural Perthshire,* illustrated by Doris Rougive (with CD of Perthshire songs, sung by Sheila Stewart, students of the RSAMD & others). Ochtertyre: Grace Note Publication, 2010.

7. *Ties that Bind and Skills that Endure: Transferable Crofting Skills of the Hebridean-Quebec Settlers / Ceanglaichean agus Sgilean a Mhaireas: Sgilean Croitearachd Luchd-tuineachaidh Innse Gall ann an Cuibeac*, (tri-lingual publication with CD and DVD). Ochtertyre: Grace Note Publication, 2010.

8. *Dileab Ailean: The Legacy of Allan MacArthur* (with 2 CDs of a 40 years recordings of one family). Ochtertyre: Grace Note Publication, 2009.

9. *'It's not the Time You Have…' Notes and Memories of Musi-making with Martyn Bennett* (Featured at Edinburgh International Book Festival, Aug. 2006). Edinburgh: Grace Note Publications, 2006.

10. *'See When You Look Back…' Clydeside Reminiscences of the Home Front, 1939–45*, with CD (Recordings of Glasgow women from Kinning Park over-60s club). Glasgow: Mitchell Library, 2005.

11. *Then Another Thing…. Remembered in Perthshire*, with Doris Rougvie. Perth: Perth & Kinross Council, Museums Dept., 2000.

12. *Oatmeal and the Catechism: Scottish Gaelic Settlers in Quebec.*(Winner of the Canadian Historical Society's Cleo Award for History, 1999.) Edinburgh: John Donald, Edinburgh and Montreal: McGill-Queen's University Press, 1998. Edinburgh: Second edition, Birlinn, 2004.

13. *The Last Stronghold: Scottish Gaelic Traditions of Newfoundland.* St. John's, Newfoundland: Breakwater Books, and Edinburgh: Canongate Publishers, , l989.

Books: Edited, introduced and annotated

1. *Dundee Street Songs, Rhymes and Games: The William Montgomerie Collection, 1952* (with CD of the complete collection, Introduced and Annotated by Margaret Bennett, Illustrated by Les McConnell). Ochtertyre: Grace Note Publications, 2021.

2. *Index to The Cregeen Journals: Pathways to Sustainability of Land-Use, Language and Culture*, Volume 10. Ochtertyre: Grace Note Publications, 2019.

3. *The Cregeen Journals: Pathways to Sustainability of Land-Use, Language and Culture*, Volumes 1–9. Ochtertyre: Grace Note Publications, 2018.

4. *Robert MacLeod: Cowdenbeath Miner Poet. An Anthology* by Arthur Nevay. Ochtertyre: Grace Note Publications, 2015.

5. *"Recollections of an Argyllshire Drover" & Other West Highland Chronicles* by Eric R. Cregeen, (Foreword by Prof. T. C. Smout). Edinburgh,: Birlinn, 2004; ochtertyre: Grace Note Publications, second edition, 2013.

Books: Select Contributions

1. 'Corbies and Laverocks and the Four and Twenty Blackbirds: The Montgomerie Legacy to Folklore and the Mother Tongue'.*Tradition Today*. Vol. 9, 1-22, july 2020. <http://centre-for-english-traditional-heritage.org/traditiontodayal.html>.

2. 'Robert Macleod: Fife Miner-Poet and Broadside-Maker' in *Street Literature and the Circulation of Songs*, ed., by David Atkinson and Steve Roud. London: The Ballad Partners, 2019.

3. 'Hamish Henderson and Martyn Bennett: Conversations and Collaborations' and 'Howard Glasser and Hamish Henderson: Creative Collaboration and Kinship' in *Anent Hamish Henderson*, ed., Ebethart Bort. Ochtertyre: Grace Note Publications, 2015.

4. 'Struileag – Guthan troimh na Linntean' – 'Voices Across the Generations' in *Cladach ri Cladach: Shore to Shore,* ed., Kevin MacNeil. Edinburgh: Birlinn, 2015.

5. 'Customs' *Cleachdaidhean*' in *Tobar an Dualchais: Ulaidh Naiseanta – Kist o Riches: A National Treasure, ed.,* Chris Wright. Sabhal Mòr Ostaig, Sleat, Isle of Skye, 2014.

6. 'The Roots of Living Tradition' (first chapter) and 'Continuing the Living Tradition' (final chapter of 15) in *The Edinburgh Companion to Scottish Traditional Literatures,* ed.,, Sarah Dunnigan & Suzanne Gilbert. Edinburgh: EUP, 2013.

7. 'The Power of Song as the Voice of the People' in *The Phenomenon of Singing,* Vol. 9 (2013): International Symposium IX, St. John's, Newfoundland, Canada, 2013.

8. 'The Singer behind the Song and the Man behind the Microphone' in *'Tis Sixty Years Since: The 1951 Edinburgh People's Festival Ceilidh and*

the *Scottish Folk Revival*, ed., Eberhard Bort. Ochtertyre: Grace Note Publications, 2011.

9. 'From Perthshire to Pennsylvania: The Influence of Hamish Henderson on Transatlantic Folklore Studies' in *Borne On The Carrying Stream: The Legacy of Hamish Henderson*, ed., Eberhard Bort. Ochtertyre: Grace Note Publications, 2010.

10. 'Quebec and the Eastern Townships of Canada: Emigration from the Outer Hebrides in the Nineteenth Century' in *Island Emigrants: The History of Emigration from the Hebrides Over the Centuries,* ed., John Randall. Isle of Lewis: Island Book Trust, 2010.

11. 'Stories of the Supernatural: From Local Memorate to Scottish Legend' in *"Fantasticall Ymaginatiounis": The Supernatural in Scottish History and Culture*, ed., Lizanne Henderson. Edinburgh: Birlinn, 2009.

12. 'It's Mony's the Race that I have Run – Interpreting Macaronic Songs', in. *Emily Lyle: The Persistent Scholar*, ed., F.J. Fischer & S. Rieuwerts. Wissenschaftlichter Verlag Trier, Manz: 2007.

13. 'From the Quebec-Hebrideans to 'les Écossais-Québecois': Tracing the Evolution of a Scottish Cultural Identity in the Eastern Townships', in *Transatlantic Scots*, ed., Celeste Ray. Univ. of Alabama Press, 2004.

14. 'Being Scottish', *in Being Scottish*, ed., Tom Devine & Paddy Logue. EUP, Edinburgh, 2002.

15. 'Calendar Customs in Scotland'; 'Courtship and Marriage in Scotland'; 'Childbirth and Infancy in Scotland" in *The Oxford Companion to Scottish History*, ed., M. Lynch. Oxford: OUP, 2001.

16. 'Céilidh', definition in *The New Grove Dictionary of Music and Musicians*. London: OUP, 2000.

17. 'From Kennedy Fraser to the Jimmy Shandrix Experience in Five Generations' in *Crosbhealach an Cheoil: Tradition and Change.* ed., Fintan Vallely, et al. Dublin: Whinstone Press, 1999.

18. 'Canntaireachd'; 'Clarsach'; 'Ossianic ballads'; 'Panegyric'; 'Psalms'; 'Puirt-a-beul'; 'Scottish Gaelic Lyrical Songs'; 'The Ireland-Scotland Link'; 'Waulking Songs', in *Companion to Irish Traditional Music*, ed., F. Vallely. Dublin: Whinstone Press, 1999.

19. Contributions to the *Dictionary of the Folklore of Plants in Britain and Ireland,* ed., Roy Vickery. London: British Museum of Natural History, 1996.

20. 'Waters of Life and Health: Well-Worshipping in Scotland', [Russian translation, summary in English], Moscow: Institute of Ethnology and Anthropology, Russian Academy of Sciences, 1995.

21. 'The Folklore of Plants in Scotland', in *Plants and People: Economic Botany in Northern Europe, 800–1800,* ed., J.H. Dickson and R.R. Mill, (Proceedings, 1993 Symposium of the Royal Botanical Society of Scotland). Edinburgh: EUP, 1994.

22. '1690–1990: Balquhidder Revisited' in *The Good People: New Fairylore Essays,* ed., Peter Narvaez. New York: Garland Publishing, l991.

23. 'Plant Lore in Gaelic Scotland' in *Flora of the Outer Hebrides* by R. Pankhurst. London: British Museum of Natural History, l991

24. 'Folkways and Religion of the Quebec Hebrideans' in *Cultural Retention and Demographic Change: Studies of the Hebridean Scots in the Eastern Townships of Quebec,* ed., Laurel Doucette. National Museums of Canada, l980.

25. 'A Codroy Valley Milling Frolic' in *Folklore Studies in Honour of Herbert Halpert: A Festschrift,* ed., K.S. Goldstein and N.V. Roseneberg. Memorial University of Newfoundland, St. John's, l980.

8. JOHN HERDMAN

Books

1. *Ghostwriting* (Gothic World Literature Editions). Edinburgh: Leamington Books], 2021.

2. *Imelda* (Gothic World Literature Editions). Edinburgh: Leamington Books, 2020.

3. *Clapperton, with The Devil and Dr Tuberose* (Gothic World Literature Editions). Edinburgh: Leamington Books, 2020.

4. *La Confession* (translation into French by Maïca Sanconie of *Ghostwriting* with a postface by Jean Berton). Paris: Quidam Editeur, 2018.

5. *Imelda* (translation into Italian by Valentina Poggi (*Scritture d'Oltremanica* 13). Canterano: Aracne editrice, 2017.

6. *Another Country*. Edinburgh: Thirsty Books, 2013.

7. *Some Renaissance Culture Wars*. Blair Atholl: Fras Publications, 2010.

8. *My Wife's Lovers: Ten Tales*. Perth: Black Ace Books, 2007.

9. *Triptych: Three Tales*. Blair Atholl: Fras Publications, 2004.

10. *The Sinister Cabaret*. Forfar: Black Ace Books, 2001.

11. *Four Tales* (with an introduction by Macdonald Daly). London Zoilus Press, 2000.

12. *Poets, Pubs, Polls and Pillar Boxes*. Kirkcaldy: Akros Publications, 1999.

13. *Cruising: A Play in Two Acts*. Edinburgh: Diehard publishers, 1997.

14. *Ghostwriting*. Edinburgh: Polygon, 1996.

15. *Imelda and Other Stories*. Edinburgh: Polygon, 1993.

16. *The Double in Nineteenth-Century Fiction*. London: The Macmillan Press, 1990; New York: St Martin's Press, 1991.

17. *Three Novellas*. Edinburgh: Polygon Books, 1987.

18. *Voice Without Restraint: Bob Dylan's Lyrics and their Background*. Edinburgh: Paul Harris Publishing, 1982; New York: Delilah Books, 1982; (Japanese translation) Tokyo: CBS/Sony Publishing, 1983.

19. *Stories Short and Tall*. Thurso: Caithness Books, 1979.

20. *Pagan's Pilgrimage*. Preston: Akros Publications, 1978.

21. *Memoirs of my Aunt Minnie / Clapperton*. Aberdeen: Rainbow Books, 1974.

22. *A Truth Lover*. Preston: Akros Publications, 1973.

23. *Descent*. Edinburgh: Fiery Star Press, 1968.

24. *Imelda* (translation. into French with a postface by Maïca Sanconie). Paris: Quidam Editeur, 2006.

Books: Edited

1. 'The Devil and Dr Tuborose' in *The Uncanny Reader: Stories from the Shadows*', ed., Marjorie Sandor. New York: St Martin's Press, 2015.

2. 'Move up, John' by Fionn MacColla (edited and introduced by John Herdman). Edinburgh: Canongate, 1994.

3. 'Third Statistical Account of Scotland: Vol. XXIII, The County of Berwick'. Edinburgh: Scottish Academic Press, 1992.

4. 'Third Statistical Account of Scotland: Vol. XXVIII, The County of Roxburgh'. Edinburgh: Scottish Academic Press, 1992.

Books: Contributions

1. 'Together Through Life', Christmas in the Hearth/Folksinger's choice' and 'Some Other Kinds of Poems' in *The Mammoth Book of Bob Dylan*, ed., Sean Egan. London: Robinson, 2011.

2. *Nineteenth Century Literature Criticism, Vol. 192* ed., Kathy D. Darrow. Gale, Cengage Learning, 2008.

3. *Short Story Criticism, Vol. 44*. Michigan: Thomson Gale, 2005–6.

4. *Bringing Back Some Brightness: 20 Years of New Writing Scotland (NWS 22)*, ed., Valerie Thornton and Hamish Whyte. Glasgow: ASLS, 2004.

5. *The Oxford Dictionary of National Biography*, ed., Colin Matthew and Brian Harrison. Oxford: Oxford University Press, 2004.

6. *The Lie of the Land: Poems and Stories from Perth & Kinross*, ed., Brian McCabe et al. Perth: Perth and Kinross Libraries, 2004.

7. *Figures of Speech: An Anthology of Magdalene Writers*, ed., M.E.J Hughes, John Mole, Nick Seddon. Cambridge: Magdalene College, 2000.

8. *The Keekin-Gless: An Anthology from Perth and Kinross*, ed., R.A. Jamieson and Carl MacDougall. Perth: Perth and Kinross Libraries, 1999.

9. *Marilynre várva: Mai skót novellák*. Hungary: Pannónia Könyvek, 1998.

10. *The Picador Book of Contemporary Scottish Fiction*, ed., Peter Kravitz. London: Picador, 1997.

11. *Nineteenth Century Literature Criticism, Vol. 40*. Detroit: Gale Research Co., 1993.

12. 'The Devil and Dr Tuberose' in *Scottish Short Stories 1991*. London: Harper Collins, 1991.